MATH TRAILBLAZERS ™

GRADE 4

SECOND EDITION

Student Guide

A Mathematical Journey Using Science and Language Arts

KENDALL/HUNT PUBLISHING COMPANY
4050 Westmark Drive   Dubuque, Iowa 52002

A TIMS® Curriculum
University of Illinois at Chicago

MATH TRAILBLAZERS™

Dedication

This book is dedicated to the children and teachers who let us see the magic in their classrooms and to our families who wholeheartedly supported us while we searched for ways to make it happen.

The TIMS Project

UIC The University of Illinois at Chicago

The original edition was based on work supported by the National Science Foundation under grant No. MDR 9050226 and the University of Illinois at Chicago. Any opinions, findings, and conclusions or recommendations expressed in this publication are those of the authors and do not necessarily reflect the views of the granting agencies.

Acknowledgments

Teaching Integrated Mathematics and Science (TIMS) Project Directors

Philip Wagreich, Principal Investigator
Joan L. Bieler
Marty Gartzman
Howard Goldberg (emeritus)
Catherine Randall Kelso

Director, Second Edition

Catherine Randall Kelso

Curriculum Developers, Second Edition

Lindy M. Chambers-Boucher
Elizabeth Colligan
Marty Gartzman
Carol Inzerillo

Catherine Randall Kelso
Jennifer Mundt Leimberer
Georganne E. Marsh
Leona Peters
Philip Wagreich

Editorial and Production Staff, Second Edition

Kathleen R. Anderson
Ai-Ai C. Cojuangco
Andrada Costoiu
Erika Larson
Georganne E. Marsh
Cosmina Menghes
Anne Roby

TIMS Professional Developers

Barbara Crum
Craig Cleve
Elizabeth Colligan
Pamela Guyton

Carol Inzerillo
Linda Miceli
Leona Peters
Jane Schlichting

TIMS Director of Media Services

Henrique Cirne-Lima

TIMS Research Staff

Catherine Randall Kelso
Barry Booton
Dibyen Majumdar

TIMS Administrative Staff

Ora Benton
David Cirillo
Enrique Puente

Principal Investigators, First Edition

Philip Wagreich, Project Director
Howard Goldberg

Acknowledgments

Senior Curriculum Developers, First Edition

Joan L. Bieler
Janet Simpson Beissinger
Astrida Cirulis
Marty Gartzman
Howard Goldberg

Carol Inzerillo
Andy Isaacs
Catherine Randall Kelso
Leona Peters
Philip Wagreich

Curriculum Developers, First Edition

Janice C. Banasiak
Lynne Beauprez
Andy Carter
Lindy M. Chambers-Boucher
Kathryn Chval
Diane Czerwinski

Jenny Knight
Sandy Niemiera
Janice Ozima
Polly Tangora
Paul Trafton

Illustrator, First Edition

Kris Dresen

Research Consultant, First Edition

Andy Isaacs

Mathematics Education Consultant, First Edition

Paul Trafton

National Advisory Committee, First Edition

Carl Berger
Tom Berger
Hugh Burkhardt
Donald Chambers
Naomi Fisher
Glenda Lappan

Mary Lindquist
Eugene Maier
Lourdes Monteagudo
Elizabeth Phillips
Thomas Post

Table of Contents

Additional student pages may be found in the *Discovery Assignment Book, Adventure Book,* or the *Unit Resource Guide.*

Table of Contents

Additional student pages may be found in the *Discovery Assignment Book, Adventure Book,* or the *Unit Resource Guide.*

Table of Contents

Additional student pages may be found in the *Discovery Assignment Book, Adventure Book,* or the
Unit Resource Guide.

Table of Contents

Additional student pages may be found in the *Discovery Assignment Book, Adventure Book,* or the *Unit Resource Guide.*

Letter to Parents

Dear Parents,

Math Trailblazers™ is based on the ideas that mathematics is best learned through solving many different kinds of problems and that all children deserve a challenging mathematics curriculum. The program provides a careful balance of concepts and skills. Traditional arithmetic skills and procedures are covered through their repeated use in problems and through distributed practice. *Math Trailblazers,* however, offers much more. Students using this program will become proficient problem solvers, will know when and how to apply the

mathematics they have learned, and will be able to clearly communicate their mathematical knowledge. Computation, measurement, geometry, data collection and analysis, estimation, graphing, patterns and relationships, mental arithmetic, and simple algebraic ideas are all an integral part of the curriculum. They will see connections between the mathematics learned in school and the mathematics used in everyday life. And, they will enjoy and value the work they do in mathematics.

The *Student Guide* is only one component of *Math Trailblazers.* Additional material and lessons are contained in the *Discovery Assignment Book,* the *Adventure Book*, and in the teacher's *Unit Resource Guides.* If you have questions about the program, we encourage you to speak with your child's teacher.

This curriculum was built around national recommendations for improving mathematics instruction in American schools and the research that supported those recommendations. The first edition was extensively tested with thousands of children in dozens of classrooms over five years of development. In preparing this second edition, we have benefited from the comments and suggestions of hundreds of teachers and children who have used the curriculum. *Math Trailblazers* reflects our view of a complete and well-balanced mathematics program that will prepare children for the 21st century—a world in which mathematical skills will be important in most occupations and mathematical reasoning will be essential for acting as an informed citizen in a democratic society. We hope that you enjoy this exciting approach to learning mathematics and that you watch your child's mathematical abilities grow throughout the year.

Philip Wagreich

Philip Wagreich
Professor, Department of Mathematics, Statistics, and Computer Science
Director, Institute for Mathematics and Science Education
The *Math Trailblazers* Team
Teaching Integrated Mathematics and Science (TIMS) Project
University of Illinois at Chicago

Unit 1

Data About Us

	Student Guide	Discovery Assignment Book	Adventure Book	Unit Resource Guide*
Lesson 1				
Getting to Know Room 204	@			
Lesson 2				
Getting to Know Room 204 a Little Better	@			
Lesson 3				
An Average Activity	@			
Lesson 4				
The Four Servants			@	
Lesson 5				
Arm Span vs. Height	@	@		@
Lesson 6				
Solving Problems About Room 204	@			

Unit Resource Guide pages are from the teacher materials.

Getting to Know Room 204

The class picture at the beginning of this unit shows Mrs. Dewey's fourth-grade class. Their classroom is Room 204 in the Bessie Coleman Elementary School in Chicago, Illinois. Mrs. Dewey's class wants to share information about themselves with their pen pals at Westmont School in Phoenix, Arizona. They also want to get to know their pen pals.

Mrs. Dewey asked her class what they would like to know about their new pen pals. Tanya said, "I'd like to know what they are interested in. I love to read. I can recommend some really good books!"

Jessie said, "I wonder if they have some really cool trails in Arizona! I love to ride my bike and roller blade!"

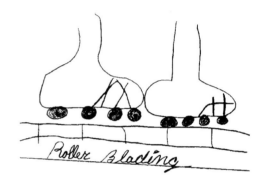

Keenya said, "I'll probably ask my pen pal to tell me about her favorite food, her favorite holiday, and her favorite color. I'll also ask if she plays an instrument. I'm learning to play a keyboard."

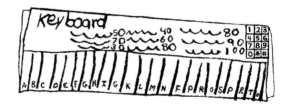

"I'll ask my pen pal about the color of his hair and eyes, and whether he is short or tall," said Jerome.

John said, "I'll ask my pen pal what his favorite sport is. I like soccer and basketball."

Values and Variables

The students in Room 204 decided to collect data they would like to share about their class. They started by making a list of things they wanted to learn about one another. They made the following chart of the variables they chose to study and possible values for each variable. A **variable** is an attribute or quantity that may have one or many different values. The possible outcomes for each variable are called **values.**

Variables and Possible Values

Variable	Possible Values
Interests	Sports, Reading, Outdoor Activities, Playing Games, Music, Animals, etc.
Eye color	Blue, Hazel, Green, Brown
Favorite food	Pizza, Tacos, Liver, Chicken

Mrs. Dewey's class decided to collect data about the variable, main interest. The main interests in Room 204 varied from student to student. Some students chose reading as their main interest, while others chose animals, sports, music, outdoor activities, or playing games. These possible outcomes are the values of the variable.

Discuss

1. What would you like to learn about the students in your class? Make a table like the one above, listing variables you can study about your classmates and possible values for each of the variables.

Room 204's Main Interests

Name	Interest
Linda	Animals
John	Sports
Tanya	Reading
Shannon	Reading
Jerome	Games
Romesh	Animals
Ana	Outdoors
Jackie	Sports
Nicholas	Animals
Ming	Sports
Luis	Music
Jacob	Reading
Jessie	Sports
Keenya	Music
Nila	Sports
Michael	Reading
Roberto	Outdoors
Irma	Reading
Maya	Sports
Lee Yah	Sports
Frank	Music
Grace	Sports

In order for the students in Phoenix to compare their class to Room 204, Mrs. Dewey's students decided to organize their data. As the class read the main interest of each child from the large data table, Maya placed a tally mark next to his or her main interest. The data in this table was then used to make a bar graph.

Main Interests Data

Main Interest	Tally	Number of Students
Animals	|||	3
Music	|||	3
Reading	ⅢⅠ	5
Outdoor Activities	||	2
Playing Games	|	1
Sports	ⅢⅠ |||	8

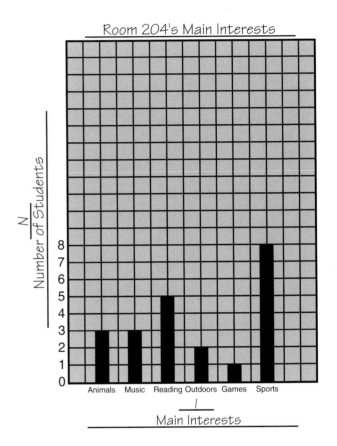

Room 204's Main Interests

2. As a class, choose a variable you wish to study that helps you describe your class. Choose from those variables you listed in Question 1.

Collect the data and organize it in a class data table.

Graph the data. Be sure you title your graph and label the axes.

3. What variable is on the horizontal axis (⟷) on your graph?

4. What variable is on the vertical axis (↕) on your graph?

5. A. Which bar is the tallest on your graph?

   B. What does the tallest bar represent?

6. A. Which bar is the shortest on your graph?

   B. What does the shortest bar represent?

7. What else does your graph tell you about your class?

8. A. Look back at Room 204's graph. Which variable did they graph on the horizontal axis?

   B. Which variable did they graph on the vertical axis?

9. What does the tallest bar on their graph represent?

10. How many more students prefer to read than play games?

Homework

You will need a sheet of *Centimeter Graph Paper* to complete Question 6.

1. Another fourth grade class at Bessie Coleman School, Mrs. Cook's class, collected data to share with their pen pals. What variable did they study?

2. What does the tallest bar on their graph represent?

3. What do the shortest bars on Room 206's graph represent?

4. How many more students speak Spanish as their primary language than Assyrian?

5. What else does this graph tell you about Mrs. Cook's class?

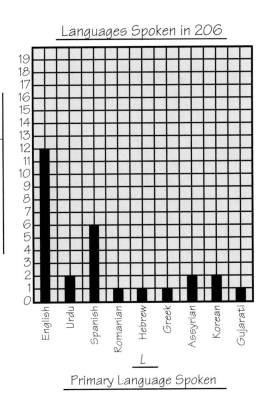

Languages Spoken in 206

---

6. Room 204's pen pals in Phoenix sent back data on their favorite subjects. Use the data to create a bar graph. Remember to label the axes and title your graph.

7. **A.** What variable is on the horizontal axis?

   B. What variable is on the vertical axis?

8. Answer the following questions based on the graph you created in Question 6.

   A. What is the most common favorite subject?

   B. What is the least common favorite subject?

   C. Which of the subjects in the data table is your favorite?

   D. How many of the Phoenix pen pals have the same favorite subject as you do?

9. How many students are in the Phoenix class? Explain how you know.

Favorite Subjects

Favorite Subject	Number of Students
Writing	2
Social Studies	3
Math	8
Reading	2
Spelling	6
Science	7

Thinking of the sun rising over the horizon helps me remember which axis is the horizontal axis.

Getting to Know Room 204 a Little Better

Here is what I am going to tell my pen pal about me. 57, 3, 1, 5, 4, 2

Frank, it would help if you told us what each of those numbers represents.

Frank continued to explain. "Well, I am 57 inches tall. I have 3 brothers and 1 sister. I live 5 blocks away from school. I have moved 4 times. I have 2 pets." Maya said, "I am 51 inches tall. I have 1 brother and no sisters. I live 4 blocks from school. I've only moved once. I have 1 pet."

In Lesson 1, Room 204 discussed what they would like to know about their pen pals. They listed **categorical** variables such as interests, favorite food, and eye color.

In this lesson, Frank discussed **numerical** variables: height, number of brothers, number of sisters, number of blocks from school, number of times moved, and number of pets. The **values** for these variables varied (or changed) from Frank to Maya.

Numerical variables have values that are numbers while **categorical variables** do not.

Numerical Variables and Possible Values

Variable	Possible Values
Height	51 inches, 57 inches, etc.
Number of brothers	0, 1, 2, 3, etc.
Blocks from school	1, 2, 3, 4, etc.

1. Think of numerical variables you would like to study about your classmates. Add these variables to the table you created in Lesson 1. List possible values for each variable.

Mrs. Dewey's class wanted to know how far the students in their class lived from school. They chose to study the variable, number of blocks from school. First they recorded and organized their data in data tables.

Number of Blocks We Live from School

Number of Blocks	Tally	Number of Students
1	///	3
2	//// //	7
3	////	4
4	//	2
5	\	1
6		0
7	/	1
8	////	4

Room 204's Data

Name	Number of Blocks
Linda	2
John	1
Tanya	3
Shannon	2
Jerome	2
Romesh	3
Ana	8
Jackie	1
Nicholas	2
Ming	8
Luis	2
Jacob	3
Jessie	7
Keenya	1
Nila	2
Michael	8
Roberto	3
Irma	2
Maya	4
Lee Yah	4
Frank	5
Grace	8

Then, Mrs. Dewey's class graphed the data in a bar graph.

2. With your class, choose a numerical variable you wish to study that helps you describe your class. Choose from those variables you listed in Question 1.

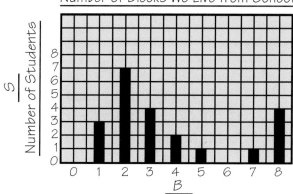

Room 204:
Number of Blocks We Live from School

Number of Blocks from School

Collect the data and organize it in a class table.

Graph the data in a bar graph. Be sure to title your graph and label the axes.

3. A. Which variable is on the horizontal axis on your graph?
   B. Is this variable a categorical or a numerical variable? How do you know?

4. A. Which variable is on the vertical axis on your graph?
   B. Is this variable a categorical or a numerical variable? How do you know?

5. A. Which bar is the tallest on your graph?
   B. What does the tallest bar represent?

6. A. Which bar is the shortest on your graph?
   B. What does the shortest bar represent?

7. **A.** Look back at Room 204's graph called Number of Blocks We Live from School. Is the variable they graphed on the horizontal axis numerical or categorical?

   B. Is the variable they graphed on the vertical axis numerical or categorical?

8. **A.** Would Room 204's graph be as easy to read if the numbers (values) on the horizontal axis were not in order? Explain.

   B. Does it matter in what order you label the horizontal axis when the variable is categorical? Refer back to Room 204's Main Interests graph in Lesson 1.

9. What story does the graph tell you about the students in Room 204?

10. **A.** How many students in Room 204 live 3 blocks or less from school?

   B. Is this more or less than half the class?

Homework

You will need one sheet of *Centimeter Graph Paper* to complete this homework.

1. Room 204's Phoenix pen pals sent back the following data on the number of times their families have moved. Use the data to create a bar graph. Remember to label the axes and title your graph.

2. Answer the following questions using the bar graph you drew in Question 1.

   A. Is the variable on your horizontal axis numerical or categorical?

   B. Is the variable on your vertical axis numerical or categorical?

   C. Which is the tallest bar on the graph? What does it tell you?

   D. What is the most number of times any student has moved?

   E. Describe the shape of your graph.

Number of Times
Families Moved

Number of Times Moved	Number of Students
0	0
1	3
2	7
3	7
4	3
5	2
6	2
7	2
8	1
9	1
10	0

3. What story does the graph tell you about the Phoenix pen pals?

4. Decide whether each of the variables below is a numerical or categorical variable. Then, name three possible values for each variable.
   A. ice cream flavors
   B. number of telephones in homes
   C. heights of tables at home
   D. favorite kind of movie
   E. weights of newborn babies
   F. foot size
   G. types of vehicles

An Average Activity

Mrs. Dewey's class was collecting data on the heights of fourth graders. She asked a doctor to talk to the class about how children grow and develop. One of the things Dr. Solinas talked about was the average height of ten-year-olds. What does "average" mean?

- "It was just an average day."
- "The doctor said my height is above average for kids my age."
- "We really need rain. Rainfall this year has been well below average."
- "My average grade in spelling is 75 percent."
- "Our soccer team averages about three goals per game."

Each sentence describes what is usual or typical for the situation.

Scientists and mathematicians use averages to help them describe data they have collected. Doctors who study how children grow measure the heights of many children. Then, they use this data to find the average height for different age groups. They use one number, an average, to represent the heights of a whole group.

The average value for any set of numbers, such as the average height of fourth graders, can be calculated in more than one way. In this lesson you will learn about one kind of average: the median. You can find the median of a set of numbers easily and use it to describe the data you collect. Later this year, you will learn to calculate another kind of average.

Finding Medians

Mrs. Dewey asked five students to stand in front of the room to show the class how to find medians. Jerome, Ana, Grace, Roberto, and Shannon stood in a line from shortest to tallest. The **median** is the number that is exactly in the middle of the data.

1. A. Which student has the median height in Jerome's group?

   B. Does it make sense to say that this student's height is the "typical" height for this group? Why or why not?

2. A. Use the information in the table to find the median height for Keenya's group. Put the numbers in order from smallest to largest. The median height will be in the middle of the data.

   B. When you have found the median, look back at the data. An **average** is one number that can be used to represent all the data. Does your answer make sense?

Keenya's Group: Our Heights

Name	Height in inches
Keenya	55 in
Nila	50 in
John	57 in
Michael	54 in
Luis	58 in
Jackie	54 in
Lee Yah	52 in

3. Keenya, Maya, Jessie, and Shannon all walk to school together.

- Jessie lives 7 blocks from school.
- Shannon lives 2 blocks from school.
- Maya lives 4 blocks from school.
- Keenya lives 1 block from school.

Jessie said, "The median number of blocks that the four of us walk to school is 3 blocks." Is she correct? Why or why not?
(*Hint:* Find the number halfway between the middle two values.)

4. Use the information in the data table to the right to find the median number of blocks the students in Linda's group live from school.

Linda's Group: Number of Blocks We Live from School

Name	Number of Blocks from School
Linda	2
John	1
Tanya	3
Michael	8
Frank	5
Luis	2

Room 204: Number of Blocks We Live from School

Number of Blocks	Tally	Number of Students
1					3
2	ⵏⵏ ||	7
3						4
4				2
5			1
6		0
7			1
8						4

5. Look at Room 204's data and graph.

A. Find the median number of blocks.

B. Explain how you found the median.

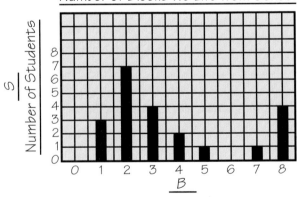

Room 204:
Number of Blocks We Live from School

6. The students in Room 204 collected data on the number of times their families had moved. The data for Ming's group is in the table to the right. Find the median number of times the students in his group have moved.

7. Jerome's baseball team has played eight games. Here are the number of runs they scored: 1, 3, 5, 3, 2, 7, 2, 4. Find the median number of runs they scored.

8. John, Shannon, and Tanya made paper airplanes. They had a contest to see who made the best airplane. Each airplane was flown three times.

   A. Find the median distance for each student's airplane.

   B. Who do you think should win the contest? Justify your choice.

Ming's Group: Number of Times We Moved

Name	Number of Times Moved
Ming	2
Irma	1
Nicholas	5
Romesh	0
Linda	3

Name	Distance in cm			
	Trial 1	Trial 2	Trial 3	Median
John	410 cm	390 cm	640 cm	
Shannon	250 cm	230 cm	290 cm	
Tanya	420 cm	590 cm	600 cm	

1. Romesh took a survey on his block and recorded his data in the table shown at the right. Find the median number of pets on his block.

2. Ana and her two brothers play soccer. They all play on different teams. Find the median number of goals for each team.

   A. Ana's team has played 6 games. Here are the number of goals her team has scored in the six games: 4, 4, 0, 3, 2, 5.

   B. David's team has played 5 games. Here are the number of goals his team has scored: 2, 1, 3, 2, 3.

   C. Tony's team has played 4 games. Here are the number of goals his team has scored: 1, 0, 3, 6.

   D. Ana claims that her team is the best. Do you agree? Why or why not?

3. A. Make a data table like the one shown below. Measure the length of your hand and the hands of your family and friends. Measure at least five hands including your own. Carefully measure from the wrist to the end of the longest finger. Measure to the nearest centimeter.

   B. Record your data in the data table.

   C. Find the median value for your hand length data.

Pets Survey

Family	Number of Pets
Bailey	2
Johnson	0
Cruz	5
Kanno	3
Holt	4
Elkins	1
Roberts	2

Hand Length Data

Name	Hand Length in cm

Arm Span vs. Height

The TIMS Laboratory Method

Irma and Jerome noticed that the Adventure Book story *The Four Servants* took place in China. All the measurements were of Chinese people. They wondered if the four servants would have found the same results if they had measured the people in Irma and Jerome's neighborhood.

I wonder if we would get a line too? The people in our neighborhood are different.

Let's try it! We can start by collecting data for our family members.

Irma and Jerome decided to use the TIMS Laboratory Method to help them solve problems involving hand length and height in their neighborhood. The four servants used this four-step method. First, Irma and Jerome **drew a picture** of the steps they would follow in the experiment. Irma's picture is shown below.

People in household

Hand Length

Height

Notice that Irma showed the people in her household, how she was going to measure hand length, and how she was going to measure height. Irma labeled the variables in her experiment, Hand Length and Height.

Irma and Jerome then **collected and organized** the data in a data table. Below is the data Jerome collected from his family:

Jerome's Family Table

Name	Hand Length (in cm)	Height (in cm)
Peter	12 cm	102 cm
Abby	13 cm	110 cm
Timothy	15 cm	124 cm
Jerome	14 cm	127 cm
Jenny	16 cm	147 cm
Mom		

Jerome **graphed** his family's data as a point graph:

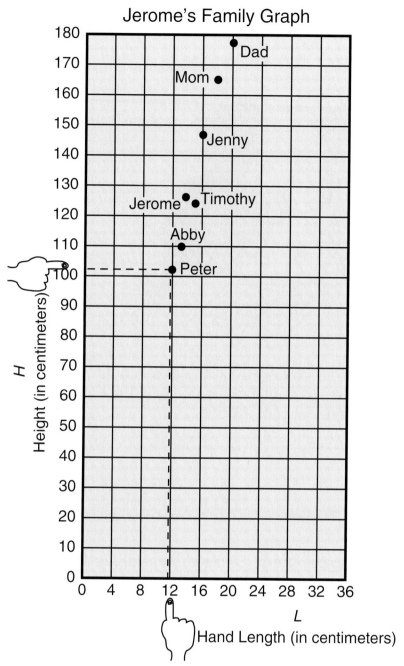

Jerome's Family Graph

Jerome graphed hand length on the horizontal axis and height on the vertical axis. To plot a point for his brother Peter's data, he first located his hand length, 12 cm, on the horizontal axis. Then he found his height, 102 centimeters, on the vertical axis.

- Make sure you see how Jerome graphed his brothers' and sisters' data.
- Use the graph to find the hand length and height of Jerome's parents.

Besides measuring their own family members, Irma and Jerome measured their classmates as well. They also collected data from other families, schoolchildren, and even teachers. When they finished graphing all the data, the graph represented Hand Length vs. Height for their neighborhood.

Finally, when their graph was finished, they **analyzed and discussed** their results.

Irma and Jerome chose to investigate the two variables, hand length and height. You, like Irma and Jerome, will investigate two variables which describe your class. The arm span and height of each student in your class will be measured. Your job is to find out whether you can predict a fourth-grade student's height if you know his or her arm span.

We never measured the principal's hand length and height.

It looks like she's in a hurry. Let's ask her if we can measure her hand. We can use our graph to predict her height.

You will begin by drawing a picture of what you will do in the experiment. Then, collect and organize data in a table. Next, you will make a graph of the data. Finally, you will explore the data by looking for patterns.

Draw a picture of the setup for your experiment. Show the variables Arm Span (*S*) and Height (*H*) in your picture. Use Irma's hand length and height picture to help you draw a picture of your *Arm Span vs. Height* experiment. Remember to label the variables.

1. A. Is arm span a categorical or a numerical variable?

    B. Is height a categorical or a numerical variable? Explain how you know.

2. What is the same about all the people you measured for this experiment?

Collect

Measure the arm span and height of each person in your group to the nearest inch. Record your group's data in a data table like the one at the right. Discuss with your group what the letters *S* and *H* stand for.

Discuss any patterns you see in the data table.

Arm Span vs. Height Data Table

Name	*S* Arm Span (in inches)	*H* Height (in inches)

Graph

- Graph your group's data. Plot arm span on the horizontal axis and height on the vertical axis. Scale your horizontal axis to at least 75 inches and the vertical axis to at least 100 inches. Remember to label each axis.

- A class graph of *Arm Span vs. Height* will provide more data for you to analyze. Plot one point, your own data, for arm span and height on the class graph.

Explore

Use your class data and your graphs to help you and your group answer the following questions. Include units with your answers. Be ready to share your answers with the entire class.

3. A. Describe your group's graph. What do you notice about the points?

   B. Describe the class graph. What do you notice about the points?

4. Compare your group's graph and the class graph. How are they alike and how are they different?

5. A. If you measured a new classmate's arm span and height, where do you think his or her data would lie?

   B. If a fourth-grader from another classroom had an arm span of 53 inches, what would you predict about his or her height?

6. A. In which part of the graph would first-grade data cluster in comparison to fourth-grade data—in the area marked A, B, or C?

   B. In which cluster would a kangaroo's data fall—in the area marked A, B, or C?

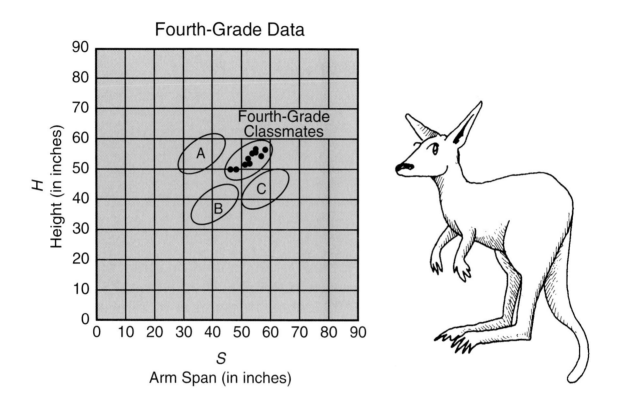

Fourth-Grade Data

Height (in inches), *H* (vertical axis)
Arm Span (in inches), *S* (horizontal axis)

Use your class graph to discuss the following.

7. Use your graph to estimate the average arm span of your classmates. (*Hint:* This is a number that represents all the arm spans in your classroom.)

8. Use your graph to estimate the average height of your classmates.

9. **A.** Find the median height in your class.

   B. Find the median arm span in your class.

   C. Compare with your estimate. Were you close?

10. **A.** Use a red pen or marker to plot the data point for the median height and arm span on your graph.

   B. Where is the data point for the median values compared to the other data points on the graph?

Homework

1. The data table shows data for three groups of students in Room 204. Graph *Arm Span vs. Height* for these groups on a sheet of *Centimeter Graph Paper*. Title the graph so that you know it is not your class data. Plot arm span on the horizontal axis and height on the vertical axis. Remember to label your axes and include units.

2. **A.** Estimate the average arm span of the groups using the graph.

   B. Estimate the average height using the graph.

   C. How does the groups' data compare to your class data?

3. If a new fourth grader who entered Mrs. Dewey's classroom had an arm span of 54 inches, what would you predict about the student's height?

4. If you measured the arm spans and heights of the parents of classmates in Mrs. Dewey's classroom, where would the data cluster? Show your answer on your graph of *Arm Span vs. Height* for the groups in Room 204.

Room 204 Arm Span and Height Data Table

Name	S Arm Span (in inches)	H Height (in inches)
Linda	51	51
Romesh	52	53
Nicholas	56	54
Jerome	49	50
Keenya	54	55
Frank	59	57
Luis	58	58
Roberto	55	57
Ana	52	52
Jacob	56	56
Grace	55	55
Lee Yah	53	52

Solving Problems About Room 204

Mrs. Dewey asked her students to solve some problems comparing Bessie Coleman School to Westmont School. She asked them to check their calculations by estimating a reasonable answer to each problem. She reminded them that sometimes using a convenient number that is easier to calculate in your head helps to make a quick estimate.

Solve the following problems Mrs. Dewey gave her class. Show how you solved each problem. Be ready to explain how you estimated your answers.

1. There are 396 students at Bessie Coleman School. At Westmont School in Phoenix, there are 509 students. How many more students go to Westmont School?

2. There are 22 students in Mrs. Dewey's fourth-grade class at Bessie Coleman School. At Westmont School, the fourth-grade class has 28 students.

   A. On the first day of school, Mrs. Dewey gave each of her students five textbooks. How many textbooks did she pass out?

   B. If each student in fourth grade at Westmont has 5 textbooks, how many textbooks do the Westmont fourth graders have in their classroom?

   C. Look back at your answers. Explain why you think they are reasonable.

3. Milk at both schools costs 25¢.

   A. If 20 students in Room 204 at the Bessie Coleman School bought milk, how much money did Mrs. Dewey collect?

   B. In the Westmont fourth-grade class, the total cost for milk was $5.25. How many students bought milk in this fourth-grade class?

4. Each of the 22 students in Mrs. Dewey's class sent a letter to their pen pal at Westmont School. Find the cost of the stamps.

5. In music class at Bessie Coleman School, Lee Yah, Roberto, Grace, and Luis lined up across the front of the room to demonstrate a folk dance. They began with their arms outstretched and their fingers just touching. They could just reach across the room. Since the average arm span of the students in Room 204 is 54 inches, about how wide is the room?

6. Bessie Coleman School begins its school day at 8:30 A.M. and ends at 3:00 P.M. Jerome stays for lunch. How long is he at school?

7. The distance between Phoenix and Chicago is 1816 miles.

   A. If you traveled from Chicago to Phoenix and back again, how many miles would you travel?

   B. Make sure your answer in Question 7A is correct. Explain how you can make a quick estimate of the total distance to see if your answer is reasonable.

Unit 2

Geometric Investigations: A Baseline Assessment Unit

	Student Guide	Discovery Assignment Book	Adventure Book	Unit Resource Guide*
Lesson 1				
Investigating Perimeter and Area	◎	◎		
Lesson 2				
Perimeter vs. Length	◎			
Lesson 3				
Letter to Myrna				◎
Lesson 4				
Helipads for Antopolis	◎			
Lesson 5				
Portfolios	◎			
Lesson 6				
Angles	◎			◎
Lesson 7				
Angles in Pattern Blocks	◎	◎		

Unit Resource Guide pages are from the teacher materials.

Investigating Perimeter and Area

In the Antopolis town square, the ants have built a beautiful fountain. In the evening, the ants come out to stroll around the perimeter of the fountain.

This diagram shows the Antopolis Town Square with the ants walking along the perimeter of the fountain.

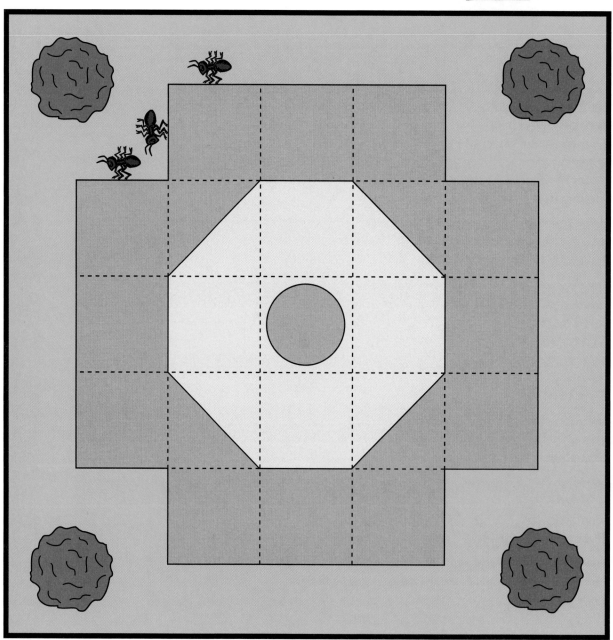

The **perimeter** is the edge all around a two-dimensional shape; it is also the distance all around the shape.

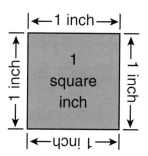

Here is a picture of a one square-inch tile.

Each side of this tile is one inch long.
The **perimeter** of the tile is 4 inches.

The **area** of the tile is one **square inch.**

Area is the amount of surface that is needed to cover something. The size of an object or shape is often measured by counting the number of unit squares that can be placed on top of the shape to cover it. This is called the area of the object.

A grid of square-inch tiles has been drawn on the diagram of the fountain. You can use it to measure the distance the ants walked to travel the perimeter of the fountain. The grid of tiles can also help you measure the square inches needed to cover the area of the fountain.

1. Find the perimeter of the fountain.

2. Find the area of the fountain.

3. Find the area of the fountain that is covered by water.

4. Find the area of the fountain that is not covered by water.

The ants of Antopolis want to build a playground with an area of 8 square inches. They have ordered enough material to build a fence around the playground that is 14 inches long.

5. Draw a design for a playground for the ants which has an area of 8 square inches and a perimeter of 14 inches. (They want the little ants inside to be able to walk from one corner of the playground to any other corner.)

6. Write a paragraph that explains how you solved the problem. Use the Student Rubric: *Telling* to help you write your paragraph.

Homework

Here are some other shapes. Their edges have already been measured for you. Calculate their perimeters.

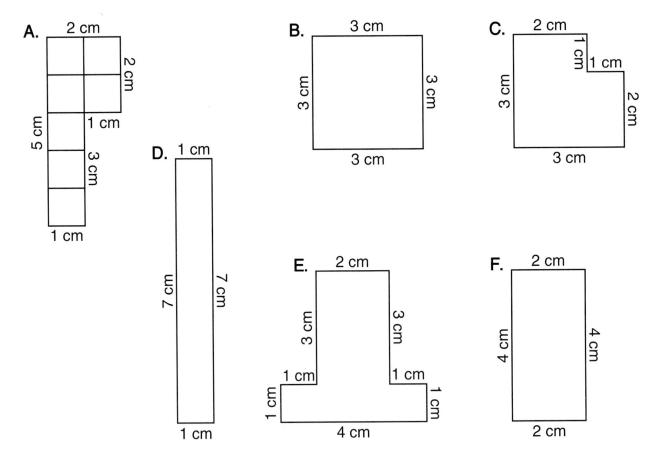

After you have found the perimeter of each shape, find the area for 3 of the shapes.

Perimeter vs. Length

Myrna Myrmidon is helping to plan a new airport for Antopolis. Myrna is in charge of the runways.

The airport plans are not done yet, so Myrna doesn't know how long the runways will be. Myrna does know what kinds of airplanes will use the airport: light planes, commuter planes, short-haul jets, long-haul jets, and heavy-transport planes. She also knows that bigger airplanes need wider runways.

The light planes are the smallest airplanes that will use the new Antopolis airport. They need runways that are 1 inch wide.

Light Plane Runway

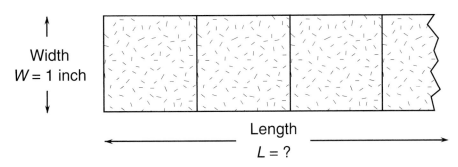

Width
$W = 1$ inch

Length
$L = ?$

The commuter planes need runways that are 2 inches wide.

Commuter Plane Runway

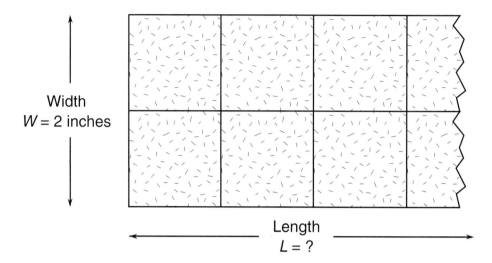

The short-haul jets need 3-inch-wide runways.

Short-Haul Jet Runway

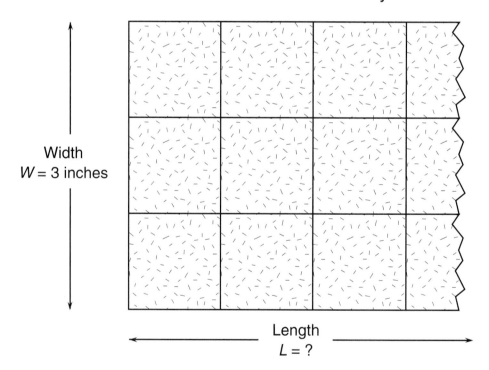

The other planes need even wider runways. The long-haul jets need 4-inch wide runways and the heavy-transport planes need runways that are 5 inches wide.

Every runway will have lights all around it. Myrna has to know how much wire is needed to connect these lights. Myrna is trying to find the **perimeter** of the runways.

For example, a runway for a light plane that is 5 inches long needs 12 inches of wire for the perimeter lights.

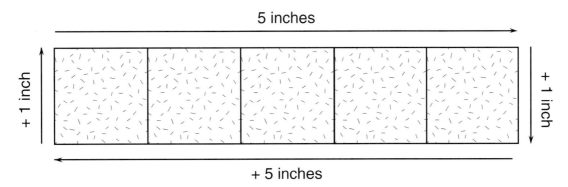

5 inches

+ 1 inch

+ 1 inch

+ 5 inches

A runway with a perimeter of 12 inches

Since Myrna doesn't know how long the runways will be, she doesn't know how much wire she needs. She has to find how much wire she needs for any kind of runway, no matter how long.

Use the TIMS Laboratory Method to help Myrna. You will work on runways for only one kind of plane. Your teacher will help you choose.

You will use square-inch tiles to make several runways for your kind of plane. For each runway, you will record the length (L) and the perimeter (P) in a data table. Then, you will graph your data and look for patterns.

1. Draw a picture of the lab.
   - Be sure to show the variables, length (L), perimeter (P), and width (W).
   - Show your kind of airplane and at least one of your runways. Show how wide your runways will be.

2. A. Which variable, length (L), width (W), or perimeter (P), will stay the same for all of your runways?
   B. Which two variables will change from runway to runway?

Collect

Use square-inch tiles to make 4–5 runways for your kind of airplane. Decide how long to make your runways. You might make one runway 1 inch long, another 2 inches long, and another 4 inches long. Or, you might make runways 2, 4, and 8 inches long. However, do not make runways that are longer than 12 inches or you may have trouble graphing your data. Discuss with your group how long your runways should be.

3. Make your runways. Find the length and perimeter of each runway. Keep track of your data in a table like this:

W Width of Runway (in inches)	L Length of Runway (in inches)	P Perimeter of Runway (in inches)

Graph

4. Draw a point graph for your data. Put length (*L*) on the horizontal axis and perimeter (*P*) on the vertical axis. (Remember to include a title for the graph, label the axes, and include units.)

5. Look at your points on the graph. Describe your points.

6. If your points form a line, use a ruler to draw a line through your data points. Extend the line in both directions.

Discuss

Questions 7–12 are for runways the same width as yours.

7. How wide are your runways?

8. What is the perimeter of a runway that is 4 inches long?

9. Use your graph to find the perimeter of a runway that is 10 inches long. Use dotted lines on your graph to show your work.

10. What is the perimeter of a runway that is 100 inches long? Explain how you found your answer.

11. Give a rule for finding the perimeter of a runway for your type of plane, no matter what the length.

12. Plot your data on the class graph and draw the line. Label the line with your type of airplane. Then, compare the different lines your class drew and answer the following questions:

   A. What is similar about the lines?

   B. How do the lines differ?

Homework

Dear Family Member:

Your child is learning about perimeters in class. Encourage your child to use a yardstick, a tape measure, a ruler, or string for these problems. Your child can use the 6-inch line below to measure 36 inches of string and then use the string like a tape measure. Thank you for your cooperation.

A 6-inch line

Bedroom Perimeter

1. Estimate, in inches, the perimeter of the room where you sleep. Explain how you made your estimate.

2. Measure the perimeter of the room where you sleep. Explain how you made your measurement. Draw a picture to help make your explanation clear.

3. What room in your home has a perimeter that is larger than your bedroom's perimeter? How did you decide?

4. What room in your home has a perimeter that is smaller than your bedroom's perimeter? How did you decide?

Runways

Use the graph to answer the following questions.

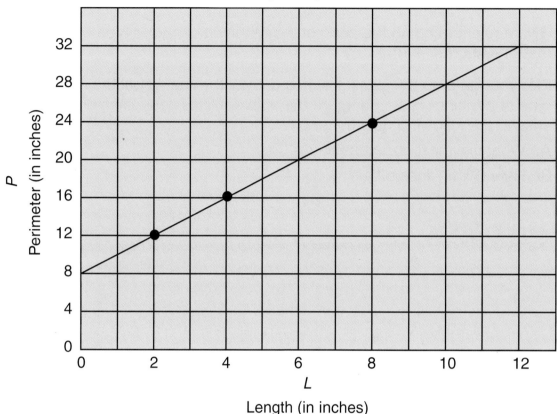

Runway Length and Perimeter

5. If the length of the runway is 6 inches, what is the perimeter?

6. If the length of the runway is 3 inches, what is the perimeter?

7. If the perimeter is 28 inches, what is the length?

8. If the perimeter is 18 inches, what is the length?

9. What is the width of the runways? Explain your answer.

Use what you have learned about lengths, widths, and perimeters of runways to answer the following questions.

10. If the length of a runway is 6 inches and the width is 3 inches, what is the perimeter? Draw a picture to help you.

11. If the length of a runway is 10 inches and the perimeter is 22 inches, how wide is the runway? Draw a picture to help you. Explain how you found your answer.

Helipads for Antopolis

Myrna Myrmidon's Aunt Penny likes to fly helicopters. When she flew to Ladybug Airport, she landed her helicopter on a helipad. The helipad at Ladybug Airport is 4 inches long and 2 inches wide.

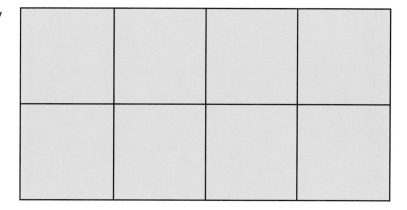

1. Ladybug Airport is building a new helipad. They are also buying new perimeter lights. The lights are attached to a wire that goes around the entire helipad. How long does the wire need to be to fit around this helipad?

2. What is the area of this helipad?

While the construction crew at Ladybug Airport waited for the lights to be delivered, they discussed the new helipad. They knew that the perimeter of the helipad could not be changed since the wire had already been ordered. However, they could change the helipad's area. The head construction worker reminded them that the helipad needed to be a rectangle made with square-inch tiles.

3. Help the construction crew.

   A. Are there other rectangles besides the one shown above that have the same perimeter as the current helipad at Ladybug Airport? Use square-inch tiles to help you.

   B. What is the area of each of the rectangles you found?

   C. Which rectangle would you recommend for the new helipad? Why?

Aunt Penny wants a helipad included in the Antopolis airport. Myrna agrees, but tells her aunt that only 24 inches of wire (for perimeter lights) can be allowed for the helipad. Myrna also says that the helipad must be a rectangle built with square-inch tiles.

4. Using square-inch tiles, find all the possible helipads with a perimeter of 24 inches. Sketch each helipad on a piece of paper showing the length and width. Be sure your helipads are rectangles.

5. What is the area of each of your helipads?

6. Penny wants the helipad to be as big as possible. Design a helipad with a perimeter of 24 inches with the largest possible area.

7. Explain why you think your helipad has the largest possible area.

Portfolios

What do you need to do to set up a portfolio? First, you will have a collection folder. After you finish a piece of work, write the date on it and then put it in the collection folder. Everything that goes in the collection folder will not go in the portfolio. From time to time, you will pick pieces from your collection folder to put in your portfolio.

Mrs. Dewey's class began organizing portfolios in its mathematics class. They decided to organize the portfolios around the idea of communication. Communication has many different meanings. This is one of the reasons the class chose it. Jackie chose a picture to include in her portfolio. Frank chose some tables and graphs.

Students in Mrs. Dewey's class chose work to include in their portfolios. They explained why each piece of work was chosen and how each showed communication. The students also wrote what they learned and what they liked about their pieces.

To keep track of all the pieces, the students in Mrs. Dewey's class made a Table of Contents. Jackie's Table of Contents is shown:

Jackie's Portfolio
Table of Contents

<u>Item</u>	<u>Description</u>	<u>Date</u>
P vs. L	I made runways of different lengths for Antopolis Airport.	September 20
Myrna Let.	I wrote about the width, length, and perimeter of runways.	October 1
Journal	My favorite mathematics activity in third grade.	October 3

Your teacher will help you select pieces for the portfolio. After you have started your portfolio, start a Table of Contents. The Table of Contents should include the name of each piece of work, a short description of the work, and the date it was finished. Add to the Table of Contents as you add to your portfolio.

Choose one of the following questions to write about. This work will be included in the portfolio.

1. What was your favorite mathematics activity last year? Why?

2. What would you like to learn in mathematics this year? Why?

Angles

Myrna's aunt, Cassandra, is in charge of designing a map for the runways at Antopolis Airport. In planning the map, she must think about several things such as how many runways are needed, how many planes will be landing at one time, and how many runways will fit in the area that is planned for the airport.

At first, Cassandra thinks the runways could be lined up in rows like the following picture:

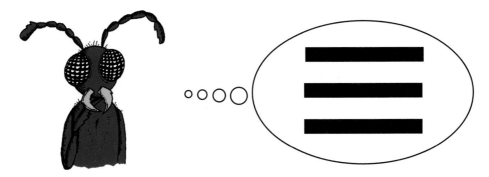

Then, she changes her mind because she knows the planes will be flying in from many different directions.

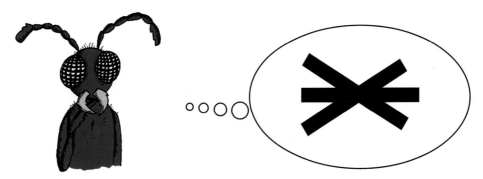

Cassandra decides to visit the airport at the nearby town, Anthill, to ask for some help. The manager of the airport asks, "Do you have any experience with angles?" Cassandra replies, "What are angles and how will they help me design the map for the runways at our airport?"

Here is what Cassandra learned.

What Is an Angle?

An **angle** is the amount of turning between two lines. The hands of a clock show turning.

The minute hand starts here:

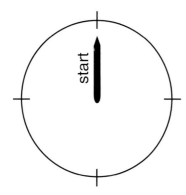

The hand turns to here:

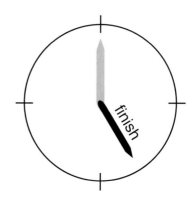

The amount of turning from start to finish shows the angle. The inside of the angle is shaded to show turning:

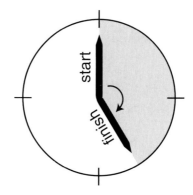

The size of the angle depends on the amount of turning. The more you turn, the larger the angle.

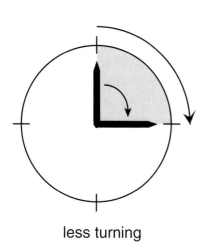

less turning

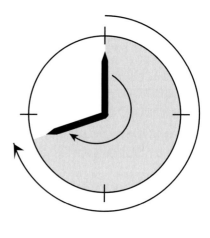

more turning

1. Compare the following pairs of shaded angles. For each pair, decide which shaded angle (the first or the second) has more turning.

A.

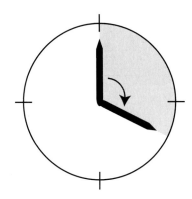 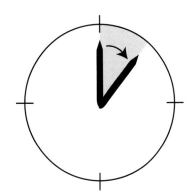

B.

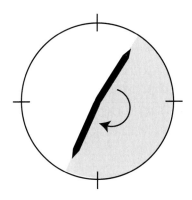 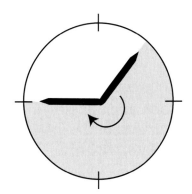

C.

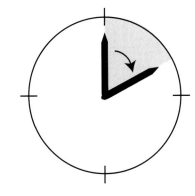 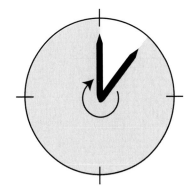

2. Mrs. Dewey's class used angle circles to make angles. For each angle circle, decide which angle, the white angle or the green angle, has more turning.

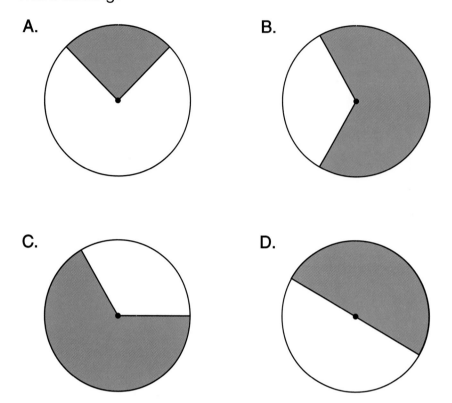

A.

B.

C.

D.

An angle with short sides can have more turning than another angle with longer sides. When you look at an angle, do not look at how long the sides are, but look at the amount of turning, or the inside of the angle. The angle on the right is bigger because it has more turning.

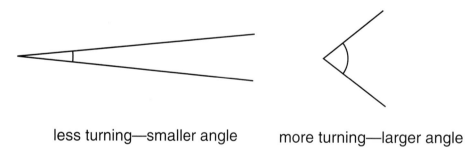

less turning—smaller angle   more turning—larger angle

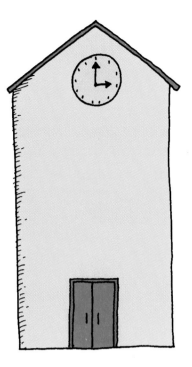

The hands of a clock on a building are much bigger than the hands of an alarm clock, but they can show the same amount of turning.

Angles in Shapes

Many shapes have angles that have already been made. Look at the cover of a book. You should see four angles on the front cover.

The figure below has five angles inside the shape.

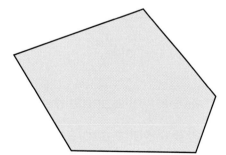

3. Look at the following shapes. How many angles do you see inside each shape?

A.

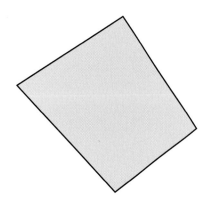

B.

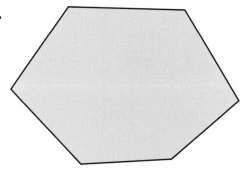

4. Look at the following shapes. How many angles do you see inside each shape?

A.

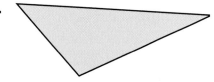

B.

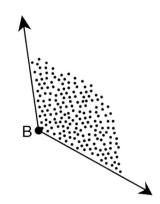

5. Look around the classroom. Find two angles in the room. Decide which of the two angles is larger. Remember, the angle with more turning is the larger angle.

Parts of an Angle

Every angle has two **sides.** We can think of the sides of an angle as the hands of a clock. The two sides of an angle meet at a point called the **vertex.** Sometimes an angle is named by its vertex.

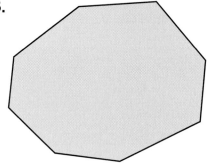

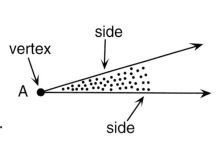

6. Use your angle circles to make a white angle that is larger than Angle A.

7. Use your angle circles to make a white angle that is smaller than Angle B.

Use a ruler to draw the following angles.

8. Draw an angle that is larger than Angle A. Label this Angle C.

9. Draw an angle that is smaller than Angle B. Label this Angle D.

10. Find an angle in the classroom that is larger than Angle A but is smaller than Angle B.

Degrees

We measure the amount of turning in angles by **degrees.** Larger angles have larger degree measures. If you turn all the way around in a circle, you have turned 360° (read as 360 degrees). The little circle (°) is an abbreviation for the word degree.

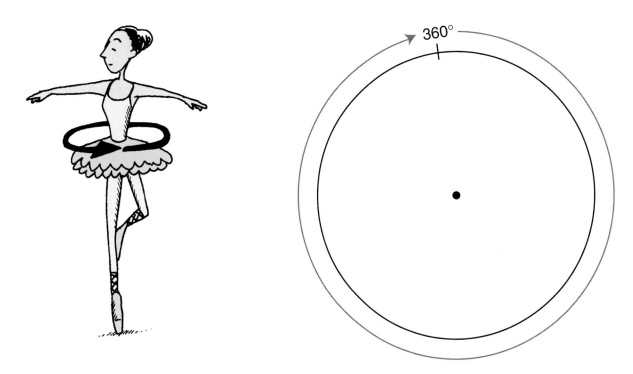

Use your calculator if needed to answer Questions 11 and 12.

11. How many degrees have you turned
when you turn halfway around a circle?

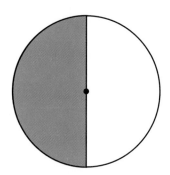

12. How many degrees have you turned
when you turn one-quarter of the way
around a circle?

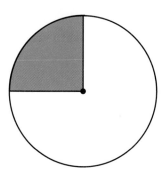

Right Angles

An angle that is easily recognized is a 90° angle
or quarter-turn. Corners of books, papers,
floors, and desks are usually right angles.
A 90° angle is called a **right angle.** Since a
right angle forms a square corner, a "box"
is often drawn at its vertex.

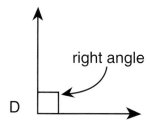

13. Make a white 90° angle with your angle circles.

14. Make a list of some right angles in your classroom.

15. Tear off one square corner from a piece of scrap paper.
Draw a box at the vertex to show a right angle.

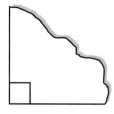

16. If a square corner of paper fits exactly in an angle, the angle is 90°. Use your piece of paper to decide if the following angles are right angles or not.

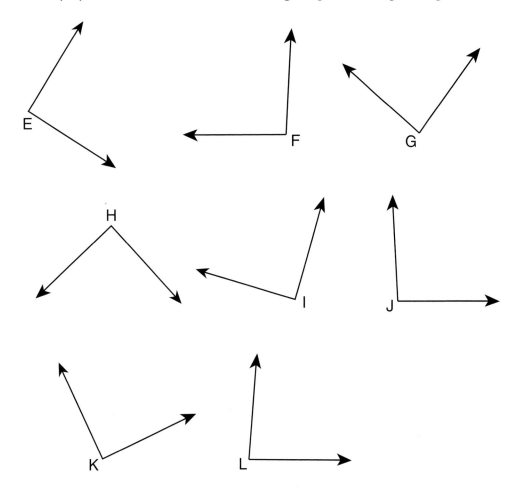

17. Use a ruler to draw an angle that is smaller than a right angle. Label the vertex with a letter. How can you show that this angle is less than 90°?

18. Use a ruler to draw an angle that is larger than a right angle. Label the vertex with a letter. How can you show that this angle is more than 90°?

19. This triangle contains a right angle. Which angle is the right angle?

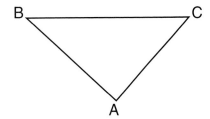

Acute Angles

These angles are **acute** angles:

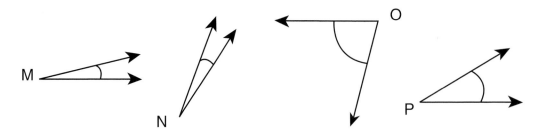

These angles are **not** acute angles:

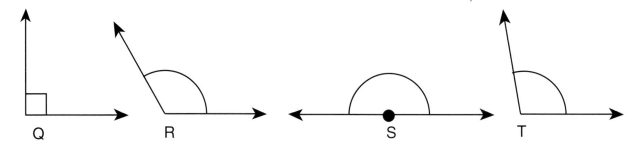

20. **A.** What can you say about the size of all of the acute angles?

    B. How would you describe an acute angle?

    C. Acute means sharp. Why is that a good name?

    D. Make an acute white angle with your angle circles.

21. Which angles in the figure below are right angles?
    Which angles are acute angles?

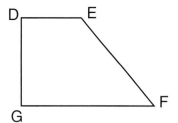

22. Tear off one square corner from a piece of scrap paper. Draw a box at the vertex to show the right angle. Fold the angle in half. What is the degree measure of the new angle? You may use your calculator if needed.

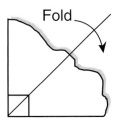

23. Use your new angle to estimate the measures of the following angles.

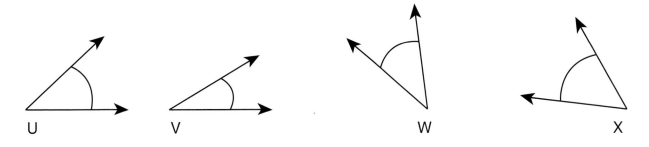

Obtuse Angles

These angles are acute angles:

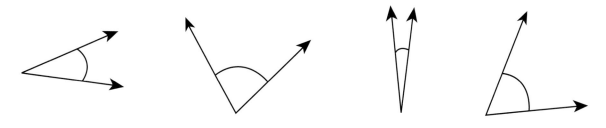

These angles are **obtuse** angles:

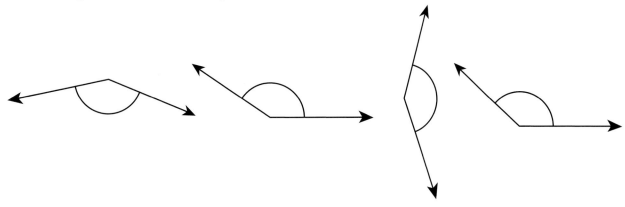

24. **A.** What can you say about the size of all of the obtuse angles?

   B. How would you describe an obtuse angle?

   C. Obtuse means dull. Why is that a good name?

   D. Make an obtuse white angle with your angle circles.

25. This triangle has an obtuse angle and two acute angles. Which is the obtuse angle?

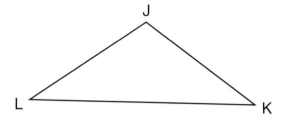

26. Here are some runway plans for Cassandra. For each plan, find the number of acute angles, obtuse angles, and right angles.

   A.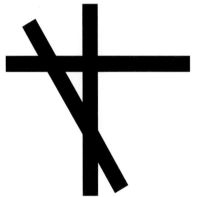

   B.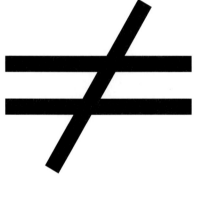

For each pair, say which is the larger angle.

1.

A.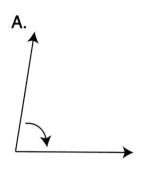

B.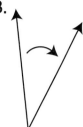

2.

A.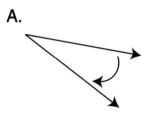

B.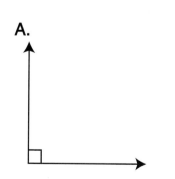

3.

A.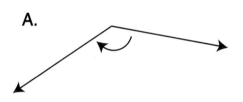

B.

4.

A.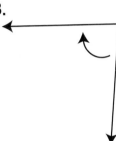

B.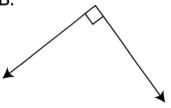

Name all the right angles, acute angles, and obtuse angles in the figures below.

5.

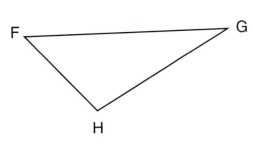

6.

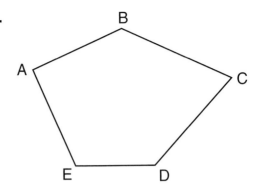

7. Draw two acute angles.

8. Draw two obtuse angles.

9. How many right angles do you have to put together to make one full turn?

10. Using a ruler, draw a shape with 4 angles.

11. Using a ruler, draw a shape with 5 angles.

Here are some more runway plans. For each plan, find the number of acute angles, obtuse angles, and right angles.

12.

13.

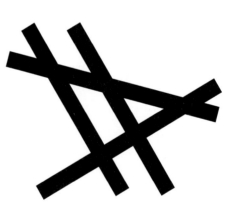

Angles in Pattern Blocks

Here are six pattern blocks and their names.

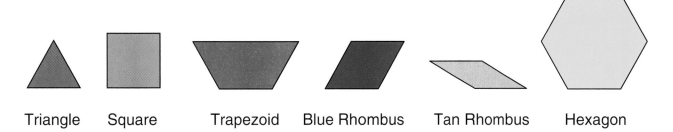

Triangle   Square   Trapezoid   Blue Rhombus   Tan Rhombus   Hexagon

1. Which shape has the smallest angle?

2. Which shape has the largest angle?

3. Which shapes have acute angles?

4. Which shapes have obtuse angles?

5. Which shapes have right angles?

6. Which shapes have both acute and obtuse angles?

7. A. Find angles in the pattern blocks that can be put together to make a right angle. Draw a picture of these pattern blocks. You may want to start by tracing a right angle. A right angle is shown here.

   B. Can you make a right angle with pattern blocks another way?

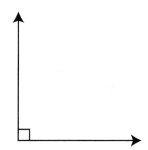

Homework

In class you explored pattern blocks and completed the table *Angle Measures in Pattern Blocks.* Use the table to answer the following questions.

1. The square has all 90° angles. Which other pattern blocks have angles that are all the same measurement?

2. A **quadrilateral** is a shape that has four sides (four angles).

    A. Make a list of the pattern blocks that are quadrilaterals.

    B. Find the sum of the angles of each of the quadrilaterals. For example, the sum of the angles for the square is 90° + 90° + 90° + 90° = 360°.

    C. What do you notice about the sum of the angles of the quadrilaterals in Question 2B?

Unit 3

NUMBERS AND NUMBER OPERATIONS

	Student Guide	Discovery Assignment Book	Adventure Book	Unit Resource Guide*
Lesson 1				
Multiplying and Dividing with 5s and 10s	◎	◎		◎
Lesson 2				
Roman Numerals	◎			
Lesson 3				
Place Value				◎
Lesson 4				
The TIMS Candy Company	◎			
Lesson 5				
Addition and Subtraction	◎			◎
Lesson 6				
What's Below Zero?	◎	◎		◎
Lesson 7				
At the Hardware Store	◎			

Unit Resource Guide pages are from the teacher materials.

Using Fact Families – Multiplying and Dividing with 5s and 10s

Jackson's Hardware Store decided to donate 30 basketballs to the schools in the neighborhood.

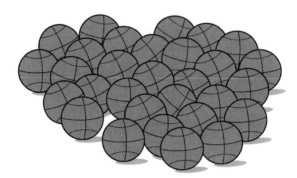

John and his father went to pick up the basketballs for Bessie Coleman school. When they arrived at the store there were people from four other schools waiting to pick up their basketballs. John helped divide the thirty basketballs into five groups.

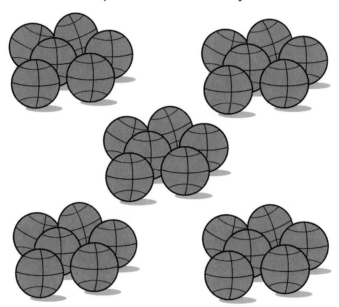

Each of the 5 schools got 6 new basketballs.

The **division sentence** for this is 30 ÷ 5 = 6. The answer to a division problem is called the **quotient.** In this sentence the quotient is six. Thirty, or the number to be divided, is the **dividend.** The **divisor** is five.

Then John told everyone that he would label all the basketballs with the correct school name. Everyone brought the new basketballs back to him for labeling, one school at a time. John added 6 + 6 + 6 + 6 + 6. He knew this was the same as five groups of six or 5 times 6, or 30 basketballs in all.

John knew that $5 \times 6 = 30$ is related to the division sentence $30 \div 5 = 6$. There are two more sentences that are related: $6 \times 5 = 30$ and $30 \div 6 = 5$. We call all four of these sentences together a **fact family.**

1. Jackson's Hardware also gave away a total of 30 soccer balls. Each school received a crate of six balls.

   A. How many schools got soccer balls? Write a number sentence to describe this.

   B. What does each number in the sentence represent?

2. John found he had 30 marbles at home and decided to give an equal number of marbles to each of his three sisters. How many marbles did John give to each sister? Draw a picture for this problem and describe it using a division sentence. Write another number sentence that is in the same fact family.

3. Nila wrote a division story for $20 \div 5$. Nila drew a picture for her story.

$20 \div 5$ There are 20 birds and 5 trees in the yard. Each tree has the same number of birds. How many birds are in each tree?

   A. What is another number sentence that is in the same fact family as $20 \div 5$?

   B. Write a division story for $50 \div 10$. Draw a picture for your story and write a number sentence. Write three more sentences that are in the same fact family.

4. Maya baked chocolate chip cookies. She counted out 45 cookies and put an equal number in each of 9 bags. Then she gave one bag of cookies to 9 friends.

   A. How many cookies did she give each friend? Write a number sentence for this story.

   B. Write a multiplication number sentence in the same fact family. What do the numbers in the multiplication sentence represent?

5. Which of the following number sentences is in the same fact family as $5 \times 8 = 40$?

   a) $40 \div 10 = 4$ **b)** $40 \div 5 = 8$ **c)** $8 \times 4 = 32$ **d)** $8 \times 5 = 40$

Solve Questions 6–15. Use fact families, manipulatives, or other strategies. Write a number sentence for each problem. Then write the other three sentences in the fact family.

6. How many dimes are in 80 cents?

7. How many nickels are in 35 cents?

8. How many nickels are in 15 cents?

9. How many nickels are in 40 cents?

10. How many dimes are in 60 cents?

11. How many nickels are in 20 cents?

12. How many dimes are in 40 cents?

13. Maya gets paid for helping her neighbor with her baby one afternoon each week. She saves all the money she gets and after five weeks, she has $25. How much money does Maya get paid each week? Write a number sentence.

14. How many weeks will Maya have to help her neighbor to make $45? Write a number sentence.

15. John lives 4 blocks from school. It takes him 20 minutes to walk to school. If John walks steadily, how long does it take John to walk one block? Write a number sentence.

Multiplying with 0 and 1

16. Think about multiplication as repeated addition of groups. Three groups of five makes fifteen. $3 \times 5 = 15$. Now think about what happens when you multiply with 1 or 0. How many groups do you have? How many are in each group? Try the following problems. You may want to use your calculator.

   A. $5 \times 0 =$

   B. $5 \times 1 =$

   C. $10 \times 0 =$

   D. $1 \times 10 =$

   E. $0 \times 98 =$

   F. $98 \times 1 =$

   G. $0 \times 5348 =$

   H. $1 \times 5348 =$

17. **A.** What can you say about multiplying numbers by 0? Explain.

   B. What can you say about multiplying numbers by 1? Explain.

Multiplication Facts and *Triangle Flash Cards*

With a partner, use the directions below and your *Triangle Flash Cards: 5s* and *Triangle Flash Cards: 10s* to practice the multiplication facts.

- One partner covers the shaded number, the largest number on the card. This number will be the answer to the multiplication problem. It is called the **product.**

- The second person multiplies the two uncovered numbers (one in a circle, one in a square). These are the two **factors.** It does not matter which of the factors is said first.
4×5 and 5×4 both equal 20.
$4 \times 5 = 20$ and $5 \times 4 = 20$ are called **turn-around facts.**

$5 \times 4 = ?$

$4 \times 5 = ?$

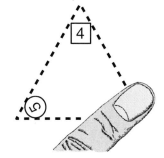

- Separate the facts into three piles: those facts you know and can answer quickly, those that you can figure out with a strategy, and those that you need to learn.

- Discuss how you can figure out facts that you do not recall right away. Share your strategies with your partner.

- Practice the last two piles again and then make a list of the facts you need to practice at home for homework.

- Circle the facts you know quickly on your *Multiplication Facts I Know* chart. Remember that if you know one fact, you also know its turn-around fact. Circle both on your chart.

- Review your answers to Question 17.

- You will continue to use *Triangle Flash Cards* to study other groups of facts. If you know one or two of the multiplication facts in a fact family, you can use those facts to help you learn the division facts.

Multiplication Facts I Know

×	0	1	2	3	4	5	6	7	8	9	10
0	0	0	0	0	0	0	0	0	0	0	0
1	0	1	2	3	4	5	6	7	8	9	10
2	0	2	4	6	8	10	12	14	16	18	20
3	0	3	6	9	12	15	18	21	24	27	30
4	0	4	8	12	16	(20)	24	28	32	36	40
5	0	5	10	15	(20)	25	30	35	40	45	50
6	0	6	12	18	24	30	36	42	48	54	60
7	0	7	14	21	28	35	42	49	56	63	70
8	0	8	16	24	32	40	48	56	64	72	80
9	0	9	18	27	36	45	54	63	72	81	90
10	0	10	20	30	40	50	60	70	80	90	100

Homework

1. How many dimes in 90 cents?

2. How many nickels in 30 cents?

3. Banks wrap dimes into packs of 50 dimes. If Nila takes 70 dimes to the bank to be wrapped, how many packs will she get? How many dollars will this be? How many dimes will be left over?

4. There are 20 Little League teams in the city. The League places 10 teams in a division. How many divisions will there be in the city? Write a number sentence for this story and all the number sentences in this fact family.

5. Write a story to show 45 ÷ 9. Draw a picture to go with your story and write a number sentence. Write all the other number sentences that are in this fact family.

6. Show two ways you can have 25 cents if you have only dimes and nickels.

7. Show three ways you can have 40 cents if you have only dimes and nickels.

8. Chewy Candies come in packs of five. Irma has 3 packs, Michael has 5 packs, Romesh has 1 pack, and Jessie has no packs.

    A. How many candies does each student have? Write a number sentence for each student.

    B. How many candies do they have altogether?

9. Jacob has 60 cents and needs $1.00 for a show. How many dimes does he need to make $1.00?

10. A pack of Chewy Candies costs 15 cents. How many packs can you buy with $1.00? Explain your solution.

Roman Numerals

One day, Mrs. Dewey started math class by asking, "How many of you speak another language besides English?"

I speak Spanish.

I speak Chinese.

I speak Russian.

Many hands went up. Roberto and Ana speak Spanish, Ming speaks Chinese, and Nila speaks Arabic. Linda speaks Tagalog, a language spoken in the Philippines, and Nicholas speaks Russian.

"That's wonderful," said Mrs. Dewey. "Did you know that there are over 220 major languages in the world? Many cultures have their own language, but almost all share the same number system. They use the digits 0, 1, 2, 3, 4, 5, 6, 7, 8, 9 to count and compute."

The number system we and many other people use is called the Hindu-Arabic number system. It was invented around the 9th century A.D. Many cultures had invented number systems well before this. One that is still used sometimes in our culture is the **Roman numeral** system. You can sometimes find Roman numerals on clocks and on buildings and in movies. Sometimes the pages in the preface of a book are numbered using Roman numerals. Often, when people want to be a little bit fancy, they use Roman numerals. For example, the Super Bowls of the National Football League are all designated with Roman numerals.

The Romans used a system that was based on counting groups similar to ours. Romans didn't only make groups of ten, they also made groups of five. Archaeologists have found evidence that their system was being used around 260 BCE. No one is really certain about where the Roman symbols for the numerals came from. They may have come from finger counting used in the market or the tally marks used to keep track of things like farm animals and soldiers. Some of the modern Roman numerals we use now came from the words Romans used.

Roman Numerals and Symbols

Early Roman Numerals	Modern Roman Numerals	Hindu-Arabic Numbers	Possible Origins	
			Finger Counting or Latin Words	Tally Marks
I	I	1		I
V	V	5		V
X	X	10		X
	L	50		
C	C	100	The Latin word for one hundred is *centum*	(X)
Ɔ	D	500		
⏀	M	1000	The Latin word for one thousand is *mille*	<|>

To write a number like 123, Romans put together their symbols for one hundred, two tens, and three ones to write the number like this:

CXXIII

At first, the Romans just used the symbols for ones, tens, hundreds, and thousands. So a number like 876 might have looked like this:

CCCCCCCCXXXXXXXIIIIII

To help make these numbers shorter, Romans began using symbols for half of ten, half of one hundred, and half of one thousand. Then, they could write 876 as:

DCCCLXXVI

1. Use the chart to help you write these Roman numerals as Hindu-Arabic numbers:

   A. LXXXVIII

   B. MDCCLXXVII

   C. MMMMMMMMCCL

2. Write the following Hindu-Arabic numbers as Roman numerals:

   A. 68

   B. 108

   C. 286

3. In the earliest Roman times, four was written as "IIII" and nine was written as "VIIII." Later, a shorter way of writing numbers was invented. Study the table below to find the pattern for the shortcut. Copy the tables, then fill in the empty boxes in the top and bottom rows.

   A.

I	II	III	IV					IX	
1	2	3		5	6	7	8		10

   B.

	XII			XV		XVII		XIX	
11	12	13	14	15	16	17	18		20

   C.

X	XX		XL		LX	LXX		XC	C
10	20	30		50			80		100

   D. What patterns did you find?

   E. Can you give a rule for the shortcuts in the table?

This pattern or rule is called the **subtractive principle.** The symbol for a smaller number is placed before a symbol for the larger number to indicate that the smaller number should be subtracted from the larger. **I** can only come in front of the **V** or **X**. **X** can only be subtracted from **L** or **C**. **C** can only be subtracted from **D** or **M**.

4. Use this pattern to write the Hindu-Arabic numbers for the following Roman numerals.

    A. XXXIV   **B.** XLIV

    C. CMXCIX   **D.** MCMXLVIII

5. Write the Roman numerals for the following Hindu-Arabic numbers in more than one way.

    A. 54   **B.** 47

    C. 192   **D.** 1996

6. Ana said, "I can think of one number we can't write in Roman numerals." What number is Ana thinking about?

7. Where do you see Roman numerals today?

Homework

Dear Family Member:

Your child is learning how to translate our numbers (Hindu-Arabic) into Roman numerals. Ask your child about Roman numerals that he or she may have seen. Then, help your child with the translations. Encourage your child to use the Roman Numerals and Symbols chart as a guide.

Thank you for your cooperation.

1. Write these numbers using Roman numerals.

    A. 12   **B.** 74

    C. 126   **D.** 239

2. Write these Roman numerals as Hindu-Arabic numbers.

    A. XIV   **B.** DXLV

    C. DCCXXIII   **D.** CMXCVIII

The TIMS Candy Company

Mr. and Mrs. Haddad own a chocolate factory that makes Chocos. The name of their company is the TIMS Candy Company. They use base-ten pieces to keep track of how much candy they make.

They use a **bit** for each Choco.

Whenever there are 10 bits, they can be packed together to make a **skinny**.

When there are 10 skinnies, they can be packaged together to make a **flat**.

A group of 10 flats makes a **pack.**

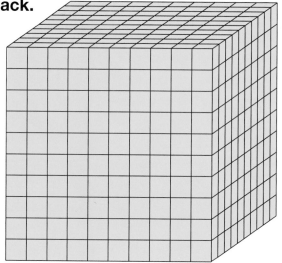

Mr. and Mrs. Haddad use a **Base-Ten Board** to show the bits, skinnies, flats, and packs. They also write the amounts in numbers on the **Recording Sheet.** For example, one day the company made 236 Chocos. This is how they recorded the candy:

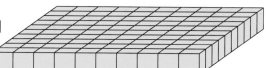

Base-Ten Board   **Recording Sheet**

	2	3	6

Rhonda and Joe work for the TIMS Candy Company.

1. Rhonda has 3 flats, 1 skinny, and 5 bits. How many pieces of candy is that?

Base-Ten Board

2. Joe has 4 packs, 2 flats, 3 skinnies, and 7 bits. How many pieces of candy is that?

Base-Ten Board

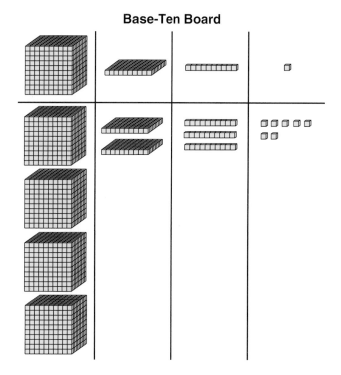

3. Rhonda had 15 bits, 3 flats, and 3 skinnies. She said this was 345 pieces of candy. Is she correct? If not, how many pieces of candy did she really have?

Base-Ten Board

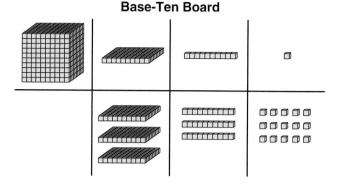

4. Joe had 5 flats, 12 skinnies, and 8 bits. He said this was 528 pieces of candy. Is he correct? If not, how many pieces of candy did he really have?

Base-Ten Board

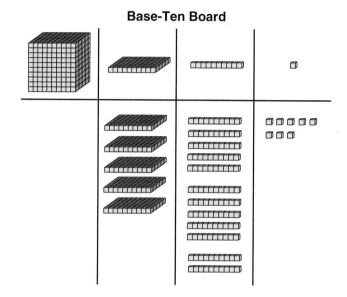

Sometimes Rhonda and Joe do not use the Base-Ten Boards. They put the blocks on a table.

5. Rhonda had 14 flats, 15 bits, and 4 skinnies. She said this was 1456 pieces of candy. Is she correct? If not, how many pieces of candy did she really have?

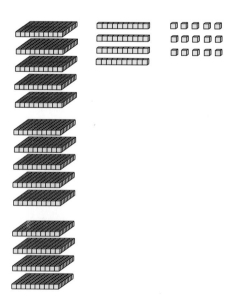

6. Joe had 2 packs, 5 skinnies, 4 flats, and 3 bits. He said this was 2543 pieces of candy. Is he correct? If not, how many pieces of candy did he really have?

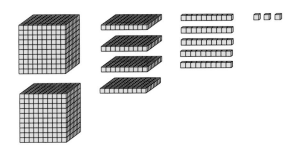

Base-Ten Shorthand

Sometimes it is useful to record your work with the base-ten pieces. Other times, base-ten pieces are not available but drawing a picture of the base-ten pieces is helpful. Mr. Haddad decided to use a shorthand for the base-ten pieces.

• = Bit   / = Skinny   ▢ = Flat   ▱ = Pack

7. Joe says there are often several ways to show an amount of candy on the Base-Ten Board. For example, 26 can be shown as:

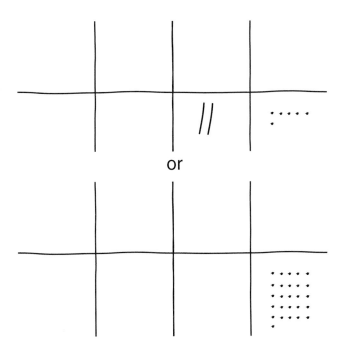

or

There is one more way 26 can be shown on the Base-Ten Board. What is this third way? Use base-ten shorthand to sketch your answer.

8. Use base-ten shorthand to show the number of candies Rhonda and Joe had in Questions 1–6.

9. Joe showed several ways of putting 32 Chocos on the Base-Ten Board by using base-ten shorthand. Some of Joe's work was erased. Fill in the missing pieces. Use base-ten shorthand to sketch your answer.

A. Here is one way to show 32.

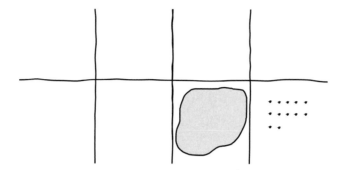

B. Here is another way to show 32.

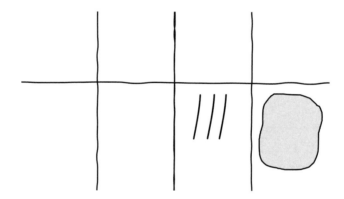

C. Here is a third way to show 32.

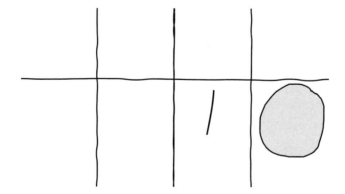

10. Rhonda made 267 pieces of candy. Fill in the missing information using base-ten shorthand and the Recording Sheet.

A. Here is one way to make 267.

Recording Sheet

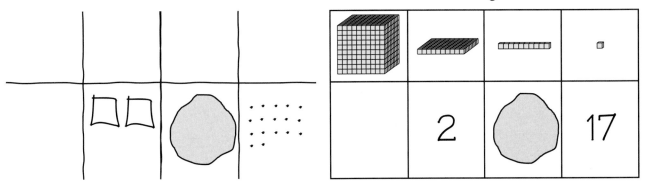

B. Here is another way to show 267.

Recording Sheet

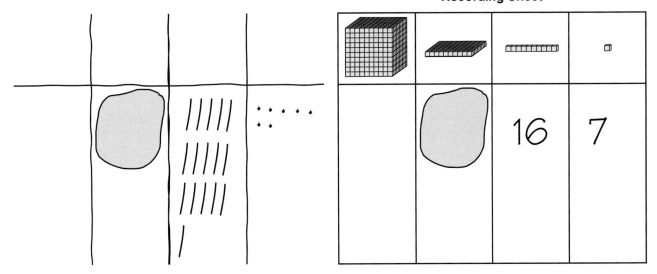

C. Here is a third way to show 267.

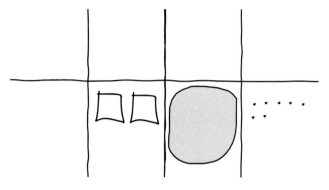

Recording Sheet

D. Here is yet another way to show 267.

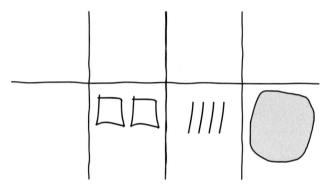

Recording Sheet

The Fewest Pieces Rule

The TIMS Candy Company decided that the best way to record the amount of candy it makes is to use the smallest possible number of base-ten pieces. The company calls this the **Fewest Pieces Rule.** For example, the best way to record 32 candies is to use 3 skinnies and 2 bits.

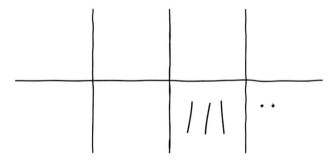

Recording Sheet

The best way to record 457 candies is to use 4 flats, 5 skinnies, and 7 bits.

Recording Sheet

	4	5	7

11. Show each number using the Fewest Pieces Rule. Record your answer by using base-ten shorthand. You do not have to sketch the columns.

   A. 236   **B.** 507   **C.** 5235   **D.** 6008

In problems 12–15:

   A. Write how many Chocos were made.

   B. Then, check if the Fewest Pieces Rule is followed. If it is not, use base-ten shorthand to show the candy using the fewest pieces possible.

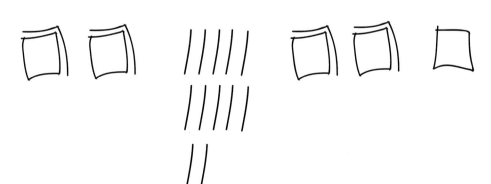

12.

13.

14.

15.

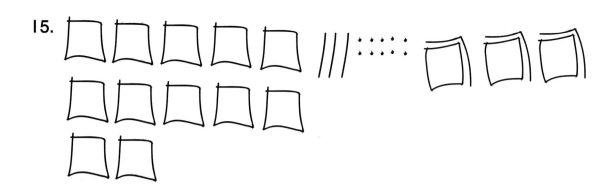

Discuss

16. The number **157** has 3 digits: the 1, the 5, and the 7. Explain the value of each of the digits. Do you have the same amount if you mix up the digits and write **571**? Explain why or why not.

Homework

Dear Family Member:

Your child is reviewing place value—the idea that the value of a digit in a number depends upon where it is placed. For example, the 2 in 329 stands for 2 tens but the 2 in 7293 is 2 hundreds.

In class your child uses base-ten pieces to represent numbers. When the pieces are not available, students are encouraged to draw pictures of the base-ten pieces. We call these drawings of the base-ten pieces base-ten shorthand. To help your child with homework Questions 1–11, you may wish to review the Base-Ten Shorthand section on the previous pages.

Thank you for your cooperation.

The sketches below show the number of Chocos made by workers at the TIMS Candy Company. Write the amount of candy using numbers.

1.

2.

3.

4.

5.

6.

The workers at the TIMS Candy Company recorded the amount of candy they made in numbers. Sketch each amount using base-ten shorthand.

7. 356

8. 4206

9. 240

10. 3005

11. One way to show 352 using base-ten shorthand is:

Sketch 352 two other ways using base-ten shorthand.

Addition and Subtraction

Addition

One day, Rhonda made 326 pieces of candy. She used the base-ten pieces to show her work. She recorded 3 flats, 2 skinnies, and 6 bits. Joe made 258 candies which he recorded as 2 flats, 5 skinnies, and 8 bits. Mrs. Haddad wanted to know how much candy they made altogether. She recorded her addition like this:

Base-Ten Board

Recording Sheet

3	2	6
2	5	8
5	7	14

Mrs. Haddad saw that she was not using the fewest base-ten pieces possible. Since there are 14 bits, she can make 1 more skinny with 4 bits left over. Mrs. Haddad recorded her work like this:

Recording Sheet

	3	2	6
+	2	5	8
	5	7^1	~~14~~
	5	8	4

1. On another day, Rhonda made 1326 candies and Joe made 575. They recorded their work by sketching the base-ten pieces using base-ten shorthand. Use your base-ten pieces to solve this problem.

Joe remembered the Fewest Pieces Rule and wrote:

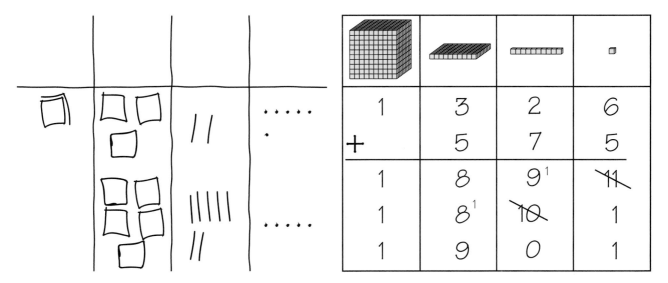

Mrs. Haddad noticed that drawing columns on the **Recording Sheet** was not necessary if she always used the Fewest Pieces Rule. Mrs. Haddad called this the **quick paper-and-pencil method for addition.** She wrote the problem like this:

$$13\overset{1}{\underset{}{2}}\overset{1}{6}$$
$$+ \ \ 575$$
$$\overline{1901}$$

At the end of one day Rhonda had made 1046, Joe had made 878, and Sam had made 767 candies. Mrs. Haddad found their total using the quick paper-and-pencil method:

$$1\overset{1}{0}\overset{1}{4}\overset{2}{6}$$
$$878$$
$$+ \ \ 767$$
$$\overline{2691}$$

2. Explain Mrs. Haddad's method for adding the three numbers.

---

3. Dominque has 325 baseball cards. Her sister Rosie has 416. About how many baseball cards do the two girls have altogether?

One way to estimate is to think about base-ten pieces. The number of baseball cards Dominque has is 3 flats and some more. The number of baseball cards Rosie has is 4 flats and some more. Together they have 7 flats and some more—or over 700 baseball cards.

Subtraction

Next to the factory, Mr. and Mrs. Haddad have a store where they sell their Chocos. They keep track of how much candy is sold using the base-ten pieces. Sometimes they have to break apart skinnies, flats, or packs to keep track of how much candy they have in the store.

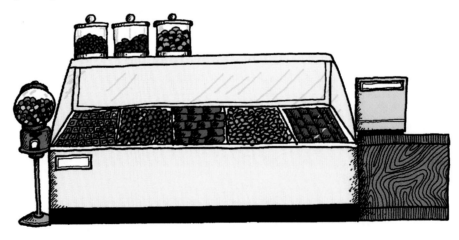

Addition and Subtraction

One morning, there were 3 flats, 6 skinnies, and 4 bits worth of candy in the store.

Base-Ten Board

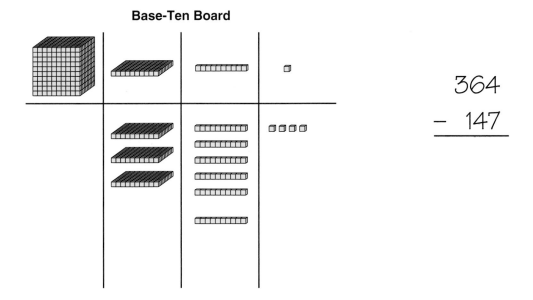

$$364$$
$$-\ 147$$

A customer came in and bought 147 pieces of candy. To find how much candy was left, Mrs. Haddad did the following:

Since 7 bits cannot be taken away from 4 bits, a skinny must be broken apart. Then there are 3 flats, 5 skinnies, and 14 bits. Now 1 flat, 4 skinnies, and 7 bits can be taken away.

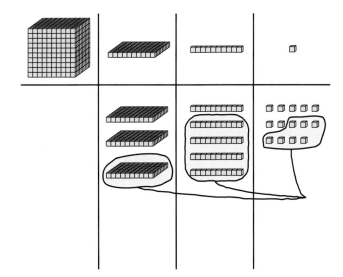

There are 2 flats, 1 skinny, and 7 bits left. Mrs. Haddad said she knew a different method to figure out how much candy is left.
This is what Mrs. Haddad did:

$$
\begin{array}{r}
3\,\overset{5}{\cancel{6}}\,\overset{1}{4} \\
-\ 1\ \ 4\ \ 7 \\
\hline
2\ \ 1\ \ 7
\end{array}
$$

4. Explain Mrs. Haddad's method in your own words.

Another day there were 1237 pieces of candy in the store. The store sold 459 pieces of candy that day. To find how much was left, Rhonda used Mrs. Haddad's method. Rhonda called this the **quick paper-and-pencil method for subtraction.**

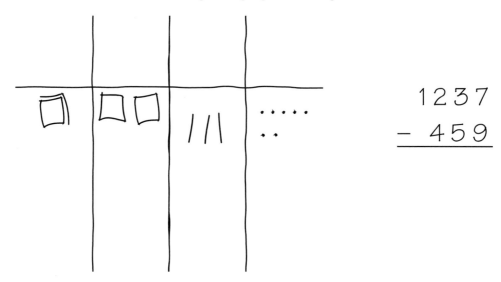

$$
\begin{array}{r}
1\,2\,3\,7 \\
-\ \ 4\,5\,9 \\
\end{array}
$$

Joe saw that he had to trade 1 skinny for 10 bits to subtract 9 bits.

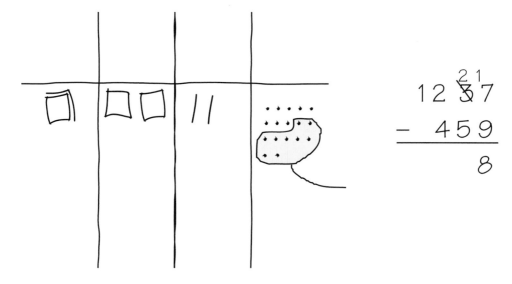

$$
\begin{array}{r}
1\,2\,\overset{2}{\cancel{3}}\,\overset{1}{7} \\
-\ \ \ 4\,5\,9 \\
\hline
8
\end{array}
$$

Joe then broke up one flat so that he had 12 skinnies and was able to subtract.

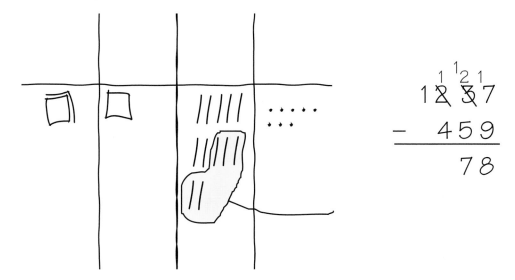

At the next step, Joe broke up his only pack so that he had 11 flats. Joe found that there were 778 pieces of candy left in the store.

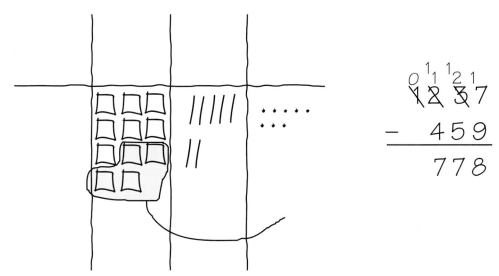

For problems 5–8:

A. Use base-ten pieces or base-ten shorthand to solve the problem.

B. Then, do the problem using paper and pencil or mental math.

5. There were 578 pieces of candy in the store (5 flats, 7 skinnies, and 8 bits). The store sold 349 pieces of candy. How many pieces of candy were left?

6. Another day there were 4443 pieces of candy and 1718 of them were sold. How many pieces of candy were left?

7. There are 2075 Chocos. The store sold 1539. How many are left?

8. There are 5204 Chocos. A customer came in and bought 565. Another customer came in and wanted to buy 4859 pieces of candy. Was there enough candy in the store so that he could buy so much?

Homework

In Questions 1 through 3, draw a picture of the problem using base-ten shorthand. Then, solve the problem using the picture to help you.

1. 364
    + 125

2. 1078
    + 2451

3. 1837
    + 2548

On Monday, Tuesday, and Wednesday, Rhonda and Joe were very busy and did not have time to compute their totals for the day. Help Rhonda and Joe compute their totals. Estimate to make sure your answer is reasonable.

Name	Monday	Tuesday	Wednesday
Rhonda	478	1003	576
Joe	589	1947	1756

4. How much candy was made on Monday?

5. How much candy was made on Tuesday?

6. Explain how you can compute the amount of candy made on Tuesday in your head.

7. How much candy was made on Wednesday?

8. How much candy did Rhonda make altogether on all three days?

9. How much candy did Joe make altogether on all three days?

10. How much candy did Rhonda and Joe make altogether on Monday, Tuesday, and Wednesday?

Solve the following problems. You may use any method you wish. Check your answer to make sure it is reasonable. Use base-ten shorthand when you need to.

11. 2357
     - 528

12. 2001
     - 432

13. 678
     + 1546

14. 1239
     - 643

15. The students from Livingston School and Stanley School are going on an outing. There are 765 students at Livingston School and 869 students at Stanley School. How many students are going on the outing?

16. To get free playground equipment, Livingston School needs to collect 4000 soup can labels by the end of the school year. In the first four months of school they collected 487 soup labels. By the end of the first semester they collected 752 more labels. How many more do they still need?

17. A high school has 2456 student desks. The principal decided that 548 of these desks should be replaced because they are not safe. How many old desks will be kept by the high school?

18. At Livingston School, Mr. Jones gave his class the following problem: Maya had 4006 stamps in her stamp collection. She sold 1658 of them. How many stamps does she have left? How would you solve this problem?

Maya thought about the base-ten pieces to solve Question 18.

John thought, "I can count up and do it in my head: 1658-2658-3658. That's 2000. Then 658-758-858-958. That's 300. Then 58-68-78-88-98 is 40. So far 2340. I have 8 more to go, so 2348 is the answer."

19. Think about John's method. Can you think of another way to do this problem? Describe your method.

What's Below Zero?

Professor Peabody, Rhonda, and Joe work for the TIMS Candy Company in Arizona. They decided to visit the TIMS Candy Company in Minnesota to check on the production of Chocos. Before traveling to Minnesota, they checked the weather report for Minnesota.

Professor Peabody, Rhonda, and Joe expect to arrive in Minnesota in approximately 6 hours.

Professor Peabody, Joe, and Rhonda decided to use a number line to check. The current temperature in Minnesota is 20°F. For the next 6 hours, the temperature will drop 5° each hour. The change in temperature is shown below on a number line.

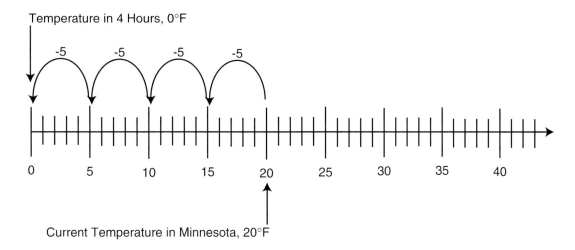

Rhonda and Joe are puzzled by the number line and the weather forecaster's prediction.

After four hours, according to our number line, there is no more temperature.

That can't be true. We need to extend the number line. The temperature is still going down according to the weather forecaster.

Rhonda and Joe need to extend the number line beyond zero. There are numbers that go to the left of zero on the number line. They are called **negative numbers.**

Historical Note: It was not until the 16th century A.D. that it was understood that there would be numbers "less than zero." Before that, if an answer was negative, it was regarded as absurd.

Negative numbers count back from zero just as **positive numbers** count up from zero. A number line with negative numbers and positive numbers is shown below.

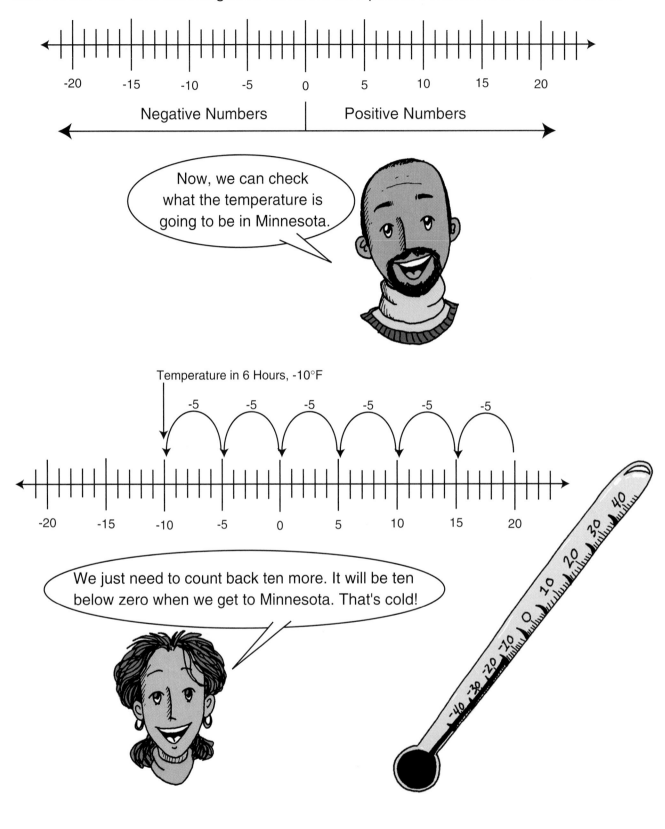

I must have forgotten my negative sign earlier when I said that the temperature would be 10°F.

It's a good thing we checked!

Discuss

You can tell the difference between negative and positive numbers by the way they are written. "Negative five" is written as "-5."

1. Check Joe and Rhonda's calculations for the temperature when they arrive in Minnesota with your calculator. Skip count backwards by subtracting 5. Start at 20 and press ⎡ − ⎤ ⎡ 5 ⎤ six times.

2. Describe what happened in your calculator's window as you subtracted five, six times.

Your calculator should show that the temperature in Minnesota in six hours will be -10°.

Joe, Rhonda, and Professor Peabody arrive in Minnesota and find that the temperature is in fact -10°F. They watch the weather report and find that the temperature will be twenty degrees warmer on Monday morning.

3. A. Use your number line to find the temperature on Monday morning if the current temperature is -10°F.

    B. Use your calculator to verify your work on the number line.

Joe, Rhonda, and Professor Peabody stay in Minnesota for a week. Professor Peabody recorded the temperature each morning and the change in temperature throughout the day.

This is shown in the data table below:

Day of Week	Temperature in Morning	Change in Temperature	Temperature in Evening
Monday	10°	drops 15°	
Tuesday	-5°	rises 35°	
Wednesday	-20°	drops 10°	
Thursday	15°	rises 20°	
Friday	20°	drops 20°	

4. Tell the temperature in the evening for each day. Use your number line and check your answer with a calculator.

5. On Friday evening, Joe, Rhonda, and Professor Peabody return to Arizona and find that the temperature is 85°F. If the temperature was -5°F when they left Minnesota, what is the change in temperature from Minnesota to Arizona? Explain.

Homework

Temperature Time

Use your number line or a calculator to find the final temperature for each of the temperature changes below.

1. It was -30°F at 10:00 this morning. The high temperature for the day was 10° higher than the temperature at 10:00 this morning. What was the high temperature for the day?

2. It was 20°F at 8:00 last night. The temperature dropped 20° overnight to reach the day's low temperature. What was the low temperature for the day?

3. The weather forecaster said that the current temperature is -15°F. The temperature is expected to drop 10 more degrees to reach the low temperature for the day. What is the low temperature expected to be?

Flying

Use a calculator to solve each of the following problems. List the keystrokes you used to solve each problem.

4. Chris was flying his plane at an altitude of 1000 feet. He decreased his altitude by 500 feet. What altitude was Chris then flying?

5. Walt took off from an airport whose altitude is 100 feet below sea level. He then flew his plane 600 feet up. What altitude was Walt then flying?

At the Bank

Show your work as you solve each of the following problems.

6. Sean opened a savings account with $50.00. He withdrew $45.00 and put it into a checking account. How much money was left in Sean's savings account?

7. Cindy opened a checking account with $5.00. She then wrote a check for $10.00. What is the balance in Cindy's account?

At the Hardware Store

Answer the following questions about the hardware store. Make sure you estimate to check if your answer is reasonable.

1. The hardware store has 576 drywall nails and 852 wood nails. How many drywall and wood nails does the store have altogether?

2. The hardware store has 217 cans of varnish. The store sold 89. How many are left?

3. The hardware store sells seed packets. It has 1145 vegetable seed packets and 2356 flower seed packets.

   A. Estimate the total number of seed packets in the store.

   B. Find the exact number of seed packets in the store.

4. On Monday morning the hardware store had 2675 flower seed packets. By Friday, 1005 of these packets had sold.

   A. How many flower seed packets were left?

   B. Explain a way to do this problem in your head.

5. The hardware store has 672 gallon cans of white indoor paint and 743 gallon cans of white outdoor paint. How many cans of white paint does the store have altogether?

6. The hardware store has 260 gallon cans of glossy white paint and 240 quart cans of glossy white paint.

   A. How many gallons is 240 quarts? Remember, there are 4 quarts in one gallon.

   B. What is the total amount in gallons of glossy white paint in the store?

7. Frank buys a 2025-foot roll of string. He cuts off 215 feet for his kite. How many feet are left on the roll?

8. A gardener goes to the hardware store to buy some bags of grass seed. He buys 2 large bags and 1 small bag. A large bag of grass seed covers about 3275 square feet. A small bag covers about 1770 square feet. About how many square feet of grass will the bags cover?

9. You need to cover 11,000 square feet of lawn with grass seed.

   A. How many bags of grass seed of each kind do you need?

   B. If a large bag costs $5.00 and a small bag costs $2.50, what does it cost to cover 11,000 square feet?

10. Frank broke open his piggy banks to go to the toy section of the hardware store. In one piggy bank he had 237 pennies. In another piggy bank, Frank had 522 pennies. In a sock in his drawer, Frank had 89 pennies.

    A. Explain a way to estimate the number of pennies Frank has altogether.

    B. Find the number of pennies Frank has.

    C. How much money does Frank have?

    D. A badminton set costs $9.51 with tax. How much more money does Frank need to buy the badminton set?

11. The hardware store sold 25 bags of seed on Monday, 32 on Tuesday, 11 on Wednesday, 9 on Thursday, and 41 on Friday. The hardware store then sold 197 bags of seed over the weekend.

    A. How many bags of seed did the hardware store sell from Monday to Friday?

    B. How many bags of seed did the hardware store sell all week?

    C. Did the hardware store sell more seeds from Monday to Friday or over the weekend?

    D. How many more bags of seed did the hardware store sell over the weekend than during the week?

Unit 4

Products and Factors

	Student Guide	Discovery Assignment Book	Adventure Book	Unit Resource Guide*
Lesson 1				
Multiplication and Rectangles	◎	◎		
Lesson 2				
Factors	◎			
Lesson 3				
Floor Tiler	◎	◎		
Lesson 4				
Prime Factors	◎			◎
Lesson 5				
Product Bingo	◎	◎		
Lesson 6				
Multiplying to Solve Problems	◎			

Unit Resource Guide pages are from the teacher materials.

Multiplication and Rectangles

Making Rectangles

I put these 12 tiles in 2 rows of 6 tiles, so 12 = 2 × 6.

I wonder if there are any other ways to arrange 12 tiles.

1. Make as many different rectangles as you can using 12 square-inch tiles. Then, complete a table like the one below to record your rectangles.

Rectangles Possible with 12 Tiles

Number of Rows	Number in Each Row	Multiplication Sentence
2	6	2 × 6 = 12

2. Draw your rectangles on *Square-Inch Grid Paper* and cut them out. Write a multiplication number sentence on each rectangle to match. Some rectangles like the 1 × 12 and 12 × 1 rectangles shown here have the same shape when you turn them sideways. You only have to cut out one of these.

3. Find all the rectangles you can make with 18 tiles. Follow the directions from Questions 1 and 2 using 18 tiles.

4. Your teacher will assign your group some of the numbers from 1 to 25.
   - For each number, arrange that many tiles into rectangles in as many ways as you can.
   - Then, draw the rectangles on *Square-Inch Grid Paper* and cut them out. Write number sentences on each rectangle to match.

5. Put your rectangles on a class chart.

6. Use the class chart of rectangles to make a table, like the one at the right, of the multiplication sentences for each of the numbers from 1–25. Use the *Rectangles* Activity Page in the *Discovery Assignment Book.*

1	2	3	4	5
1 × 1	2 × 1	3 × 1	4 × 1 2 × 2	5 × 1

Multiples

Use the rectangles the class made to answer the following questions:

7. Which numbers have rectangles with 2 rows? List them from smallest to largest.

8. Which numbers have rectangles with 3 rows? List them from smallest to largest.

A number is a **multiple** of 2 if it equals 2 times another whole number. If you can make a rectangle with 2 rows for a number then it is a multiple of 2.

Numbers that are multiples of two (2, 4, 6, 8, etc.) are called **even numbers.** Numbers that are not multiples of 2 (1, 3, 5, 7, etc.) are called **odd numbers.**

When you skip count, you say the multiples of a number. For example, skip counting by 3 gives the multiples of 3. The multiples of 3 are 3, 6, 9, 12, and so on. They are all the numbers that have rectangles with 3 rows.

9. Which numbers on the chart are multiples of 4 (have a rectangle with 4 rows)? List them from smallest to largest.

10. Which numbers on the chart are multiples of 5? List them from smallest to largest.

Prime Numbers

11. **A.** How many different rectangles can you make with 5 tiles?

    B. How many with 7 tiles?

Numbers that are larger than one and have only one rectangle have a special name. They are called **prime numbers.** For example, 5 and 7 are prime numbers.

12. List the prime numbers between 1 and 25.

13. Are all odd numbers prime? Explain.

Square Numbers

The number nine is special because it has a rectangle that is a square that has three rows and three columns.

14. Which other numbers have rectangles that are squares? These numbers are called **square numbers.**

15. Find the next largest square number after 25.

16. Another way mathematicians write 3×3 is 3^2. This is read "three to the second power" or "three squared." The raised 2 is called an **exponent.** Here are some more examples:

$$1^2 = 1 \times 1 = 1$$
$$2^2 = 2 \times 2 = 4$$
$$3^2 = 3 \times 3 = 9$$
$$4^2 = 4 \times 4 = 16$$

    A. What is 5^2?

    B. What is 6^2?

Arrays and Fact Families

17. My rectangle has a total of 18 square tiles. It has 3 rows of tiles.

   A. How many tiles are in each row? Write a number sentence for this rectangle.

   B. What are the other three sentences that are in this same family? Explain how all these sentences fit with this rectangle. Use the total number in each column in your explanation.

18. Another rectangle has 3 rows of tiles and a total of 24 square tiles.

   A. Write a number sentence to fit this rectangle.

   B. What are all the other number sentences in the same fact family?

19. A. Write a multiplication number sentence for a rectangle with 4 tiles in all and 2 tiles in each row.

   B. Can you write a different multiplication sentence for this rectangle? Why or why not?

   C. Write a division sentence for this rectangle.

   D. Can you write a different division sentence for this number?

20. A rectangle is made of 9 tiles and has 3 tiles in each row.

   A. How many different number sentences can you write for this rectangle?

   B. Look at the rectangles for the other square numbers. How many facts are in their fact families?

21. A. Write all the number sentences in the fact family for 5×2.

   B. Write all the number sentences in the fact family for 5^2.

You can draw pictures of rectangles on *Square-Inch Grid Paper* to help you solve these problems.

1. John built rectangles with 20 tiles, but some of his work was erased. Help John fill in the missing numbers.

Rectangles Possible with 20 Tiles

Number of Rows	Number in Each Row	Multiplication Sentence
1		$1 \times ? = 20$
	10	$? \times 10 = 20$
4		$4 \times ? = 20$
5		$5 \times ? = 20$
	2	$? \times 2 = 20$
20		$20 \times ? = 20$

2. **A.** Is 36 an even number? How do you know?

   B. Is 36 a square number? How do you know?

3. Find multiples by skip counting.

   A. Multiples of 2: Start at zero and skip count by 2s to 50.

   B. Multiples of 3: Start at zero and skip count by 3s to 48.

   C. Multiples of 5: Start at zero and skip count by 5s to 50.

   D. Multiples of 6: Start at zero and skip count by 6s to 48.

4. Tell whether the following numbers are even or odd.

   A. 10   **B.** 17   **C.** 21   **D.** 44

5. Jane says that any number that ends in 2, like 12, 72, and 102, is an even number. What other digits can even numbers end in?

6. A. Which of the following are multiples of 5?

    20   34   45   56   60   73   35

    B. Can you tell whether a number is a multiple of 5 by looking at the last digit? If so, tell what digits the multiples of 5 end in.

7. A. Which number in each of the following pairs is a multiple of 3?

    11   21 (last digit 1)
    12   22 (last digit 2)
    23   33 (last digit 3)
    14   24 (last digit 4)
    15   25 (last digit 5)
    16   36 (last digit 6)
    17   27 (last digit 7)
    18   28 (last digit 8)
    39   19 (last digit 9)

    B. Can you tell whether a number is a multiple of 3 by looking at its last digit? If so, tell what digits multiples of 3 end in.

8. Write the following multiplication problems using exponents. Then multiply.

    A. 2×2 **B.** 5×5 **C.** 7×7 **D.** 10×10

9. Rewrite the following without using exponents. Then multiply.

    A. 8^2 **B.** 3^2 **C.** 9^2

10. Ming has 32 rocks in his rock collection. He wants to buy a rectangular display box with one square compartment for each rock. At the store he found boxes with 6 rows and 6 columns, 8 rows and 4 columns, 2 rows and 16 columns, and 3 rows and 10 columns. Which boxes will hold his collection with no empty compartments?

Factors

Tile Problems

Use *Square-Inch Grid Paper* or tiles to help you solve these problems. Write a number sentence to go with each problem.

1. Shannon made a rectangle with 32 tiles. If there were 4 rows, how many tiles were in each row?

2. Roberto made a rectangle with 6 rows and 5 tiles in each row. How many tiles did he use?

3. Jackie made a rectangle with 21 tiles. There were 7 tiles in each row. How many rows were there?

4. A rectangle of 12 tiles has 3 different colors. There is an equal number of each color. How many of each color are there?

Finding Factors

Jacob wondered whether he could arrange 24 tiles into 5 rows. He used his calculator to divide 24 into 5 groups.

Hmm. 24 ÷ 5 equals 4.8, so that means $4\frac{8}{10}$ tiles would go in each row. That's not possible, since I can't cut the tiles.

The **factors** of a number are the whole numbers that can be multiplied to get the number. For example, $3 \times 8 = 24$, so 3 and 8 are factors of 24. All the factors of 24 are 1, 2, 3, 4, 6, 8, 12, and 24, because we can multiply pairs of numbers to get 24 in the following ways: 1×24, 2×12, 3×8, and 4×6.

The factors of a number can also be described as the whole numbers that divide the number evenly. Two is a factor of 24 because $24 \div 2 = 12$. But 5 is not a factor of 24 because $24 \div 5 = 4.8$ which is not a whole number.

The factors of a number tell us which numbers of rows are possible in rectangles made with that number of tiles. Jacob couldn't make a rectangle with 5 rows and 24 tiles because 5 is not a factor of 24.

5. A. Is it possible to make a rectangle with 24 tiles and 6 rows? If so, how many tiles would be in each row? Use your calculator to check.

　　 B. Is it possible to make a rectangle with 24 tiles and 7 rows? Use your calculator to check. Explain.

6. A. Is 5 a factor of 38? Why or why not?

　　 B. Is it a factor of 35? Why or why not?

7. A. Is 8 a factor of 32? Why or why not?

　　 B. Is it a factor of 36? Why or why not?

8. The band leader at Coleman School wants to arrange the 48 members of its marching band into rows with an equal number of students in each row.

   A. Can he arrange them into 6 rows? Is 6 a factor of 48?

   B. Can he arrange them into 7 rows? Is 7 a factor of 48?

   C. Can he arrange them into 8 rows? Is 8 a factor of 48?

9. A. Make a table like the one at right to show all of the rectangles that can be made with 20 tiles. Use a calculator or multiplication facts to help you divide.

   B. Use your table to help you list the factors of 20.

   C. Look back at Lesson 1, Question 1 in the Homework section on page 100. What do you notice about the table in Lesson 1 and this table? What is the same and what is different?

Rectangles Possible with 20 Tiles

Number of Rows	Number in Each Row	Division Sentence
1	20	$20 \div 1 = 20$
2	10	$20 \div 2 = 10$

10. A. Make a table like the one in Question 9 to show all of the rectangles that can be made with 36 tiles.

    B. Use your table to help you list the factors of 36.

11. Find the factors of:

    A. 12   B. 16   C. 18

A **prime number** is any number greater than one that has only two factors—itself and one. Thirteen is a prime number because its only factors are 13 and 1. Fourteen is not a prime number because it has four factors: 1, 2, 7, and 14.

12. Which of the following are prime numbers? Explain.

    A. 35   B. 27   C. 41

Homework

More Tile Problems

Use *Square-Inch Grid Paper* to help you solve these problems. Write a number sentence to go with each problem.

1. Irma made a rectangle with 28 tiles. If there were 7 rows, how many tiles were in each row?

2. Keenya made a rectangle with 8 rows and 5 tiles in each row. How many tiles did she use?

3. Romesh made a rectangle with 42 tiles. There were 6 tiles in each row. How many rows were there?

4. A rectangle of 18 tiles has 3 different colors. There is an equal number of each color. How many of each color are there?

More Finding Factors Problems

5. **A.** Make a table like the one at right to show the rectangles that can be made with 28 tiles. You can use a calculator, multiplication facts, or *Square-Inch Grid Paper* to help you divide.

   B. Use the table to help you list the factors of 28.

Rectangles Possible with 28 Tiles

Number of Rows	Number in Each Row	Division Sentence
1	28	28 ÷ 1 = 28
2	14	28 ÷ 2 = 14

6. **A.** Make a table similar to that in Question 5 to show the rectangles that can be made with 40 tiles.

   B. List the factors of 40.

7. **A.** Is 3 a factor of 27? How do you know?

   B. Is 7 a factor of 32? How do you know?

8. List all the factors of:

   A. 6

   B. 30

   C. 32

Factors

9. Help the Sunny Fruit Company design a rectangular-shaped box for shipping four dozen oranges. (How many oranges are in four dozen?) How many layers will your box have, how many rows of oranges will be in each layer, and how many oranges will be in each row? (There is more than one way to do this.)

10. Which of the following are prime numbers? How do you know?

A. 39

B. 51

C. 67

11. Challenge question: Find all the prime numbers between 25 and 50. Explain what you did to find your answer.

Floor Tiler

This game can be played by two or more players.

Materials

- $\frac{1}{2}$ sheet of *Centimeter Grid Paper*
- *Spinners 1–4 and 1–10* Activity Page
- A clear plastic spinner or a paper clip and pencil
- A crayon or marker for each player

Rules

1. The first player makes two spins so that he or she has two numbers. The player may either spin one spinner twice or spin each spinner once.

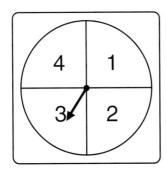 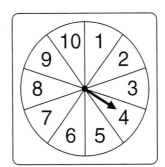

2. The player must then find the **product** of the two numbers he or she spun. For example, $3 \times 4 = \mathbf{12.}$ 12 is the product. The product is the answer to a multiplication problem.

3. After finding the product, the player colors in a rectangle that has the same number of grid squares on the grid paper. For example, he or she might color in 3 rows of 4 squares for a total of 12 squares. But the player could also color in 2 rows of 6 squares or 1 row of 12 squares. (Remember, the squares colored in must connect so that they form a rectangle.)

4. Once the player has made his or her rectangle, the player draws an outline around it and writes its number sentence inside. For example, a player who colored in 3 rows of 4 squares would write "3 × 4 = 12." A player who colored in 2 rows of 6 squares would write "2 × 6 = 12."

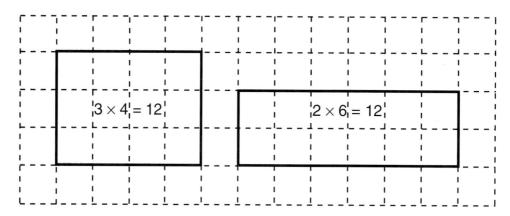

5. Players take turns spinning and filling in their grids.

6. If a player is unable to fill in a rectangle for his or her spin, that player loses the turn, and the next player can play.

7. The first player to fill in his or her grid paper completely wins the game.

Prime Factors

Multiplying Three Factors

Mrs. Dewey asked her class to multiply $3 \times 4 \times 5$.

David multiplied 3×4 first.

③ × ④ × 5

12 × 5

60

Arti multiplied 4×5 first.

3 × ④ × ⑤

3 × 20

60

Lin multiplied 3×5 first.

③ × 4 × ⑤

15

4 × 15

60

1. When you find a product like $3 \times 4 \times 5$, you can only multiply 2 numbers at a time. It does not matter which two you multiply first. Multiply the following at least two different ways.

   A. $2 \times 2 \times 3 =$

   B. $2 \times 3 \times 3 =$

2. Find the products. You may use mental math, a calculator, or your multiplication tables.

   A. $2 \times 2 \times 5 =$ **B.** $2 \times 3 \times 5 =$

   C. $3 \times 3 \times 3 =$ **D.** $2 \times 5 \times 5 =$

   E. $4 \times 2 \times 5 =$ **F.** $4 \times 3 \times 2 =$

   G. $5 \times 6 \times 3 =$ **H.** $3 \times 6 \times 2 =$

Finding Prime Factors

Mrs. Dewey asked her class to write 24 as the product of at least three factors. Students had many different answers:

Luis:	$24 = 3 \times 4 \times 2$
Nicholas:	$24 = 3 \times 2 \times 2 \times 2$
Michael:	$24 = 6 \times 2 \times 2$
Nila:	$24 = 2 \times 3 \times 2 \times 2$

Which of these four ways show factors for 24 that are all prime?

The class noticed that all the factors Nicholas found were prime numbers. They are called the **prime factors** of 24. Nila found the same prime factors, but wrote them in a different order. There are many ways to factor a number, but only one way (not counting the order in which they are written) in which all the factors are prime numbers.

Nicholas showed how he found the prime factors of 24. He wrote: $24 = 3 \times 8$.

Then, he replaced the 8 with 4×2: $24 = 3 \times \mathbf{4 \times 2.}$

Next, he replaced the 4 with 2×2: $24 = 3 \times \mathbf{2 \times 2} \times 2$.

He stopped because none of the factors could be replaced. They were all prime.

Mrs. Dewey showed another way to write Nicholas's solution. She used a **factor tree.**

She factored 24 into 3 × 8. She circled the 3 because it cannot be factored anymore (it is prime). She factored 8 into 4 × 2 and circled the 2 because it is prime. She factored 4 into 2 × 2 and circled the 2s. She multiplied the circled numbers and got the same answer as Nicholas: 24 = 3 × 2 × 2 × 2.

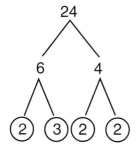

Nila decided to use a factor tree to show her solution. She factored 24 into 6 × 4. She decided not to write the multiplication signs in her factor tree. That was O.K.

She factored 6 into 2 × 3 and 4 into 2 × 2. She circled the 2s and the 3 because they were prime and could not be factored anymore.

She multiplied the prime numbers she had circled and got: 24 = 2 × 3 × 2 × 2.

Nila's answer was the same as Nicholas's, even though her factor tree was different.

3. John started the following factor tree for 24. Continue building his tree until all the numbers are prime. What factorization does your tree give you of 24?

Prime Factors

4. Complete the following factor trees for 36. Write 36 as a product of its prime factors.

A.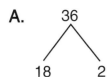
36
18   2

B.
36
12   3

C.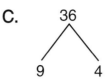
36
9   4

D.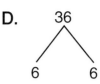
36
6   6

5. Use factor trees to factor each of the following numbers into primes. Write number sentences to show your answers.

   A. 18
   B. 12
   C. 56
   D. 90

6. I am a prime number between 10 and 20. I am one more than a square number. What number am I?

7. I am a multiple of 3. I am a square number. I am less than 20. What number am I?

8. I am a multiple of 5. Two is not one of my factors. I am not prime and I am not square. I am less than 30. What number am I?

Did You Know?

Some mathematicians study ways to factor large numbers. This is part of a branch of mathematics called number theory. Mathematicians study number theory because it is fun and interesting. Many of the discoveries that mathematicians made about number theory later turned out to be very useful. For example, factoring is important in making and breaking secret codes.

Exponents

Lee Yah factored 45 into prime factors. She wrote $45 = 5 \times 3 \times 3$. Linda found the same prime factors of 45 but wrote them using an exponent: $45 = 5 \times 3^2$.

John factored 32. He wrote $32 = 2 \times 2 \times 2 \times 2 \times 2$. He wondered whether there was a shortcut for writing this. Mrs. Dewey showed how exponents can be used as a shortcut for writing products of the same factor:

$2 \times 2 \times 2 = 2^3$ (We read this as "2 cubed" or "two to the third power.")

Three is the **exponent.** Two is the **base.** The exponent tells us to multiply by 2, three times.

$2 \times 2 \times 2 \times 2 = 2^4$ (We read this as "two to the fourth power.")

$2 \times 2 \times 2 \times 2 \times 2 = 2^5$ (We read this as "two to the fifth power.")

How would you use this shortcut to write $3 \times 3 \times 3 \times 3$?

Jerome factored 72. He wrote $72 = 3 \times 3 \times 2 \times 2 \times 2$. Then, he wrote this with exponents: $72 = 3^2 \times 2^3$.

Prime Factors

9. Rewrite the following factorizations using exponents:

   A. $600 = 2 \times 2 \times 2 \times 3 \times 5 \times 5$

   B. $378 = 2 \times 3 \times 3 \times 3 \times 7$

   C. $250 = 2 \times 5 \times 5 \times 5$

   D. $99 = 3 \times 3 \times 11$

10. Use exponents to rewrite each factorization you found in Question 5.

11. Write each of the following products without using exponents. Then multiply.

    A. $2^3 \times 3$

    B. $3^2 \times 5$

    C. 2×5^2

    D. $7^2 \times 2$

12. Find the prime factors of each of the following numbers. Write your answers using exponents.

    A. 100

    B. 40

    C. 80

    D. 500

Homework

1. Find the products. You may use mental math, a calculator, or your multiplication table.

   A. $2 \times 3 \times 3 =$ **B.** $3 \times 2 \times 3 =$

   C. $2 \times 2 \times 2 =$ **D.** $3 \times 3 \times 5 =$

   E. $3 \times 3 \times 3 =$ **F.** $2 \times 2 \times 5 =$

   G. $3 \times 2 \times 5 =$ **H.** $7 \times 3 \times 2 =$

   I. $5 \times 4 \times 3 =$ **J.** $3 \times 4 \times 2 =$

2. Determine which of the following are prime numbers. If a number is prime, tell how you know. If it is not prime, write it as the product of prime factors.

   A. 6
   B. 17
   C. 12
   D. 39

3. Use factor trees to factor each of the following numbers into primes. Write multiplication sentences to show your answers.

   A. 20
   B. 28
   C. 60
   D. 48
   E. 54
   F. 72
   G. 100
   H. 42

4. I am a multiple of 2. I am not a multiple of 3. I am greater than 10 but less than 20. I am not a square number. What number am I?

5. I am between 6 and 35. I am one more than a square number. Five is one of my factors. What number am I?

6. I am the smallest square number that has the factors 2 and 3. What number am I?

7. Write your own number puzzle, similar to the ones in Questions 4–6. Use some of the following words: multiple, factor, prime number, square number.

8. Rewrite the following factorizations using exponents:

   A. $200 = 2 \times 5 \times 5 \times 2 \times 2$
   B. $600 = 2 \times 3 \times 2 \times 5 \times 2 \times 5$
   C. $1200 = 2 \times 2 \times 3 \times 2 \times 2 \times 5 \times 5$
   D. $1500 = 2 \times 5 \times 2 \times 5 \times 5 \times 3$

9. Write each of the following products without exponents. Then multiply.

   A. $2^2 \times 3^2$
   B. $3^3 \times 4^2$
   C. $2^2 \times 5^2$
   D. $2^4 \times 3$

10. Find the prime factorizations of each of the following numbers. Write your answers using exponents.

    A. 50
    B. 66
    C. 96
    D. 300

Prime Factors

Product Bingo

This is a game for five players. You need a clear plastic spinner and beans or something else to use as markers. If you don't have a spinner, you can use a pencil and a paper clip.

One player is the Caller. The other players each choose a game board from the *Product Bingo Game Boards* Game Page in the *Discovery Assignment Book.*

The Caller spins the spinner twice. If the product of the spun digits is on your game board, then put a marker on it. The Caller should keep track of all digits spun by writing multiplication sentences on a piece of paper.

The first player with four markers in a row or a marker in each corner is the winner. (The **P** space, for **P**roduct, is a free space.)

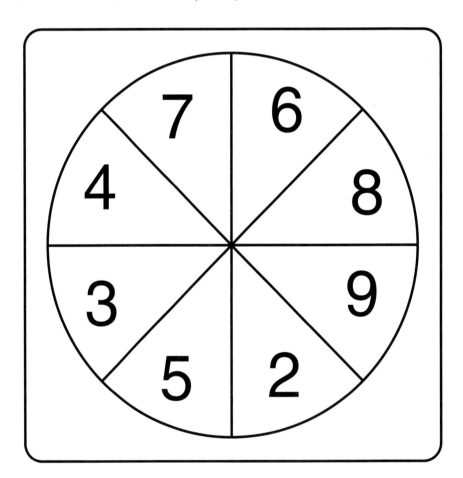

Answer these questions after you have played *Product Bingo.*

1. Which game board is the best?

2. Which game board is the worst?

3. Why is the best game board better than the worst one?

4. Design your own *Product Bingo* game board.

   A. First, draw an empty game board:

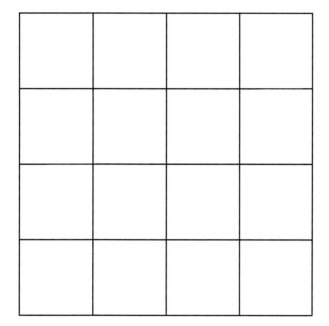

   B. Second, write products of the numbers 2 through 9 in all the squares except one.

   C. Finally, put a **P** in the last square.

5. Play *Product Bingo* using your game board. Did you win or not? Explain why.

Multiplying to Solve Problems

Use paper and pencil, calculators, your multiplication tables, mental math, or manipulatives to solve the following problems.

1. A movie theater has 20 rows with 10 seats in each row. How many seats are in the theater?

2. Twelve yards of fabric were used to make 4 dresses. How many such dresses can be made with 15 yards of fabric?

3. Jacob and his sister gave their mother a box of candy for Mother's Day. The box had 2 layers. Each layer had 5 rows with 8 pieces in each row. How many pieces of candy were in the box?

4. Jessie went to the Post Office to buy a block of 30 stamps. (Stamps usually come in rectangular blocks.) What are the possible rectangles of a block of 30 stamps? Tell how many rows and how many stamps are in each row.

5. Maya bought a box of paint at the hardware store. If the box had 3 levels of gallons of paint with 3 rows of 4 gallons of paint in each row, how many gallons of paint were in the box?

6. A. In the morning, 80 new math books were delivered to the school in 10 identical boxes. How many books were in each box if each box had the same number of books?

   B. In the afternoon, 48 more math books were delivered in the same size boxes. How many boxes of books were delivered in the afternoon?

Unit 5

Using Data to Predict

	Student Guide	Discovery Assignment Book	Adventure Book	Unit Resource Guide*
Lesson 1				
Predictions from Graphs	◎	◎		
Lesson 2				
Another Average Activity	◎			
Lesson 3				
The Meaning of the Mean	◎			◎
Lesson 4				
Bouncing Ball	◎			
Lesson 5				
Two Heads Are Better Than One			◎	
Lesson 6				
Professor Peabody Invents a Ball				◎
Lesson 7				
Speeds at the Indianapolis 500	◎			
Lesson 8				
Midterm Test				◎

Unit Resource Guide pages are from the teacher materials.

Predictions from Graphs

Graphs can tell stories. The following graph tells a story about the men's long jump competition in the Olympics. Contestants in the long jump try to jump as far as possible with a running start.

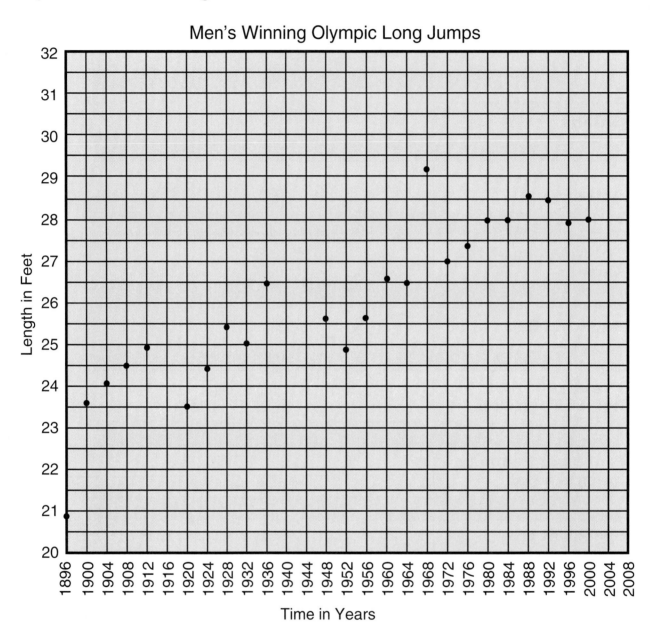

Men's Winning Olympic Long Jumps

I. **A.** What variable is on the horizontal axis?

  B. What variable is on the vertical axis?

---

2. Jesse Owens won the long jump competition in 1936.
   A. How far did he jump?
   B. Is the distance Jesse Owens jumped longer or shorter than the length of your classroom?
   C. How many years passed before someone jumped farther than Jesse Owens in the Olympics?

3. A. Describe the graph. What does it look like?
   B. If you read the graph from left to right, do the points tend to go uphill or downhill?
   C. What does the graph tell you about the winning long jumps in the Olympics?

4. In 1968 Bob Beamon of the United States won the long jump competition.
   A. How far did Beamon jump?
   B. What is unusual about this point on the graph?
   C. Do you think the winner in 2008 will jump as far as Bob Beamon jumped in 1968? Why or why not?

Here is another graph. It shows the history of the mile run in college championship races. Runners do not run the mile anymore in these track meets because the distances are measured using the metric system. Contestants now run 1500 meters, which is a little shorter than a mile.

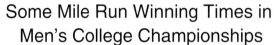

Some Mile Run Winning Times in
Men's College Championships

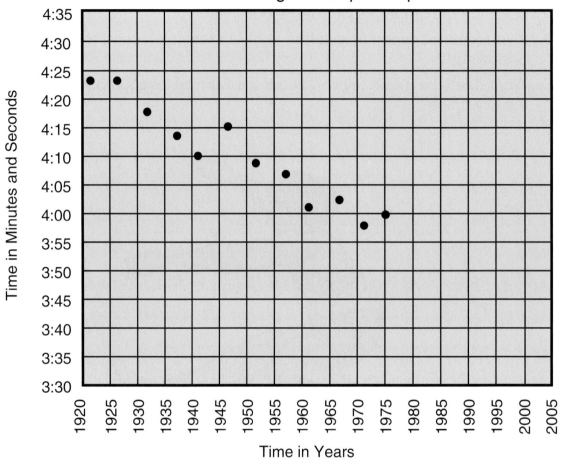

5. **A.** What variable is on the horizontal axis?

   B. What variable is on the vertical axis?

6. What was the winning time for running the mile in 1941?

7. Find the data point which shows a time for the mile race which is less than 4 minutes. What is the year for this data point?

8. **A.** Describe the graph. What does it look like?

   B. If you read the graph from left to right, do the points tend to go uphill or downhill?

   C. What does the graph tell you about the winning times for the mile run?

If the points on a graph lie close to a line, you can draw a line to help you make predictions. This line is called the **best-fit line.**

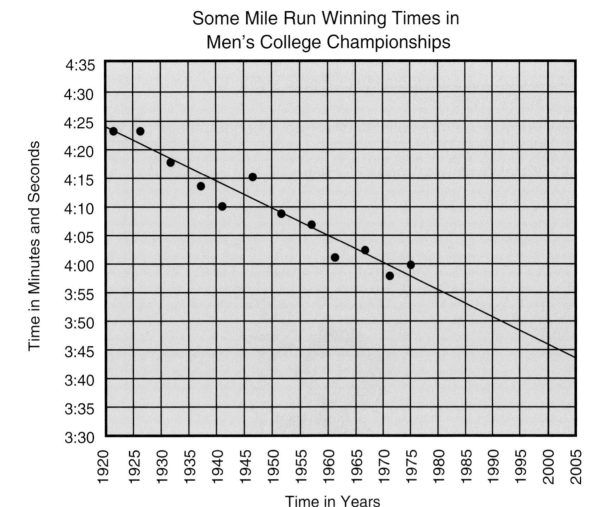

Some Mile Run Winning Times in
Men's College Championships

9. **A.** Why do you think the line drawn on the graph is called a best-fit line?

   B. How many points on the graph are above the line?

   C. How many points are on the line?

   D. How many points are below the line?

10. Use this graph to estimate the winning time for the mile run in 1955.

11. If the mile were run in the college championships in the year 2005, predict the winning time. Explain how you made your prediction.

Using the graph to estimate distances which lie between two points on the graph is called **interpolation.** "Inter" means between points.

Using the graph to predict distances which lie beyond the data points on the graph is called **extrapolation.** "Extra" means beyond or outside the points on the graph.

12. **A.** Did you use interpolation or extrapolation to estimate the winning time in 1955?

    B. Did you use interpolation or extrapolation to predict the winning time in 2005?

    C. Which is more accurate? Explain.

Another Average Activity

Every week the students in Room 204 take a spelling test of 10 words. Each student records the number of words he or she spells correctly in a table. Mrs. Dewey reports the average score to the parents.
Here are Ming's scores:

Ming's Scores

Test	Words Correct
Test #1	7
Test #2	9
Test #3	7
Test #4	7
Test #5	10

My median score is 7 words correct, so that is my average score. I guess you could say that 7 is a typical score, but it seems that the 9 and 10 should help bring my grades up.

Discuss

1. **A.** Do you agree that 7 words correct is Ming's median score?

   B. How do you find the median of a set of numbers?

2. In Unit 1, you learned that an **average** is one number that represents a set of data. For this data, the median number of words correct is 7. Is 7 a good number to represent all of Ming's scores? Why or why not?

3. Averages can also be used to make predictions. Do you think 7 words correct is a good prediction for the typical score on Ming's next five spelling tests? Why or why not?

The **median** is a useful average because it is often easy to find. Since it is the number that is exactly in the middle of the data, it can be used to describe what is normal or typical for that data. However, we can also use another kind of average to represent a set of data. This average is called the **mean.**

Mrs. Dewey showed Ming how to use the mean to average his spelling scores. She used connecting cubes. She said, "Each cube represents one spelling word. Make a tower of cubes to represent each of your spelling test scores. For example, the first tower will have 7 cubes because you spelled 7 words correctly on that test."

After Ming made these five towers, Mrs. Dewey said, "Using just the cubes in your towers, even them out so that each of the five towers has the same number of cubes."

When the towers are evened out, the number of cubes in each of your towers is the mean.

Then my mean score is 8, and I can say that my average score is 8.

4. Is 8 a good number to represent all of Ming's scores? Why or why not?

5. How did the scores of 9 and 10 affect the mean score for Ming's tests?

Mrs. Dewey showed all the students in Room 204 how to find the median and the mean using connecting cubes. Students worked in pairs to complete the activity. Irma and Tanya's work is described on the following pages. Work with a partner to follow their example.

Irma and Tanya took turns pulling a handful of cubes from a paper bag and then building towers with the cubes. Together they made the five towers shown in the picture.

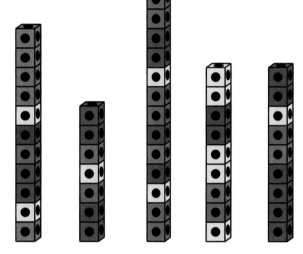

6. With your partner, build towers with the same numbers of cubes as in the picture.

Mrs. Dewey asked students to use one number, an average, to describe all of the towers. One way to do this is to find the median. To do this, the girls lined up their towers from shortest to tallest.

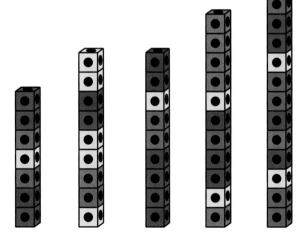

7. Line up your towers as shown in the picture.

8. The number of cubes in the middle tower is the median. What is the median number of cubes?

To find the mean, the girls tried to "even out" the towers so that they all had the same number of cubes.

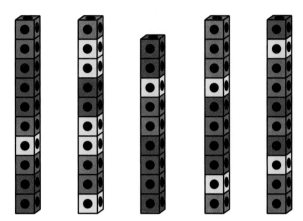

9. Even out your towers. (*Hint:* You can only use the cubes that are already in your towers and you must keep the same number of towers.)

10. Now each tower has about the same number of cubes. This number is the mean. What is the mean?

11. The median number of cubes in Tanya and Irma's towers was nine. Do you agree that nine cubes is a normal handful for Irma and Tanya? Why or why not?

12. The mean number of cubes in the girls' towers was ten. Do you agree that this number can also describe a normal handful? Why or why not?

13. Scientists use averages to make predictions. Predict the number of cubes Tanya or Irma would pull, if they pulled another handful.

14. With your partner, complete the same activity that Irma and Tanya did.

    A. Return the cubes to your bag. Be sure they have all been separated.

    B. Pull out one handful of cubes and build a tower with the cubes in your hand. Take turns with your partner until you have built five towers.

    C. Find the median number of cubes in your towers.

    D. Draw a picture of your towers. Record the median on your drawing.

    E. Find the mean number of cubes. Record the mean on your drawing. (Remember, you must keep the same number of towers. Do not add any more cubes from the bag or put any cubes back in the bag.)

Using Cubes to Solve Problems

Solve the following problems. Use towers of cubes to help you.

15. Jacob surveyed five families on his block. He filled in the following data table. Jacob found the median and the mean number of people in a household using towers.

    A. Jacob built five towers. Why?
    B. What did each tower stand for?
    C. What did each cube stand for?
    D. Use towers to find the median.
    E. Use towers to find the mean. (*Hint:* Use the closest number for your answer.)

Jacob's Data

Family	Number of People in Household
Scott-Haines	2
Thomas	6
Molina	3
Chang	5
Green	3

16. When Mrs. Dewey was in the fourth grade, she took a math quiz each week. Every quiz had ten problems. She got 10 problems right the first week, 7 problems right the second week, 8 problems right the third week, and 4 problems right the fourth week. Use towers to find the median and mean.

    A. How many towers will you build?
    B. What does each tower stand for?
    C. What does each cube stand for?
    D. Find the median. (*Hint:* What number is halfway between the number of cubes in the middle two towers?)
    E. Even out the towers to find the mean. (You must use the same number of towers as in 16A.)

17. When Rita, a new Girl Scout leader, was introduced to her group of girls, she asked them how old they were. Keenya, Shannon, Ana, Grace, and Maya all said they were 10 years old.

    A. What one number can be used to describe the age of the girls?
    B. What is the median age for this group of Girl Scouts?
    C. What is the mean?

18. How are the two kinds of averages alike? (*Hint:* What do they tell us?)

19. How are the mean and the median different? (*Hint:* How do you find each one?)

20. Which average is easier to find?

21. Roberto rolled a toy car down a ramp and measured the distance it rolled. The first time it rolled 13 cm; the second time it rolled 14 cm; and the third time it rolled 18 cm.

   A. Find the median distance the car rolled.

   B. Find the mean.

   C. Which number, the mean or the median, better describes the distance the car rolls? Explain your answer.

Homework

Dear Family Member:

In class, students used towers of cubes to learn how to find two kinds of averages: the mean and the median. You can look back at the previous pages in this section to see how this is done. In the next lesson, students will learn how to compute an average using calculators.

Use pennies or small building blocks to build towers to solve the following problems. You will need about 30 pennies or blocks.

1. Linda counted the number of plants her mom has in each room in the house. She filled in the following data table.

   A. Find the median number of plants in the house.

   B. Find the mean.

Linda's Data

Room	Number of Plants
Kitchen	5
Living Room	8
Family Room	7
Linda's Room	1
Bathroom	2
Dining Room	2
Mom's Room	3

2. John wanted to see how many free-throws he could make in one minute. The first minute he made 6 baskets. The second minute he made only 3. The third minute he made 6 baskets again. The fourth minute he made 9.

   A. Find the median number of baskets.

   B. Find the mean.

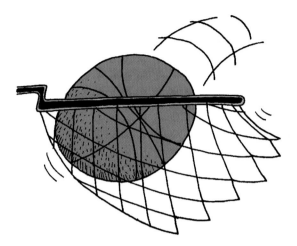

3. The students in Mrs. Dewey's class record the number of books they read each week. Here is Jerome's data.

Jerome's Data

Week	Number of Books
Week #1	3
Week #2	2
Week #3	5
Week #4	2
Week #5	2

   A. Find the median.

   B. Use towers to find the mean. Give your answer to the nearest whole book.

   C. Which average (the median or the mean) do you think better represents the number of books that Jerome read? Why?

The Meaning of the Mean

The students in Mrs. Dewey's class are preparing for the Bessie Coleman School Olympic Day. The class wants to wear sweatbands around their heads during the races. To order the headbands, they need to know the average head circumference of the students in the class.

The class first worked together in groups of four students. They measured the distance around each person's head. Then, they found the mean circumference for each group.

Finding the Mean Circumference

Work with a group of four people to complete the same activity:

Measure head circumference with strips of paper:

- For each member of the group, wrap adding machine tape around the student's head.
- Mark the distance around the head with a crayon.
- Cut the adding machine tape at the crayon mark to make a strip that is the same length as the circumference of the student's head.
- Check the strip. Wrap it around the student's head again. The ends of the strip should just touch each other.

- Measure to the nearest centimeter.
- Make a data table like the one shown.

Group 1's Data

Name	Circumference of Head (in cm)
Michael	52 cm
Ming	56 cm
Shannon	50 cm
Roberto	54 cm

Even out the strips to find the mean:

- Tape the four strips together end-to-end to make one long strip. Be careful not to let the strips overlap.

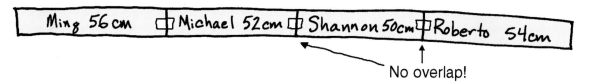

Ming 56 cm Michael 52cm Shannon 50cm Roberto 54cm

No overlap!

- Fold the long strip into four equal parts. (Fold strip in half, then in half again.)

- Measure the length of one-fourth of the long strip to the nearest centimeter. This length is the mean.
- Write the mean for your group at the bottom of your data table.

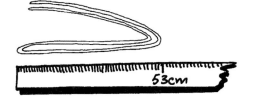

53cm

When the students in Group 1 finished "evening out" the length of their strips, they found that one-fourth of the long strip measured 53 cm. This is the mean length of their strips. They reported to the class that on average the circumference of their heads is 53 cm.

1. Report to the class the average circumference of the heads of the students in your group. Give the mean.

2. Compare the means for all the groups. What can you say about them?

3. Estimate the average circumference for the whole class using the means for each group.

4. **A.** How would you find the mean if there were five people in your group?

   B. Three people?

5. How could you use a calculator to find the mean? (*Hint:* What steps did you go through to find the mean using the strips?)

Using a Calculator to Find the Mean

Michael's group used a chart to think through its answer to Question 5.

Finding the Mean

Steps with adding machine tape	Steps on the calculator
1. We taped the strips together.	1. Add the lengths of the strips together. 56 + 52 + 50 + 54 = 212 cm
2. We folded the long strip into 4 equal parts.	2. Divide the total length by the number of people in our group. 212 ÷ 4 = 53 cm
3. The length of one-fourth of the long strip is 53 cm.	3. The mean is 53 cm. On average, the circumference of our heads is 53 cm.

These are the keystrokes that Michael's group used. Try them on your calculator.

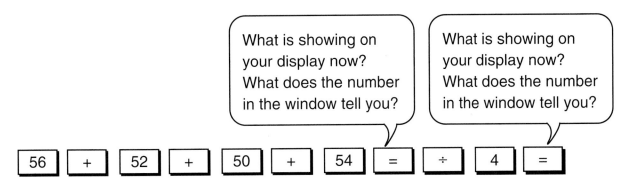

What is showing on your display now? What does the number in the window tell you?

What is showing on your display now? What does the number in the window tell you?

56 + 52 + 50 + 54 = ÷ 4 =

Michael's group found the mean by adding the values for each head circumference and dividing by the number of students in the group. The **mean** for any data set is an average that is found by adding the values in the set of data and dividing by the number of values.

6. The data for Group 2 is shown below.

Group 2's Data

Name	Circumference of Head (in cm)
Jacob	60 cm
Tanya	57 cm
Maya	56 cm
Jessie	54 cm

They used a calculator to find the mean for their data.
The display on their calculator read 56.75.

A. Write calculator keystrokes for finding the mean for Group 2.

B. Is 56.75 cm closer to 56 cm or 57 cm?

56.75 cm

C. Give the mean to the nearest whole centimeter.

7. A. Use your data table and your calculator to find the mean circumference for your group. Give your answer to the nearest centimeter. (*Hint:* Use a meterstick to help you find the nearest centimeter.)

B. Compare the number you found on your calculator for the mean to the number your group found by measuring the folded strip. Are the numbers close?

8. Groups 3 and 4 only had three students.

A. Find the mean for each data set. Give your answer to the nearest centimeter.

B. Show the calculator keystrokes you used for finding the mean.

C. Find the median for each set of data.

Group 3's Data

Name	Circumference of Head (in cm)
John	58 cm
Jerome	59 cm
Roberto	54 cm

Group 4's Data

Name	Circumference of Head (in cm)
Keenya	53 cm
Grace	53 cm
Ana	51 cm

9. Each day for a week, students in Room 204 recorded the temperature outside at noon.

   A. Find the mean temperature. Show your calculator keystrokes. Give your answer to the nearest whole degree.

   B. Find the median temperature.

Temperature Data

Day	Temperature at Noon in °F
Monday	47°
Tuesday	38°
Wednesday	37°
Thursday	43°
Friday	46°

10. In the first six soccer games of the season, Jackie's team scored 2, 3, 4, 0, 1, and 2 goals.

    A. Find the mean number of goals.

    B. Find the median number of goals.

    C. Look back. Do your answers make sense? Are the averages you found typical scores for Jackie's team?

11. Each week a fourth grade class has a test on 20 spelling words. A student got 13 right the first week, 19 right the second week, 12 right the third week, 20 right the fourth week, and 11 right the fifth week.

    A. On average, how many words did the student get right?

    B. Did you use the median or the mean? Why?

You will need a calculator to complete this homework.

1. The data table for a group of students from the experiment *Arm Span vs. Height* is shown below.

   A. Find the mean arm span for Jerome's group to the nearest inch. Show your calculator keystrokes.

   B. Find the median arm span.

   C. Find the mean height to the nearest inch.

   D. Find the median height.

   E. Look back at your answers. Do they make sense? Are they typical arm spans and heights for fourth graders?

Jerome's Group

Name	S Arm Span (in inches)	H Height (in inches)
Jerome	49	50
Keenya	54	55
Frank	59	57
Luis	58	58
Roberto	55	57

2. The students in Room 204 collected data on the number of times students have moved. Here is the data that one group collected: Shannon has moved 7 times, Linda has moved 3 times, Grace has moved 0 times, and Romesh has moved 2 times. Shannon said, "The average number of times we have moved is 12 times." Is Shannon correct? Why or why not?

3. John, Jackie, Nicholas, Irma, Maya, and Michael all walk to school together.

   John lives 1 block from school.
   Nicholas lives 2 blocks from school.
   Maya lives 4 blocks from school.

   Jackie lives 1 block from school.
   Irma lives 2 blocks from school.
   Michael lives 8 blocks from school.

   A. Find the median number of blocks the students live from school.

   B. Find the mean number of blocks.

   C. Michael lives much farther away from school than the other children. How does that affect the mean?

Bouncing Ball

Ana and Tanya wanted to play jacks at lunch time. Tanya brought jacks from home, but forgot the ball. Mrs. Dewey told the girls that they could look for a ball in the closet where the class keeps playground equipment. They found an old tennis ball and a Super ball.

Ana said, "I'll use the Super ball and you can use the tennis ball."

"No, that wouldn't be fair," said Tanya. "The balls won't bounce the same. We have to use the same ball."

"Oh, you're right. Which one should we use?" Ana began to bounce the balls to try them out. "They both bounce pretty well when I drop them from here, but when we play jacks we are sitting down."

Mrs. Dewey said, "You girls better go outside and get your game started or lunch will be over. Experiment with both of the balls before you start to play. You've given me an idea for an experiment we can do in class."

After lunch, Mrs. Dewey asked Tanya and Ana to let her have the tennis ball and the Super ball. She asked the class, "Can you predict how high the tennis ball will bounce if I drop it from 1 meter?"

Students answered:

"One meter."

"Yeah, one meter."

"Half as high. 50 centimeters."

"Higher than a meter."

Mrs. Dewey said, "Are you guessing? Or, can you give a reason for your answers? How can we make accurate predictions?"

Jessie said, "We'd have to try it out. We'd have to write down where we want to drop the ball. Then, drop the ball and measure how high it bounces."

Mrs. Dewey said, "Here is the challenge: If I give you a drop height, can you predict the bounce height? Can you make a prediction that is close to the actual bounce height?"

You will use the TIMS Laboratory Method to carry out two experiments: one with a tennis ball and one with a Super ball. Using the results of your experiments, you should be able to accurately predict the bounce height of either ball, if you know the drop height.

Identifying the Variables

One of the first tasks in setting up an experiment is identifying the variables. The two main variables in these two experiments are the drop height (D) and the bounce height (B).

We have special names for the two main variables in any experiment. The variable with values we know at the beginning of the experiment is called the **manipulated variable.** We can often choose the values of the manipulated variable. The variable with values we learn by doing the experiment is called the **responding variable.**

The values for the manipulated and responding variables change during an experiment. In these experiments, good values for the drop height (D) are 40 cm, 80 cm, and 120 cm. Each time you change the drop height, you measure the bounce height (B).

Each experiment should tell you how much the bounce height changes when you change the drop height. Usually there are other variables involved in an experiment. Look at the experimental setup. Try bouncing a ball on the floor a few times. What could change the bounce height, besides the drop height? List some.

The variables in your list should remain the same during an experiment, so that the only thing that affects the bounce height is the drop height. These variables are called **fixed variables.** The results of a carefully controlled experiment will help you make accurate predictions.

1. What is the manipulated variable in both the tennis ball experiment and the Super ball experiment?

2. What is the responding variable?

3. What are the fixed variables in each of the experiments?

4. **A.** Is the bounce height a categorical or numerical variable?

   B. Is the drop height a categorical or numerical variable?

   C. Is the type of ball a categorical or numerical variable?

5. Mrs. Dewey's class dropped the ball three times from each drop height and measured the bounce height each time. Why is it a good idea to do three trials?

Draw a picture of the lab. Show the tools you will use. Be sure to label the two main variables. A student from another class should be able to look at your picture and know what you are going to do during the lab.

Collect

Work with your group to collect the data for each experiment. You will need two data tables, one for each type of ball.

- Tape two metersticks to the wall. Your teacher will show you how.
- Fill in the values for the drop height before starting. Follow the example.
- For each drop height, do three trials. Find the average bounce height for each trial. Record the average in the data table.

Tennis Ball

D Drop Height (in cm)	B Bounce Height (in cm)			
	Trial 1	Trial 2	Trial 3	Average
40				
80				
120				

Graph

- Make a point graph of your data for each experiment. Use two pieces of graph paper.
- Put the drop height (*D*) on the horizontal axis. Put the bounce height (*B*) on the vertical axis.
- Use the same scales on both graphs. Leave room for extrapolation.
- Remember to title the graphs, label the axes, and include units.
- Plot the average bounce height for each drop height.

6. **A.** If the drop height were 0 cm, what would the bounce height be?

   B. Put this point on your graphs.

7. Describe your graphs. Do the points lie close to a straight line? If so, use a ruler to draw best-fit lines.

8. Suppose you drop your tennis ball from 60 cm.

   A. Use your graph to predict how high it will bounce. $D = 60$ cm, predicted $B = ?$ Show your work using dotted lines on your graph.

   B. Did you use interpolation or extrapolation to find your answer?

   C. Check your prediction by dropping the tennis ball from 60 cm. What is the actual bounce height? $D = 60$ cm, actual $B = ?$

   D. Is your prediction close to the actual bounce height?

9. Suppose you want your tennis ball to bounce 75 cm.

   A. From what height should you drop it? $B = 75$ cm, predicted $D = ?$

   B. Did you use interpolation or extrapolation to find your answer?

   C. Check your prediction by dropping the tennis ball from your predicted drop height. What is the actual bounce height?

   D. Was the actual bounce height close to 75 cm?

10. Suppose you drop your tennis ball from 180 cm.

   A. Predict the bounce height. $D = 180$ cm, predicted $B = ?$

   B. How did you make your prediction?

   C. Check your prediction by dropping the tennis ball from 180 cm. What is the actual bounce height? $D = 180$ cm, actual $B = ?$

   D. Is your prediction close to the actual bounce height?

11. Suppose you drop your Super ball from 1 meter.

    A. Use your graph to predict the bounce height. $D = 1$ m, predicted $B = ?$

    B. Did you use interpolation or extrapolation to find your answer?

    C. Check your prediction by dropping the Super ball from 1 m. What is the actual bounce height? $D = 1$ m, actual $B = ?$

    D. Is your prediction close to the actual bounce height?

12. Suppose you want your Super ball to bounce exactly 2 m. From what height should you drop the ball? Explain how you found your answer.

13. Compare the graph for the tennis ball with the graph for the Super ball. How are they alike? How are they different?

14. You find a strange ball on the playground. Because you have been investigating bouncing balls, you drop the ball from a height of 50 cm. It bounces back to a height of 18 cm. Is it more like the tennis ball or the Super ball? How did you find your answer?

15. Maya brings in a ball which is not as lively as a tennis ball. Is the line for Maya's ball Line X or Line Y?

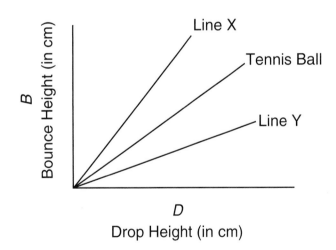

You will need a piece of *Centimeter Graph Paper* and a ruler to complete this homework.

Here are the results of an experiment using a ball Frank found on the way to school:

1. Make a point graph of this data. Put the drop height (*D*) on the horizontal axis and the bounce height (*B*) on the vertical axis. The scale on the horizontal axis should go to at least 150 cm. The scale on the vertical axis should go to at least 100 cm.

2. A. If the drop height were 0 cm, what would be the bounce height?

   B. Put this point on your graph.

3. Draw a best-fit line.

4. Frank dropped his ball from 150 cm.

   A. Use your graph to predict the bounce height of the ball. Show how you found your answer on your graph. *D* = 150 cm, predicted *B* = ?

   B. Did you use interpolation or extrapolation to find your answer?

5. Frank dropped his ball and it bounced 25 cm.

   A. From what height was it dropped? Show how you found your answer on your graph. *B* = 25 cm, predicted *D* = ?

   B. Did you use interpolation or extrapolation to find your answer?

Frank's Data

D Drop Height in cm	*B* Bounce Height in cm
30	11
60	18
120	44

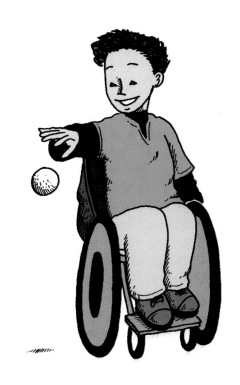

6. Frank wants his ball to bounce to a height of 100 cm. From what height should he drop the ball? Explain how you found your answer.

Speeds at the Indianapolis 500

The Indianapolis 500 is a famous car race that takes place every Memorial Day weekend in Indianapolis, Indiana. The cars race around an oval track until they have gone 500 miles. The graph shows the average speed in miles per hour for the winner of each race.

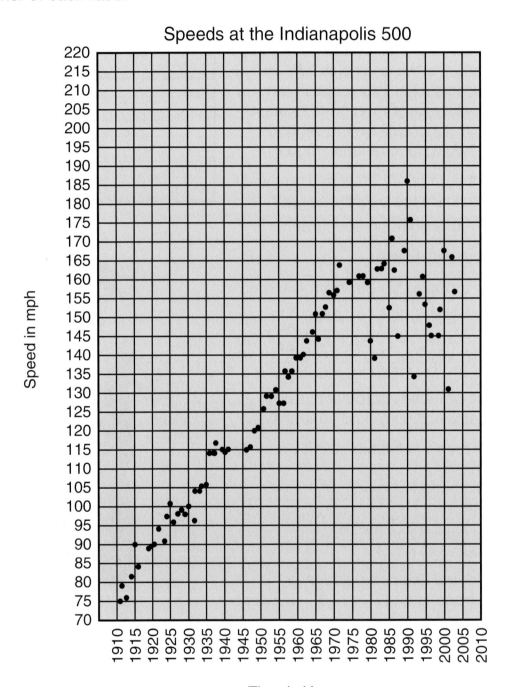

The drivers go as fast as possible unless they are given a yellow light. This is a signal that the track is dangerous due to an accident or rain. The cars must slow down and maintain their race position until the track is safe again. When the drivers must drive slower, their average race speeds go down.

1. In 1920 the winner of the race, Gaston Chevrolet, won the race with a winning speed of 89 miles per hour. Fifty years later, Al Unser won with a winning speed of 156 miles per hour. What is the difference in the two speeds?

2. In 1993 the winning speed was 157 miles per hour.
   A. In 1911 the winning speed was 75 miles per hour. About how many times faster did the winner drive in 1993 than in 1911?
   B. The speed limit on freeways in cities is usually 55 miles per hour. About how many times faster did the winning 1993 car travel during the race than a car travels on a freeway?

3. When Jessie's family went on a trip in their car, they drove about 50 miles each hour. How long did it take Jessie's family to drive 500 miles?

4. There were no races in 1917 or 1918 during World War I.
   A. Can you use the graph to estimate the winning speed if there had been a race in 1917? If so, what is your estimate?
   B. Did you use interpolation or extrapolation to make your estimate?

5. There were no races from 1942–1945 during World War II.
   A. Can you use the graph to estimate the winning speed if there had been a race in 1943? If so, what is your estimate?
   B. Did you use interpolation or extrapolation to make your estimate?

6. Can you use the graph to make an accurate prediction about the winning speed in 2010? Why or why not?

   A. If so, what is your prediction?

   B. Did you use interpolation or extrapolation?

7. Write a short paragraph that tells the story of the graph. In your paragraph, describe the graph. What does the graph tell you about the speeds of the winning cars over the years?

8. Here is part of the graph. This part shows the winning speeds from 1980 to 2003.

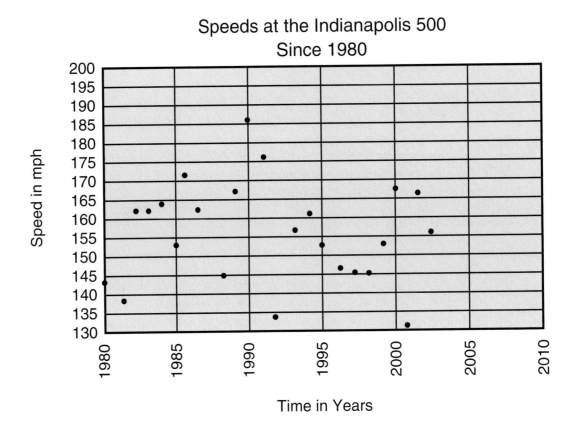

A. Describe this part of the graph.

B. Can you make predictions about the speed of the winner using only this data? Why or why not?

Unit 6
Place Value Patterns

	Student Guide	Discovery Assignment Book	Adventure Book	Unit Resource Guide*
Lesson 1				
Newswire	◎	◎		
Lesson 2				
Doubles	◎			
Lesson 3				
Big Base-Ten Pieces	◎	◎		
Lesson 4				
News Number Line	◎			
Lesson 5				
Close Enough	◎	◎		
Lesson 6				
Using Estimation	◎			◎
Lesson 7				
9 to 5 War	◎	◎		

Unit Resource Guide pages are from the teacher materials.

Newswire

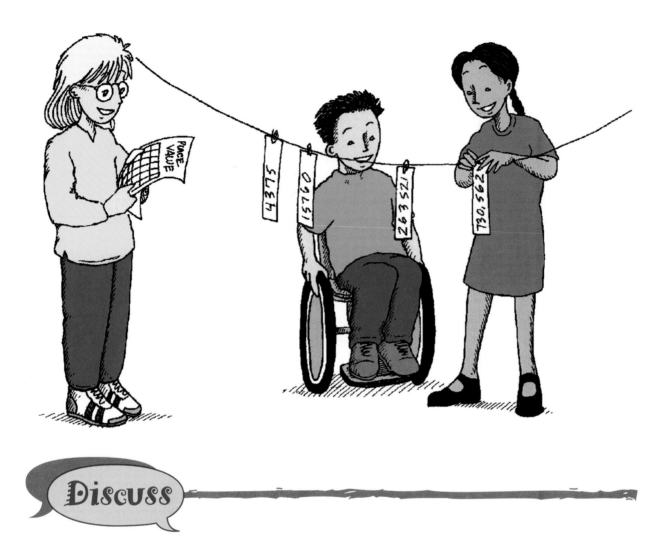

Discuss

The students in Mrs. Dewey's class used a place value chart to help them compare numbers they found in newspaper articles. Using the place value chart helped them put the numbers in order on a wire.

Shannon found two large numbers. She wrote the numbers on her place value chart.

Millions' Period			Thousands' Period			Ones' Period		
4	2	3	1	7	6	3	2	1
	4	5	2	1	8	7	0	3

Then, she read the first number out loud, "Four hundred twenty-three million, one hundred seventy-six thousand, three hundred twenty-one." Shannon noticed that there is a repeating pattern. Can you describe the pattern?

Each repeating core pattern is called a **period** on the *Place Value Chart.*

- The first three-digit group on the right is the **ones' period.** It is made up of ones, tens, and hundreds.

- The second group is the **thousands' period.** It is made up of thousands, ten thousands, and hundred thousands.

- The third group is the **millions' period.** It is made up of millions, ten millions, and hundred millions.

When you say a number, you say each period just the way you do when you read a number in the ones' period and then you add the name of the period. For example, to read Shannon's second number, say, "Forty-five million, two hundred eighteen thousand, seven hundred three." When writing numbers, a comma or a space is placed between each period to make reading easier: 45,218,703.

Jacob found these numbers in the *National Parks Gazette*:

National Parks Numbers

Crater Lake in Oregon **183,224 acres**	Kobuk Valley National Park in Alaska **1,750,736 acres**	Glacier National Park in Montana **1,013,572 acres**	Canyonlands National Park in Utah **337,570 acres**	Voyageurs National Park in Minnesota **218,200 acres**
Extraordinary blue lake in crater of extinct volcano encircled by lava walls 500 to 2000 feet high.	Caribou and black bears; archaeological sites indicate that humans have lived there for over 10,000 years.	Superb Rocky Mountain scenery, numerous glaciers, and glacial lakes.	At junction of Colorado and Green Rivers; extensive evidence of prehistoric Indians.	Abundant lakes, forests, wildlife, and canoeing.

1. Put the numbers in bold in order from smallest to largest on your *Place Value Chart*. Then, write each number in word form on a separate sheet of paper.

For example, the smallest National Park in this table is Crater Lake in Oregon.

Millions			Thousands			Ones		
			1	8	3	2	2	4

Crater Lake National Park has one hundred eighty-three thousand, two hundred twenty-four acres.

2. Which of the national parks in the table National Parks Numbers has an area closest to 1 million acres?

3. Rhode Island has an area of about 777,000 acres.

   A. Which of the national parks has an area that is about half the area of Rhode Island?

   B. Which of the national parks has an area which is about twice the area of Rhode Island?

Homework

To complete the homework, you need to take home your *Place Value Chart*.

Nila found these numbers in the *National Parks Gazette*.

More National Parks Numbers

Yellowstone National Park in Idaho, Montana, and Wyoming	Olympic National Park in Washington	Gates of the Arctic National Park in Alaska	Glacier Bay National Park in Alaska	Big Bend National Park in Texas
2,219,791 acres	**922,651 acres**	**7,523,898 acres**	**3,224,840 acres**	**801,163 acres**
The first national park; has the world's greatest geyser area, spectacular waterfalls, impressive canyons, and bears and moose.	Mountain wilderness containing the finest remnant of Pacific Northwest rain forest, active glaciers, Pacific shoreline, and rare elk.	The largest national park. Huge tundra wilderness, with rugged peaks and steep valleys.	Rugged mountains, with glaciers, lakes, sheep, bears, and bald eagles.	Desert land amid rugged Chisos mountains on the Rio Grande River; dinosaur fossils.

1. Put the numbers in bold in order from smallest to largest and write each number in word form. Use your *Place Value Chart* as a guide if you need it.

2. Which two of these national parks have areas closest to 1 million acres?

3. Find one number written in symbols (not words) greater than 1000 in a newspaper or magazine. Cut out the paragraph that contains the number. Highlight or circle the number. Bring the article and the number to school and place it on the class newswire.

> **Acre.** An acre is a unit of measure for area. We use acres to measure land area. An acre is equal to 43,560 square feet. There are 640 acres in a square mile. A football field is a little larger than one acre.

Doubles

A Double Reward

There is an old story about the man who invented the game of chess. His name was Sissa Ben Dahir (da-here) and he was the Grand Vizier (viz-ear) of King Sirham of India. King Sirham was so pleased when Sissa Ben Dahir showed him his new game that he offered a great reward. "Choose your prize," said the king after he had played his first game of chess. The vizier's reply seemed very foolish to the king: "Today, place one grain of wheat on the first square of the chessboard. Tomorrow, place two grains of wheat on the second square. On the third day, place four grains on the third square. Continue the pattern by doubling the number of grains each day. In this manner, give me enough grains to cover all 64 squares." The king was glad to grant what he considered to be a small request, so he ordered a bag of wheat brought to the vizier.

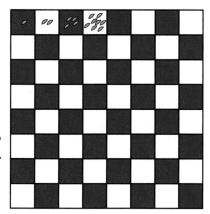

However, when the counting began, it became clear that one bag of wheat was not nearly enough. On the first day, one grain of wheat was placed on the chessboard, two grains on the second day, four on the third day, and so forth. As the days passed, the king realized that he could not possibly keep his promise. Some say Sissa Ben Dahir did not insist on receiving his full reward, and the king was again greatly impressed by his wisdom. Others say that the king was so angry that he could not fulfill the request that he cut off Sissa Ben Dahir's head.

Discuss

1. Estimate how much wheat Sissa Ben Dahir asked for. More than 100 grains? More than 1000 grains? More than 1,000,000 grains?

2. **A.** One way to find out how much he requested is to make a data table. Copy the following data table in your journal or on a piece of paper. Complete the data table for eight days.

   B. Look for patterns.

Writing numbers using exponents in the second column may help you see more patterns. Each of the numbers in the second column of the data table are **powers of two.** For example, $2 \times 2 \times 2 = 2^3$ is read "two to the third power." We say that 2^3 is the "third power of two." Follow the examples to write the powers of two using exponents in your data table. Use a calculator to help you. (*Hint:* You may need to stop writing $2 \times 2 \times 2 \ldots$ after several rows.)

Doubling Data Table

D Time in Days	N Number of Grains of Wheat Added	T Total Number of Grains of Wheat
1	1	1
2	$2 \times 1 = 2$	3
3	$2 \times 2 = 2^2 = 4$	7
4	$2 \times 2 \times 2 = 2^3 = 8$	15

3. Describe any patterns you see.

4. **A.** How many grains of wheat will be added on the eighteenth day?

   B. How many total grains of wheat are needed by the eighteenth day?

5. Use the patterns to help you predict when the total number of grains of wheat on the chessboard will reach 1 million.

6. Check your prediction. Complete your data table until the total number of grains of wheat reaches a million.

Graph

7. Make a point graph for the first two columns in your data table on *Centimeter Graph Paper*. Put the time in days (*D*) on the horizontal axis. Scale the horizontal axis by ones. Put the number of grains of wheat added each day (*N*) on the vertical axis. Scale the vertical axis by fours.

   A. Do the points form a straight line? If so, draw a best-fit line through the points.

   B. If the points do not form a line, describe the shape of the graph.

Use the *Solving* and the *Telling* Rubrics to help you organize your work for the following problems. Explain your strategies and show your work.

Biological Parents

Biological Grandparents

Tanya

1. You have two biological parents, four biological grandparents, and eight great-grandparents. How many great-great-great-great-great-grandparents do you have? Write this number using an exponent.

2. Suppose your pay for a job is one penny on the first day you work, two pennies on the second day, four pennies on the third day, eight pennies on the fourth day, etc.

   A. How much money will you earn on the tenth day?

   B. What is your total pay for the first ten days? (Give your answer in dollars and cents.)

   C. How long will you have to work to make a total of $1000?

3. You won the lottery! The lottery committee has given you a choice: get paid a cool $1 million in cash or get paid 1 cent on the first day, two on the second, four on the third, and so on for 1 month (30 days). What is your choice? Explain why you made the choice you did.

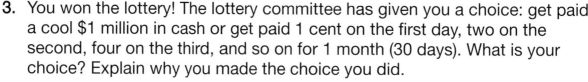

Big Base-Ten Pieces

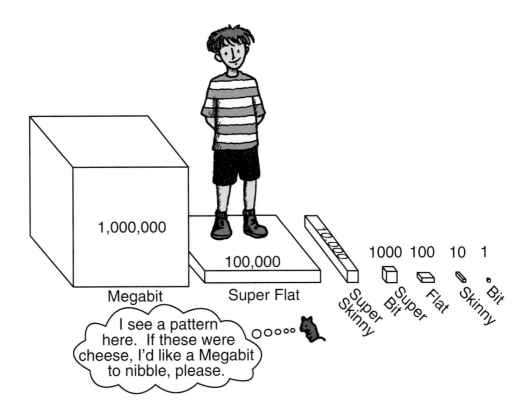

1,000,000
Megabit

100,000
Super Flat

1000 100 10 1

Super Skinny Super Bit Flat Skinny Bit

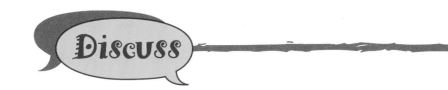
I see a pattern here. If these were cheese, I'd like a Megabit to nibble, please.

Patterns in the Base-Ten Pieces

Discuss

The base-ten pieces are one model of the place value system. You have built models of base-ten pieces for numbers up to 1,000,000. We have given special names to the base-ten pieces to help us talk about the patterns in our base-ten number system. Starting in the ones' place we use the names: bit, skinny, flat, super bit, super skinny, super flat, and megabit.

1. What patterns do you see in the shapes of the base-ten pieces?

2. The sizes of the pieces also form a pattern.

   A. How many bits make a skinny?

   B. How many skinnies make a flat?

   C. How many flats make a super bit?

   D. Describe the pattern. Do all the pieces follow the pattern?

We can write the value of each piece using the powers of 10. For example, $100 = 10 \times 10$ and it can be written as 10^2. This is read as 10 to the second power or 10 squared. $1000 = 10 \times 10 \times 10$ and it can be written as 10^3. This is read as 10 to the third power. The following chart helps to show these patterns.

3. Draw the chart on your paper and fill in the missing spaces.

Base-Ten Chart

Base-Ten Piece	Written as a Power of 10	Value
Bit	1	1
Skinny	$1 \times 10 = 10^1$	
Flat		100
Super Bit	$10 \times 10 \times 10 = 10^3$	
Super Skinny		10,000
Super Flat		
Megabit		

Each repeating core pattern is called a period on the *Place Value Chart*.
The bit-skinny-flat group makes up the **ones'** period.
The super bit-super skinny-super flat group makes up the **thousands'** period.
The megabit begins the **millions'** period.

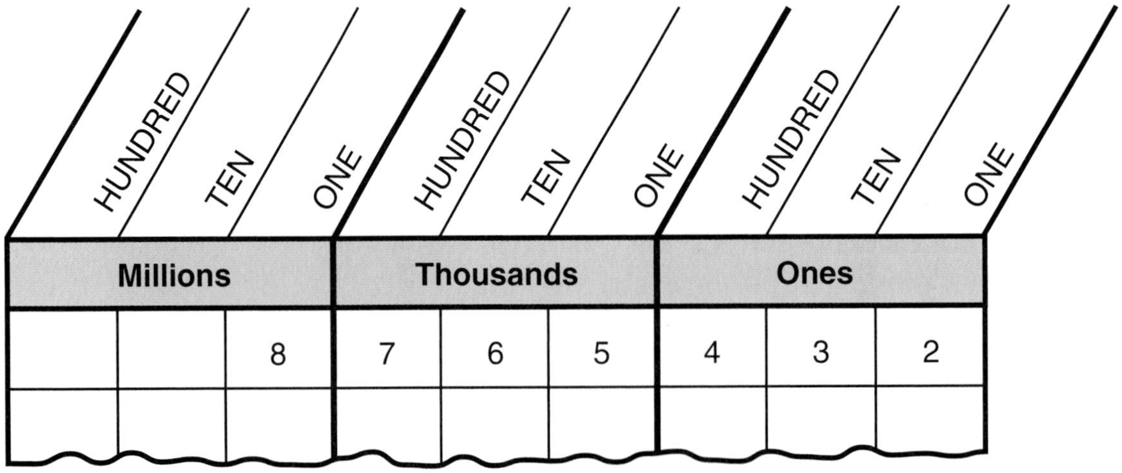

		HUNDRED	TEN	ONE	HUNDRED	TEN	ONE	HUNDRED	TEN	ONE
	Millions				Thousands			Ones		
			8	7	6	5	4	3	2	

To make reading large numbers easier, each period takes its name from the number that the cube represents in that period. In Lesson 1, you learned that a comma or space is placed between each period to make reading easier. Remember, the comma or space alerts you to say the period name. For instance: 8,765,432 is read as eight **million,** seven hundred sixty-five **thousand,** four hundred thirty-two.

Draw, Place, and Read

Play *Draw, Place, and Read*. Follow the directions that are written on the game page in the *Discovery Assignment Book*.

Tanya and Irma played *Draw, Place, and Read*. After all seven digit cards had been drawn, Tanya's number looked like this: 5,369,210. Irma's number looked like this: 6,935,021. Read each number.

4. Which of the girls recorded the larger number?

Homework

Play *Draw, Place,* and *Read* at home with your family.

News Number Line

How Big Is One Million?

1. Use your calculator to count by 10,000s to 1 million. If you count out loud, how many numbers will you say?
Begin this way, "ten thousand, twenty thousand, thirty thousand, . . ."

2. Use your calculator to count by 100,000s to 1 million. If you count out loud, how many numbers will you say?
Begin this way, "one hundred thousand, two hundred thousand, three hundred thousand, . . ."

3. A pencil manufacturer donates 1,000,000 pencils to your school. Your principal divides the pencils evenly among the students. How many pencils will each student get?

    A. What do you need to know before you can solve the problem?

    B. Use your calculator to find the answer.

Taking Attendance

Museum Attendance in 2001 and 2002

Museum	Attendance in 2001 and 2002	
	2001	2002
Science Museum	1,890,227	1,985,609
Institute of Art	1,338,266	1,295,321
Children's Museum	1,295,755	1,227,062
Aquarium and Oceanarium	1,858,766	1,789,222
Museum of the Stars	577,997	458,156

1. Put the 2001 attendance numbers in order from smallest to largest.

2. Name the most popular museum in 2001.

3. Which museum's attendance was closest to 1,000,000 in 2001?

4. Which museum had fewer visitors in 2001 than it had in 2002?

5. Put the 2002 attendance numbers in order from smallest to largest.

6. Name the least popular museum in 2002.

7. Write the 2002 attendance for each museum in words.

Making Mystery Jars

The next three problems prepare for the next lesson, *Close Enough*. If your class is not going to do Lesson 5, you may skip these questions.

8. Here is a picture Linda made using a computer.

There are about 15 animals in the small picture at the right. Use this number as a reference number to help you estimate the number of animals in the picture above.

In the next lesson, you will use the same idea you used in Question 8 to estimate the number of objects in jars.

9. Bring in a mystery jar of objects to use in the activity.

   - Find a clear, clean jar with a lid.
   - Fill (or partly fill) the jar with one kind of object such as beans, pasta, or small building blocks. The objects should be small, and each object should be about the same size.
   - Count the objects in your jar. Write the number of objects on a small piece of paper. Tape the paper to the inside of the lid and put the lid on the jar so that no one can see the number.
   - Put your name on the outside of the lid.

One way to make good estimates is to compare the mystery jar to another jar or bag with a known number of objects. The picture below shows Ana's mystery jar of marbles and a bag with 50 marbles. Other students can use the 50 marbles as a reference to estimate the number of marbles in the mystery jar.

10. Bring in a number of objects in another jar or in a plastic bag. Your classmates will use this number as a reference to help them estimate the number of objects in your mystery jar.

   - Count out a convenient number of objects. Use the same objects that are in your mystery jar. (10, 25, 50, or 100 objects work well.)

   - Place them in another jar or a clear plastic bag.

   - Label the jar (or bag) with your name and the number of objects so your classmates can see this number.

Close Enough

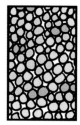

Look at the picture of the basketball game below. Do you think there are more or less than 100 people in the crowd? Do you think there are more or less than 500 people? more or less than 1000 people? more or less than 2000 people?

Use the small picture on the left to help you estimate. There are about 80 people in the small picture.

1. Estimate the number of people watching the game. How did you decide on your estimate?

The students in Mrs. Dewey's room made mystery jars for homework and brought them to class. Three of the jars the students brought to class are shown in the picture. Mrs. Dewey made a mystery jar of centimeter connecting cubes.

Linda and Romesh estimated the number of objects in each jar and recorded their estimates in data tables. Here are their estimates:

Linda's Data Table

Object	Estimate
marbles	130
marshmallows	50
beans	350
cubes	500

Romesh's Data Table

Object	Estimate
marbles	120
marshmallows	35
beans	375
cubes	600

2. The actual number of marbles is 142. The actual number of marshmallows is 38.

   A. What is the difference between Linda's estimate of the number of marbles and the actual number?

B. What is the difference between Linda's estimate of the number of marshmallows and the actual number?

C. Is Linda's estimate for the number of marbles better than her estimate for the number of marshmallows? Why or why not?

Mrs. Dewey said: "Let's say that an estimate is 'close enough' if it is within ten percent. Ten percent (10%) means 10 out of every 100. That's the same as 1 out of every 10 or $\frac{1}{10}$. So, to find out which numbers are within 10% of 142, we have to find $\frac{1}{10}$ of 142. How can we do that?"

Linda chose to find $\frac{1}{10}$ of 142 by dividing the marbles into 10 equal groups. When she finished, each group had 14 marbles and two marbles were left over. She decided that $\frac{1}{10}$ of 142 is about 14.

Romesh used a calculator to find $\frac{1}{10}$ of 142. He divided 142 by 10. Since the display read 14.2, he agreed with Linda. 10% of 142 is about 14.

Any prediction in the range between 128 and 156 is within 10% of 142, since:

$$142 - 14 = 128$$
and
$$142 + 14 = 156.$$

3. A. Look back at Linda's and Romesh's estimates listed in the data tables. Which of the estimates for the jar of marbles is within 10% of 142?

B. Do you agree that this estimate is close enough?

4. A. Find 10% of 38. Check your answer by finding 10% of 38 in a different way.

B. Look back at Linda's and Romesh's estimates listed in the data tables. Which of the estimates for the jar of marshmallows is within 10%?

5. Draw the following data table on your paper. Complete the table.

Object	N Actual Number	N ÷ 10	10% of the Number	Range
marbles	142	14.2	About 14	128–156
marshmallows	38			
beans	351			
cubes	526			

6. A. Is Linda's estimate for the number of beans within 10%? Why or why not?

   B. Is the estimate Romesh made for the number of beans within 10%? Why or why not?

7. A. Is Linda's estimate for the number of cubes within 10%? Why or why not?

   B. Is the estimate Romesh made for the number of cubes within 10%? Why or why not?

8. Estimate the height of the door to your classroom to the nearest cm.

   A. Record your estimate and share it with your class.

   B. Measure the height of the door to the nearest cm.

   C. Which estimates are within 10% of the actual measurement?

9. A carpenter is making a door. The opening is 75 cm wide. If the carpenter measures the width of the door to within 10%, will the measurement be close enough? Why or why not?

Homework

Dear Family Member:

The students have learned to find 10% of various objects by finding one-tenth of the number. They can divide the number of objects into ten equal groups and count the number of objects in one group, or they can use a calculator to divide the number by ten. Ask your child to describe how he or she finds 10% of a number.

1. Here is part of the *10% Chart* the students in Mrs. Dewey's class made. Complete the table.

Object	N Actual Number	N ÷ 10	10% of the Number	Range
blocks	51			
macaroni	632			
pennies	198			
Super balls	15			

2. **A.** Is an estimate of 60 blocks within 10% of the actual number? Show how you know.

   B. Is an estimate of 650 macaroni pieces within 10% of the actual number? Show how you know.

   C. Is an estimate of 175 pennies within 10% of the actual number? Show how you know.

   D. Is an estimate of 18 Super balls within 10% of the actual number? Show how you know.

3. Tanya is working on the *Bouncing Ball* experiment. She predicts that the tennis ball will bounce to a height of 50 cm if it is dropped from a height of 100 cm. She checks her prediction and the ball actually bounces to a height of 54 cm. Is her prediction of 50 cm within 10% of the actual bounce height of 54 cm? Why or why not?

4. The average height of students in Room 204 is 55 inches. Nila is 48 inches tall. Is her height within 10% of the average height?

5. Keenya goes to the store with $32 for groceries. As she shops, she estimates the cost of the groceries so that she will have enough money when she goes to the cash register. She estimates that the groceries in her cart will cost about $32.

   A. The actual cost of the groceries is $34.52. Is her estimate within 10% of the actual cost?

   B. Is her estimate close enough? Explain.

Using Estimation

It's About...

Jerome brought in an article for the number newswire. Mrs. Dewey asked him to share the numbers he found. "My article says that 407,997 people visited the planetarium during 2001 and 458,156 people visited during 2002," said Jerome.

"Can anyone estimate the total number of people who visited the planetarium during these two years?" asked Mrs. Dewey.

Round numbers are often used when estimating because they are convenient to think about. Round numbers such as tens, hundreds, or thousands end in zeros. They are one type of convenient numbers. A number line can help you when you round a number.

1. **A.** Jerome estimated where 407,997 would be on the number line. He knew that it would be between 400,000 and 500,000 so he chose these two numbers as his **benchmarks.** Locate the mark Jerome made on the number line showing 407,997.

   B. Is 407,997 closer to 400,000 or 500,000?

   C. Round 407,997 to the nearest 100,000.

2. **A.** Using the same two benchmarks, Jerome estimated where 458,156 is on the number line. Find the mark Jerome made for 458,156 on the number line.

   B. Is it closer to 400,000 or 500,000?

   C. Round 458,156 to the nearest 100,000.

3. Ana did not round 458,156 to the nearest hundred thousand. She rounded 458,156 in two other ways. She used these two number lines.

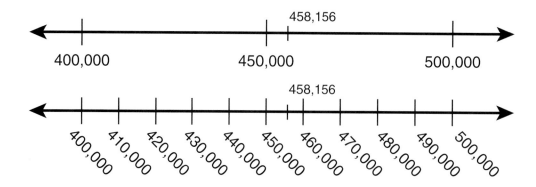

Using these two number lines, give two ways to round 458,156.

4. A. Ana used the second number line in Question 3 to round 407,997 to the nearest 10,000. What is her estimate?

   B. What benchmarks did she use?

5. Jerome estimated the total number of people who visited the planetarium over the last two years as 900,000. Ana's estimate was 870,000 people.

   A. Write a number sentence to show how Jerome found his estimate.

   B. Write a number sentence to show how Ana found her estimate.

   C. Which student is correct?

6. The museum estimated how much the attendance grew from 2001 to 2002. Use rounded numbers to estimate the increase in attendance.

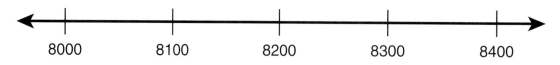

Practice rounding the numbers in each problem below.

7. A. Use this number line to round 8207 to the nearest thousand.

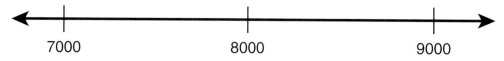

   B. What two benchmarks did you use?

8. A. Round 8207 to the nearest hundred using this number line.

8000	8100	8200	8300	8400

B. What two benchmarks did you use?

C. Compare this rounded number with the rounded number you found in Question 7. Which one is closer to the exact number?

D. Last year, 8207 people attended a high school play. The school play committee is expecting about the same number to attend this year's show. If the committee members are trying to plan refreshments for this year's show, which rounded number would be best to use?

9. A. Use this number line to round 36,736 to the nearest thousand.

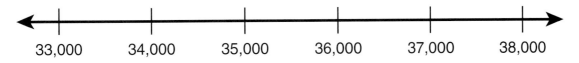

33,000   34,000   35,000   36,000   37,000   38,000

B. What two benchmarks did you use?

C. Round 36,736 to the nearest 10,000. Draw a number line showing the benchmarks that you would use.

D. Last year 36,736 tickets were sold at a fun fair during a summer festival. The planning committee is getting ready to order tickets for this summer's fun fair. Tickets are sold in rolls of 1000. If the planning committee expects about the same number of tickets to be sold, which rounded number should they use when ordering the tickets?

Estimating Sums and Differences

Ming and Keenya were researching the national parks in the United States. They found that Yellowstone National Park, established in 1872, was the world's first national park. Since then, more than 50 national parks have been set aside by the American government.

Ming organized some of the national park information they found in a table.

National Parks

National Park	State	Established	Area
Acadia	Maine	1929	46,051 acres
Badlands	South Dakota	1978	242,756 acres
Carlsbad Caverns	New Mexico	1930	46,776 acres
Denali	Alaska	1980	4,740,911 acres
Everglades	Florida	1934	1,398,902 acres
Grand Canyon	Arizona	1919	1,217,403 acres
Mammoth Cave	Kentucky	1941	52,830 acres
Mesa Verde	Colorado	1906	52,122 acres
Petrified Forest	Arizona	1962	93,533 acres
Rocky Mountains	Colorado	1915	265,769 acres
Wind Cave	South Dakota	1903	28,295 acres

10. **A.** Ming estimated that about 1,300,000 acres of land have been set aside in Arizona as national park land. Ming wrote this number sentence showing the convenient numbers he chose:

    1,200,000 + 100,000 = 1,300,000 acres of land set aside

    Explain how Ming arrived at his estimate.

    B. Find another estimate for the amount of land set aside in Arizona as national park land. Explain your thinking.

Use Ming and Keenya's table to answer Questions 11–13. Write a number sentence showing the convenient numbers you chose to use.

11. Estimate the amount of land that has been set aside in Colorado as national park land.

12. Which state, Arizona or Colorado, has more national park land? Estimate the difference.

13. Mammoth Cave is the longest known cave network in the world. Estimate the difference in size between Mammoth Cave National Park and Wind Cave National Park.

Using Estimation

Making Money

The Parent-Teacher Club at Bessie Coleman School wants to purchase computer hardware for the school computer lab over a two-year period. The club's goal is to purchase hardware for 25 computer lab stations. Club members made a table to show what they wanted to buy:

Quantity	Item	Total Cost ($)
25	14-inch color monitor	7469.00
25	extended keyboards	3127.00
25	personal computers	30,716.00
25	color printers	14,054.00

14. Use estimation to set a goal for the amount of money the Parent-Teacher Club needs to earn. Write a paragraph explaining how you arrived at your goal. Use the Student Rubric: *Knowing* to help you write your paragraph.

Homework

1. Find at least two ways to round each of these numbers.
   - Draw a number line for each rounded number.
   - Label your line with the benchmarks you chose.
   - Estimate the location of the actual number on the number line.

   A. 5599   B. 24,681   C. 18,260

   D. 764,296   E. 206,492   F. 6,847,000

Use this number line to answer Questions 2–4.

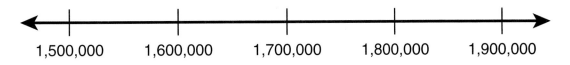

1,500,000   1,600,000   1,700,000   1,800,000   1,900,000

2. According to an article Linda hung on the newswire, 1,858,766 people visited the aquarium last year. Use the number line to round 1,858,766 to the nearest hundred thousand.

3. 1,510,063 people visited the Sears Tower Skydeck in one year. Use the number line to round 1,510,063 to the nearest hundred thousand.

4. During one season a total of 1,697,398 people attended home games for the Chicago White Sox. Use the number line to round 1,697,398 to the nearest hundred thousand.

Addition and Subtraction Practice with Paper and Pencil

Solve the following problems using paper and pencil. Find exact answers. Show all your work. Use estimation to look back and see if your answers are reasonable.

5. 9436
  + 4831

6. 4302
  + 3005

7. 7407
  − 3822

Estimate the answers to the following problems. Show the round numbers you used.

8. 23,065
  − 9,638

9. 94,378
  − 76,893

10. 80,025
  − 9,559

11. The United States has 12,383 miles of coastline along four different oceans. The Atlantic coast is 2069 miles long, the Arctic coast is 1060 miles long, and the coast of the Gulf of Mexico is 1631 miles long. About how long is the Pacific coast of the United States?

12. The United States has a total area of 3,787,319 square miles. Water covers 251,041 square miles. About how much of the United States area is land?

9 to 5 War

This is a card game for two players.

Materials

Both players need two stacks of cards: one stack of 9s and 5s and another stack of cards with other digits.

Getting Ready

- Each partner cuts out the cards on both of the *9 to 5 War Cards* Activity Pages in the *Discovery Assignment Book.* Mix up your cards and place your stack face down in front of you.
- Prepare a second stack of cards with other numbers:
    Each player uses 20 *Digit Cards* (0–9). Mix up your digit cards and place them in a stack in front of you.

    Or, use a deck of playing cards. Remove all the face cards. The ace will be one. Mix up the rest of the cards and divide them equally. Put your share in a stack face down in front of you.

Playing the Game

- Each player turns over two cards, one from the 9s and 5s pile, and one from the other pile.
- Each player should say a number sentence that tells the product of his or her two cards. Whoever has the greater product wins all four cards.
- If there is a tie, then each player turns over two more cards. The player with the greater product of the second pairs wins all eight cards.

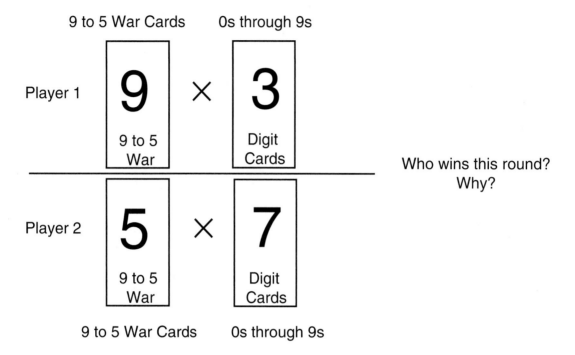

Goal

Play for ten minutes or until the players run out of cards. The player with more cards at the end is the winner.

Variations

1. Whoever has the *smaller* product takes the cards.

2. Play with more than two players.

3. Each player is given only one pile of cards (playing cards with face cards removed or *Digit Cards*). Each player takes the top two cards from his or her pile and multiplies the numbers. The player with the larger product wins all four cards. This game practices all the facts—it does not just focus on the 9s and 5s.

Unit 7

PATTERNS IN MULTIPLICATION

	Student Guide	Discovery Assignment Book	Adventure Book	Unit Resource Guide*
Lesson 1				
Order of Operations	@			
Lesson 2				
Divisibility Rules	@			@
Lesson 3				
Oh, No! My Calculator Is Broken	@			@
Lesson 4				
Multiplying by 10s	@			
Lesson 5				
Multiplication	@			
Lesson 6				
Estimation	@			
Lesson 7				
Multiplying Round Numbers	@			@
Lesson 8				
A Camping Trip	@			

Unit Resource Guide pages are from the teacher materials.

Order of Operations

An operation is work that someone or something does. When a surgeon takes out an appendix, he or she performs an *operation.* People who use cranes and bulldozers *operate* heavy machinery. If a pop machine is broken, then we say it is not *operating.*

Things that are done to numbers are also called **operations.** The four basic operations are addition, subtraction, multiplication, and division. People have agreed on a certain **order of operations** for arithmetic problems. The order in which you perform operations in an arithmetic problem is very important. You can see why in the problem below.

Mrs. Dewey brought raisins to the class picnic. There are six boxes of raisins in each snackpack.

After the picnic was over, there were 3 individual boxes of raisins and two unopened snackpacks left over. How many boxes of raisins were left?

Jessie said that there were 3 boxes and 2 snackpacks left over. She wrote this number sentence: $3 + 2 \times 6$. But, she didn't know whether to multiply or add first. Try both ways.

If you add $3 + 2$ first, the answer is 30 boxes of raisins. If you multiply 2×6 first, the answer is 15 boxes of raisins. Which is the correct answer?

There were three boxes and two snackpacks of raisins left over. This amount is shown below.

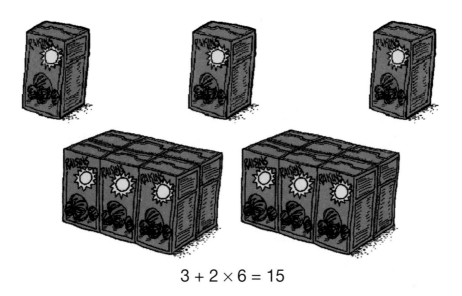

$$3 + 2 \times 6 = 15$$

If you count up all the boxes, you will see that the correct answer is 15 boxes of raisins left over. So, you need to multiply first in the problem: $3 + 2 \times 6$.

You cannot simply work from left to right when you solve problems like $3 + 2 \times 6$. Mathematicians have agreed on the following rules for the order of operations: First, do all the multiplications and divisions. If there are several multiplications and divisions, solve them from left to right.

When you finish all the multiplying and dividing, then do the additions and subtractions. Work from left to right. Some examples are shown below.

Do the multiplication first. Then, add.

$7 + (3 \times 4) = ?$
$7 + 12 = 19$

Do the division and multiplication first. Then, add.

$(6 \div 2) + (8 \times 2) = ?$
$3 + 16 = 19$

Order of Operations

Calculator Order of Operations

For each of these problems, first find the answer. Then, if possible, check your answer using a calculator that follows the order of operations.

1. $4 - 2 + 1$
2. $15 - 8 + 6 - 4$
3. $4 + 3 \times 2$
4. $4 + 9 - 3 \times 2$
5. $5 \times 2 + 3$
6. $3 + 5 \times 2$
7. $5 + 2 \times 3$
8. $6 \div 3 \times 2$
9. $4 \times 4 - 4 \div 4$
10. $4 + 4 \times 4 - 4$
11. $4 \times 4 - 4 - 4$
12. $4 \times 4 \div 4 - 4$
13. $10 + 6 \times 8$
14. $10 - 24 \div 6$
15. $8 \times 7 - 6$

Operation Target

This is a cooperative contest for two or three people. The goal is to use four digits and four operations (+, −, ×, and ÷) to make as many different whole numbers as you can. You need paper, a pencil, and a calculator.

You must use each of the four digits exactly once. You can use operations more than once or not at all. (All division operations must give whole numbers. For example, $9 ÷ 2 = 4.5$ is not allowed.)

16. Use 9, 5, 2, and 1 and +, −, ×, and ÷ to make as many whole numbers as you can. For example, $9 + 5 × 2 − 1 = 18$. List the numbers you make and show how you made them.

    A. What is the largest whole number you can make?

    B. What is the smallest whole number you can make?

    C. How many whole numbers less than 10 can you make? Write number sentences for each number.

    D. What whole numbers can you make in more than one way? Show at least two number sentences for each.

17. Pick four different digits. Make as many whole numbers as you can using your four new digits and +, −, ×, and ÷. List the numbers you make and show how you made them.

18. Nila used 1, 2, 3, and 4 to make 10. How do you think she did it? Can you think of another way?

19. Luis used 1, 2, 3, and 4 to make 24. How could he have done it?

20. Romesh used 1, 3, 5, and 7 to make 8. How could he have done it?

21. Make up your own problem like Questions 18, 19, and 20.

Divisibility Rules

Is It Divisible by 2?

Shannon, Roberto, and Ming are talking about good books to read. Shannon shows Roberto and Ming the book she is reading. She plans to read the book this weekend.

I want to read half of this 318-page book on Saturday and the other half on Sunday. How many pages should I read each day?

Divide 318 by 2 on the calculator. 318 ÷ 2 = 159 2 divides 318 evenly.

Of course, 318 is even.

Shannon checked Ming's answer by multiplying 159 by 2 on the calculator. She got 318 as her answer—159 × 2 = 318. Since 2 is a **factor** of 318, 318 is **divisible** by 2. A number is divisible by 2 if 2 divides it evenly, that is, if the answer is a whole number.

Shannon plans to read 159 pages each day. What if the book Shannon plans to read had 319 pages? On your calculator, press: [319] [÷] [2] [=] Your calculator window should show:

$$159.5$$

The ".5" in the calculator window tells us there is a remainder. If the book had 319 pages, Shannon could read 159 whole pages each day—Saturday and Sunday. But if she did that, she would only read 159 × 2 or 318 pages. There would be a remainder of one page. Shannon could divide the leftover page in half. (The decimal .5 is the same as $\frac{1}{2}$.) She could read $\frac{1}{2}$ page on Saturday and $\frac{1}{2}$ page on Sunday.

Since 2 does not divide 319 evenly (we do not get a whole number answer), 319 is not divisible by 2.

1. On a copy of the *100 Chart*, use a blue crayon or pencil to circle all the **multiples** of 2. Then, describe any patterns you see. Save your copy of the *100 Chart* for later use.

2. Shannon's book is 318 pages long. In which column would 318 be if the 100 chart kept going beyond 100?

3. **A.** Which of the following numbers are divisible by 2? Why do you think so? Check your predictions using a calculator.

109	213	216	275	784
1000	1358	2462	6767	8091

    B. Write a multiplication sentence and a division sentence for each number that is divisible by 2. For example: 216 ÷ 2 = 108 and 108 × 2 = 216

4. How can you tell if a number is divisible by 2?

Is It Divisible by 3?

12 is divisible by 3.
  4 × 3 = 12
  12 ÷ 3 = 4

21 is divisible by 3.
  7 × 3 = 21
  21 ÷ 3 = 7

30 is divisible by 3.
  10 × 3 = 30
  30 ÷ 3 = 10

3 is a factor of 12, 21, and 30. A factor of a number can be divided evenly into the number, that is, the answer (or quotient) is a whole number. Since 12, 21, and 30 can be divided by 3 evenly, we say that 12, 21, and 30 are divisible by 3.

5. Use your copy of the *100 Chart* that you used earlier (the multiples of 2 should be circled in blue). Using a red crayon or pencil, mark all the multiples of 3 with an "X." Your *100 Chart* should look like the one below.

1	(2)	X̶3̶	(4)	5	(6̶)	7	(8)	9̶	(10)
11	(12̶)	13	(14)	1̶5̶	(16)	17	(1̶8̶)	19	(20)
2̶1̶	(22)	23	(2̶4̶)	25	(26)	2̶7̶	(28)	29	(3̶0̶)

6. Describe any patterns you see.

7. Use your copy of the *100 Chart* and your calculator to help you answer the following questions:

   A. Is 27 a multiple of 3? Write a multiplication sentence.

   B. Is 27 divisible by 3? Write a division sentence.

   C. Is 51 a multiple of 3? Write a multiplication sentence.

   D. Is 51 divisible by 3? Write a division sentence.

8. A. Is 14 a multiple of 3? How do you know?

   B. If 14 is divided by 3, what is the remainder? Write a multiplication or division sentence. Remember to include the remainder.

   C. Use your calculator. Press: $\boxed{14}\ \boxed{\div}\ \boxed{3}\ \boxed{=}$
   How does your calculator show whether 14 is divisible by 3?

9. Is 74, 75, or 76 divisible by 3? Use your copy of the *100 Chart* or a calculator to decide. Write a division sentence showing which number is divisible by 3.

10. Look carefully at your *100 Chart*. Write in more numbers below it if you need to.

    A. Predict: Is 101 divisible by 3? Check your prediction with a calculator.

    B. Predict: Is 102 divisible by 3? Check your prediction with a calculator.

    C. Predict: Which of the following is divisible by 3? 116, 117, or 118? Why do you think so? Check your prediction with a calculator.

11. Mrs. Dewey started listing numbers from the *100 Chart* that were divisible by 3. Ming saw a pattern. Do you? Explain.

Number	Sum of Digits
18	1 + 8 = **9**
42	4 + 2 = **6**
51	5 + 1 = **6**
84	8 + 4 = **12**
99	9 + 9 = **18**

12. Name a number greater than 125 that is divisible by 3. Check your prediction.

13. Name a number greater than 200 that is divisible by 3. Check your prediction.

14. Use the numbers below to make predictions for Questions 14A–14C. Then, check your predictions with a calculator.

126	209	342	177	1664
1002	991	297	8770	8775

    A. Which of the numbers are divisible by 3?

    B. Which are divisible by 2?

    C. Which are divisible by 2 and 3?

15. Is 12,345,678 divisible by 2? Divisible by 3? Check using your calculator.

Is It Divisible by 6?

16. A. Find out which numbers in Question 14 are divisible by 6. Use a calculator.

    B. How can you determine if a number is divisible by 6? Find the multiples of 6 by skip counting by 6s on your *100 Chart*. What do you notice?

    C. Based on the patterns you see, predict whether 12,345,678 (from Question 15) is divisible by 6. Check your prediction.

17. A. Give a number greater than 150 that is divisible by 6.

    B. Give a number greater than 225 that is divisible by 6. Explain how you found your number.

Is It Divisible by 9?

18. Copy and complete the list of facts for 9. Then, write the products in a column, one on each line.

$$1 \times 9 =$$
$$2 \times 9 =$$
$$3 \times 9 =$$
$$4 \times 9 =$$
$$5 \times 9 =$$
$$6 \times 9 =$$
$$7 \times 9 =$$
$$8 \times 9 =$$
$$9 \times 9 =$$
$$9 \times 10 =$$

19. What patterns do you see? What can you say about the sum of the digits of the products?

20. Use your calculator to find more multiples of 9. Find the products below.

   A. $9 \times 634 =$ **B.** $9 \times 23 =$

   C. $9 \times 37 =$ **D.** $9 \times 73 =$

   E. $9 \times 143 =$ **F.** $9 \times 444 =$

   G. $9 \times 754 =$ **H.** $9 \times 4421 =$

21. Go back and add the digits of each product in Question 20.
    For example: $9 \times 634 = 5706$
    Add the digits in 5706: $5 + 7 + 0 + 6 = 18$
    Now, add the digits in 18: $1 + 8 = 9$
    Describe what happens when you add the digits of a multiple of 9.

22. **A.** Predict which numbers below are divisible by 9. Show how you decided.

    B. Then, check using a calculator.

    C. Finally, write a multiplication and division sentence for each multiple of 9 you identify.

172	144	743	747	1007
2556	4906	8721	9908	12,987

You will need a clean copy of the *100 Chart* to complete this homework.

1. Which numbers below are divisible by 2? Tell how you decided.

345	980	1369	1197	3288
9036	2273	1035	8665	2073

2. Which numbers are divisible by 3? Tell how you decided.

3. Which numbers are divisible by 6? Tell how you decided.

4. Which numbers are divisible by 9? Tell how you decided.

5. Are any of the numbers divisible by 2, 3, 6, and 9? Which one(s)?

6. Use a clean copy of a *100 Chart* and a calculator to explore the following.

    A. Skip count by 5s on the *100 Chart.* Mark each multiple of 5. Then, skip count by 10s and mark the multiples of 10.

    B. Describe how you know a number is divisible by 5. In your description, include:
       - Examples of numbers that are divisible by 5.
       - Multiplication sentences and division sentences for those numbers.
       - Descriptions of patterns you see on the *100 Chart.*
       - Any keystrokes you used on the calculator.

    C. Describe how you know a number is divisible by 10. In your description, include:
       - Examples of numbers that are divisible by 10.
       - Multiplication sentences and division sentences for those numbers.
       - Descriptions of patterns you see on the *100 Chart.*
       - Any keystrokes you used on the calculator.

Use the order of operations.

7. $6 \times 7 - 4 \times 8 =$

8. $1 + 48 \div 8 =$

9. $4 + 7 \times 8 =$

10. $4 \times 7 - 24 \div 6 =$

Oh, No! My Calculator Is Broken

Multiplication

What's the matter with this calculator?

Mrs. Dewey passed out calculators to her class. She asked the class to use the calculators to do 6 × 8. John pressed: | 6 | × | 8 | = |.

He soon realized the | 8 | key on his calculator was broken. Both Keenya and Grace tried their calculators. They each found that the | × | keys on their calculators were broken. In fact, all of the calculators in the class had keys that didn't work. Mrs. Dewey said, "Some of the keys on these calculators have been disconnected. Think about how you can use your calculator to multiply 6 × 8."

John knew that he could break apart 8 into 5 + 3. He could then multiply 6 × 5 and 6 × 3 and add the two products together to get 6 × 8. To show his solution, John recorded the following keystrokes:

| 6 | × | 5 | + | 6 | × | 3 | = |

Since the $\boxed{\times}$ key was broken on Keenya's calculator, she decided to turn 6×8 into an addition problem. Keenya recorded the following keystrokes:

$$\boxed{8}\ \boxed{+}\ \boxed{8}\ \boxed{+}\ \boxed{8}\ \boxed{+}\ \boxed{8}\ \boxed{+}\ \boxed{8}\ \boxed{+}\ \boxed{8}\ \boxed{=}$$

Grace knew that 6×8 would be twice the answer to 3×8. "Since $3 \times 8 = 24$, I can use my calculator to add $24 + 24$ to find the answer for 6×8." She recorded these keystrokes:

$$\boxed{24}\ \boxed{+}\ \boxed{24}\ \boxed{=}$$

With your calculator try each of the strategies suggested by Grace, John, and Keenya. Do you get the same answer with each strategy?

1. **A.** Pretend you are using Keenya's calculator and the $\boxed{\times}$ key is broken. Give a different list of keystrokes to find 6×8. Record your keystrokes on your own paper.

   B. Pretend you are using John's calculator and the $\boxed{8}$ key is broken. Give a different list of keystrokes to find 6×8. Record your keystrokes on your own paper.

Use a calculator to do the problems below two different ways. For each problem, record the keystrokes you pressed.

2. Imagine that the $\boxed{6}$ key on your calculator is broken.

   A. $6 \times 7 =$ **B.** $6 \times 4 =$

3. Imagine that the $\boxed{7}$ key on your calculator is broken.

   A. $7 \times 8 =$ **B.** $6 \times 7 =$

4. Imagine that the $\boxed{2}$ key on your calculator is broken. Use your calculator to find the answer to this problem in two ways: $4 \times 2 \times 7 =$. Record your keystrokes.

5. Imagine that the $\boxed{\times}$ key on your calculator is broken. Use your calculator to find the answer to each problem in two ways. Record your keystrokes.

   A. $9 \times 6 =$ **B.** $9 \times 7 =$

Discuss

There are many strategies for doing multiplication problems. Some strategies are easier to use without a calculator.

Maya found a strategy for multiplying 9 × 4. She said, "First I will multiply 10 × 4, then if I subtract 4 from 40, I will get 9 × 4."

$10 \times 4 = 40$
$40 - 4 = ?$

6. **A.** Why is Maya multiplying 10 × 4?

   B. Why is she subtracting 4?

7. How would you explain Maya's strategy to a friend?

8. Use Maya's strategy to solve 9 × 7. Explain your thinking.

9. What are some strategies you could use to solve 12 × 8?

Addition and Subtraction

Shannon found an old calculator. When she tried the calculator, she found that only the clear key and these keys worked:

She found that she could get the number 2 on her display by pressing:
, but she wondered if she could figure out a way to get the number 1 on her display.

10. Help Shannon think of a strategy she could use to get a 1 on her calculator display.

11. What keystrokes can Shannon use to get the number 55 on her calculator display? Remember, you can only use the 6 keys that work.

Multiplying by 10s

On Monday, ten of the candy machines at the TIMS Candy Company were working. Each machine can make four Chocos in one minute. On Monday, how many Chocos were made every minute at the company?

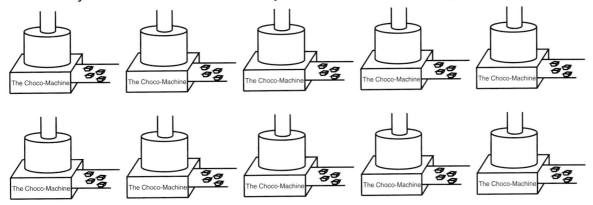

A number sentence for this question is $4 + 4 + 4 + 4 + 4 + 4 + 4 + 4 + 4 + 4 = n$.

Another way to write this is $10 \times 4 = n$. What number must n be to make the sentences true?

The value of n is 40 (or $n = 40$) since 40 is 10 groups of 4.

$4 + 4 + 4 + 4 + 4 + 4 + 4 + 4 + 4 + 4 = 40$ and $10 \times 4 = 40$.

We can also say this as $4 \times 10 = 40$. This is the same as 4 groups of 10.

Complete Questions 1 and 2. You may use your calculator.

1. There are 10 polar bears at the Greenville Zoo. Each bear eats 6 pounds of fish a day. How many pounds of fish are eaten by polar bears at the Greenville Zoo every day? Write an addition sentence for this problem and solve. Write a multiplication sentence for the problem and solve.

2. Tanya has 10 friends who wrote her letters when she was away at camp. Each friend wrote Tanya 3 letters. How many letters did Tanya receive? Draw a picture of the problem and write a multiplication sentence.

3. Luis says that multiplication by multiples of 10 is easy.

   A. Do the following problems. You may use your calculator if necessary.

10	20	40	30	70	40	80	20	90
× 6	× 3	× 3	× 7	× 2	× 6	× 2	× 9	× 8

   B. Do you notice a pattern in multiplying by multiples of 10? Describe it.

4. Do the following problems. You may use your multiplication table.

60	70	40	20	50	50	90
× 4	× 5	× 7	× 2	× 6	× 5	× 3

5. Frank said one of the problems in Question 4 was tricky. He almost got it wrong. Which one do you think Frank is talking about and why is it tricky?

6. Irma found some more patterns on her calculator. Describe the patterns.

   $7 \times 1 = 7$ $7 \times 4 = 28$
   $7 \times 10 = 70$ $7 \times 40 = 280$
   $7 \times 100 = 700$ $7 \times 400 = 2800$
   $7 \times 1000 = 7000$ $7 \times 4000 = 28,000$
   $7 \times 10,000 = 70,000$ $7 \times 40000 = 280,000$

7. Find the products. You may use a calculator if necessary.

   A. $6 \times 1 =$
      $6 \times 10 =$
      $6 \times 100 =$
      $6 \times 1000 =$
      $6 \times 10,000 =$

   B. $6 \times 3 =$
      $6 \times 30 =$
      $6 \times 300 =$
      $6 \times 3000 =$
      $6 \times 30,000 =$

   C. $6 \times 5 =$
      $6 \times 50 =$
      $6 \times 500 =$
      $6 \times 5000 =$
      $6 \times 50,000 =$

8. For the following problems, make a prediction of what you think the answer will be. Then, do the problem on your calculator to check.

   A. 8×30 **B.** 40×5 **C.** 200×3 **D.** 5×600

   E. 7×2000 **F.** 90×4 **G.** 600×2

9. Predict what number n must be to make the number sentence true. Check your work on a calculator.

   A. $200 \times 5 = n$ **B.** $60 \times n = 120$ **C.** $5000 \times n = 15,000$

   D. $n \times 40 = 80$ **E.** $n \times 700 = 4900$ **F.** $6 \times n = 6000$

   G. $n \times 6 = 3600$ **H.** $2 \times n = 1400$

10. Can you find a rule that makes multiplying numbers that end in zeros easy?

Homework

For the following problems, make a prediction of what you think the answer will be. Then, do the problem on your calculator to check.

1. 8×3
   8×30
   8×300
   8×3000
   $8 \times 30,000$

2. 9×6
   9×60
   9×600
   9×6000
   $9 \times 60,000$

3. 7×6
   7×60
   7×600
   7×6000
   $7 \times 60,000$

4. $30 \times 7 = n$

5. $500 \times 8 = n$

6. $300 \times 9 = n$

7. $7 \times 200 = n$

8. $4 \times 6000 = n$

9. $\begin{array}{r} 3000 \\ \times\ 4 \\ \hline \end{array}$ 10. $\begin{array}{r} 5000 \\ \times\ 7 \\ \hline \end{array}$ 11. $\begin{array}{r} 100 \\ \times\ 9 \\ \hline \end{array}$ 12. $\begin{array}{r} 400 \\ \times\ 3 \\ \hline \end{array}$ 13. $\begin{array}{r} 600 \\ \times\ 2 \\ \hline \end{array}$

14. A zoo has 10 displays of turtles. Each display has 4 turtles. How many turtles are at the zoo? Draw a picture. Write an addition sentence and a multiplication sentence. Solve.

15. There are 10 elevators in an office building. There can be up to 9 people in an elevator at one time. How many people can ride the elevators at the same time?

16. There are 3 juice boxes in a juice pack. If Roberto's mother buys 10 juice packs, how many juice boxes is that?

17. A juice pack costs $2.00. How much will 8 juice packs cost? How much will 10 juice packs cost?

18. There are 30 desks in every fourth-grade classroom at Holmes School. If there are 5 fourth-grade classes, how many desks are there for fourth graders?

19. There are 8 granola bars in a package. A school buys 40 packages. How many granola bars is that?

20. A large bottle of ketchup costs $3.00. The head cook at Stanley School buys 40 bottles. How much money does he spend on ketchup?

Predict what number _n_ must be to make the number sentence true. Check your work on a calculator.

21. $200 \times n = 600$

22. $n \times 2 = 800$

23. $2 \times n = 600$

24. $2 \times n = 20{,}000$

25. $n \times 7000 = 42{,}000$

26. $n \times 800 = 3200$

27. $60 \times 7 = n$

28. $n \times 8 = 320$

29. $n \times 400 = 2800$

Multiplication

Mrs. Haddad noticed that 4 of the workers at the TIMS Candy Company each made 32 Chocos in one hour. To find the total number of Chocos made, Mrs. Haddad used base-ten pieces and wrote 32 + 32 + 32 + 32. She said this could be an addition problem or a multiplication problem.

Base-Ten Board

Mrs. Haddad used the **all-partials method** to solve the problem by multiplication. Since there are 4 groups of 2 bits, there are 8 bits total.

Recording Sheet

	3	2
×		4
		8

Since there are 4 groups of 3 skinnies, this makes 12 skinnies or 1 flat, 2 skinnies, and 0 bits or 120 bits. The workers made a total of 128 Chocos in 1 hour.

Recording Sheet

		3	2
	×		4
			8
1	2	0	
1	2	8	

One of the employees at the TIMS Candy Company solved the problem a little differently. His work is shown here. He first found that 4 groups of 3 skinnies makes 120 bits. Then, he found that 4 groups of 2 bits makes 8 bits total. The answer matches Mrs. Haddad's answer—128 Chocos.

Recording Sheet

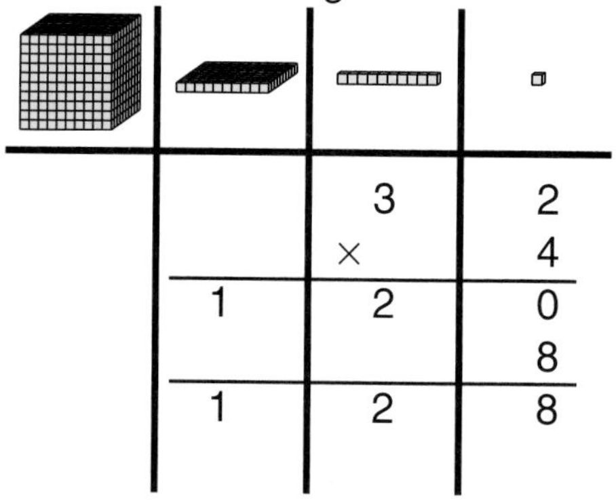

	3	2
×		4
1	2	0
		8
1	2	8

1. On another day, 3 workers at the TIMS Candy Company each made 26 pieces of candy in one hour.

Base-Ten Board

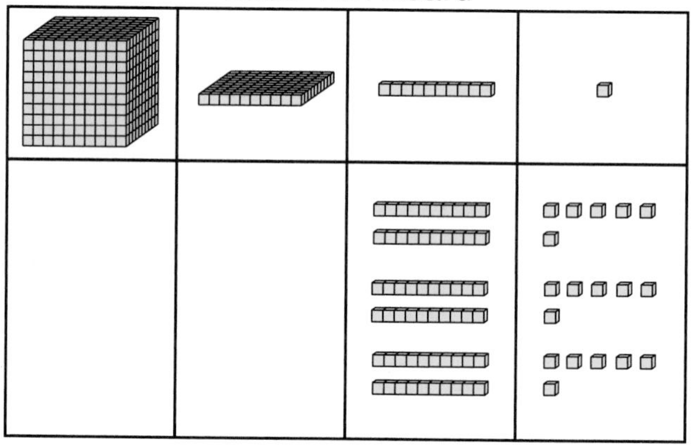

A. Fill in the missing numbers. Since there are 3 groups of 6 bits, there are ____ bits or ____ skinny and ____ bits.

We write this as shown on the *Recording Sheet* to the right.

Recording Sheet

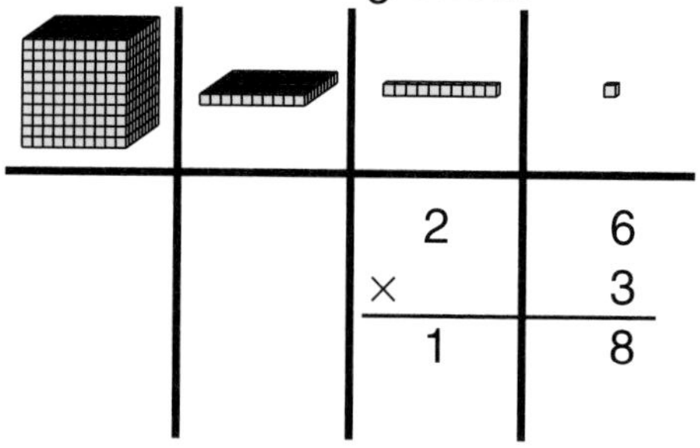

	2	6
×		3
	1	8

Multiplication

B. Since there are 3 groups of 2 skinnies, there are ____ skinnies. This is the same as ____ skinnies and ____ bits.

We write this as shown on the *Recording Sheet* to the right.

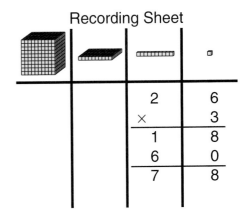

Recording Sheet

		2	6
	×		3
		1	8
		6	0
		7	8

C. What is the total number of candies made by the workers at the TIMS Candy Company?

Use base-ten pieces and the all-partials method to do the following problems:

2. 12
×3

3. 61
×4

4. 26
×4

5. 57
×4

6. 83
×9

Homework

Solve the following problems. You may use your multiplication table. You may also check your work on a calculator.

1. 20
×8

50
×3

90
×4

60
×7

40
×9

70
×6

80
×6

2. 100
×5

30,000
×7

700
×5

200
×4

40,000
×6

700
×8

3. Find *n* for each of the problems.

A. $5 \times 60 = n$

B. $70 \times 2 = n$

C. $n = 3 \times 600$

D. $n = 100 \times 5$

E. $n \times 70 = 140$

F. $500 \times n = 4000$

G. $80 = n \times 20$

H. $700 = 7 \times n$

I. $7 \times 800 = n$

Write a number sentence for each problem and solve. You may also want to draw a picture.

4. A sailboat can travel about 30 miles in 1 hour. How far can the sailboat travel in 6 hours?

5. There are about 50 crackers in a box. If 5 children share the box, how many crackers does each child get?

6. Mr. Thoms drove for 3 hours without stopping. He drove about 50 miles every hour (50 miles per hour or 50 mph). About how far did he drive?

Fill in the missing numbers in the multiplication problems. You may use base-ten shorthand if it is helpful. You may also use your multiplication table.

7. 13
    × 7
    ___
    21
    70
    ___
    ◯

8. 42
    × 6
    ___
    ◯
    240
    ___
    252

9. 51
    × 4
    ___
    4
    ◯
    ___
    204

10. Solve the problems. You may use base-ten shorthand if it is helpful. You may also use your multiplication tables.

A. 14	B. 21	C. 52	D. 25	E. 41
× 2	× 6	× 3	× 3	× 6

F. 65	G. 83	H. 76	I. 78	J. 67
× 6	× 7	× 9	× 6	× 4

11. There are 32 students in Miguel's class. For his birthday, Miguel's mother baked cookies to bring to school. If he wanted to give each student 4 cookies, how many cookies must his mother bake?

12. At Livingston School there are 3 fourth-grade classes. If there are 26 students in each class, how many fourth graders are there at Livingston School?

13. A zoo has 22 lions. Each lion eats 8 pounds of meat a day. How much meat must the zookeeper bring to the lion exhibit each day?

14. The Rodriguez family is having a big party. Mrs. Rodriguez knows she should have 70 cans of soda. Ana buys 3 cases of soda. Each case contains 24 cans of soda. Will this be enough soda? Why or why not?

15. The array below has 6 rows of 13 tiles. How many tiles are in the array?

16. An array has 7 rows of 46 tiles. How many tiles in all are in the array?

17. An array has 9 rows of 58 tiles. How many tiles in all are in the array?

18. An array has 7 rows of 99 tiles. How many tiles? Explain a way to do this problem in your head.

Estimation

Nicholas wants to buy two books that each cost $5.79. He **estimates** the cost of the two books to get a good idea of how much he will have to spend. In order to find the estimate, Nicholas uses a **convenient number.** He thinks, "$5.79 is close to $6.00 but $6.00 is easier to work with than $5.79." He multiplies $2 \times \$6$ in his head and comes up with an estimate of $12.00.

As Nicholas waited in line at the cashier, he shared his estimate with Lee Yah. She estimated the total too and then said, "Your estimate is close to mine. I doubled $5.80. I knew $2 \times \$5$ is $10 and $2 \times 80¢ = \$1.60$. My estimate is $11.60."

Nicholas chose the number 6 when estimating because it was a convenient number to work with in his head. He rounded $5.79 to the nearest whole dollar, $6. Rounded numbers are one type of convenient number. Lee Yah chose the convenient number $5.80 because she could double $5.80 in her head more easily than $5.79. Remember, a number that is convenient for one person might not be convenient for another.

1. A. Keenya has a bag of 25 oatmeal cookies to share with her friends. There are 6 girls altogether. How might Keenya decide on the number of cookies each girl gets?

   B. Keenya thinks, "I have about 24 cookies. Since 6×4 is 24, each of us gets 4 cookies." What is Keenya's convenient number? How did she pick it?

2. Jackie's Girl Scout troop is planning a hike. The troop needs to know how heavy the supplies will be. Jackie weighs a bottle of water and finds that it weighs 4.1 kg. About how much will 3 bottles of water weigh?

We find estimates when we need to have a good idea about how big or small a number is, but we do not need to know exactly. Sometimes it is impossible to know an exact answer. We use estimates in many different situations.

For example:
You can estimate how far you live from Boston or Chicago.
You can estimate how many people are watching a Little League game.
You can estimate how much you will pay for a full cart of groceries.

When we estimate, we find a number or answer that is reasonably close to the actual number. It may be bigger or smaller than the actual number, depending on the problem. To make an estimate, we sometimes need to do some number operations in our head. To make these computations easy to do in our heads, we often choose **convenient numbers** to make our estimates. Convenient numbers are really estimates as well.

Which of the answers in Questions 3 and 4 are reasonable estimates? There may be more than one reasonable answer. When is one estimate better than another? Which answers are unreasonable?

3. Mrs. Borko buys 4 jackets for her children. Each jacket costs $47. About how much will all 4 jackets cost?

   A. $100   B. $20   C. $160   D. $2000   E. $200

4. There are about 27 students in each fourth-grade class at Hill Street Elementary School. If there are 6 fourth-grade classes, how many fourth-graders are there at the school?

   A. 120   B. 1200   C. 150   D. 180   E. 300

5. Keenya and her sister went to a concert in the park with her parents. People sat in rows on benches. Keenya counted 12 people in the first row. There were 9 rows.

   A. Keenya thought, "There are about 10 people in each of the 9 rows. There are about . . ." Finish Keenya's statement using 10 as a convenient number.

   B. Keenya's sister thought, "There are about 10 rows and about 10 people in each row. I'd say there are about . . ." Finish her statement. What convenient numbers did Keenya's sister use to make her estimate?

6. At the grocery store, Jackie and her brother pick some grapes and weigh them. The grapes weigh 3 pounds and 7 ounces. Grapes are on sale for 49¢ a pound (1 pound = 16 ounces). Jackie and her brother estimate the price of the grapes.

   A. Jackie thinks, "3 pounds and 7 ounces is about 4 pounds. 4 pounds of grapes, at 50¢ a pound, would be . . ." Finish Jackie's statement. Will the actual price be higher or lower than this estimate?

B. Jackie's brother thinks, "3 pounds of grapes cost 3 × 50¢ or $1.50. 7 ounces is about $\frac{1}{2}$ pound. If 1 pound costs 50¢, $\frac{1}{2}$ pound costs about 25¢. The grapes we picked should cost about . . ." Finish his statement.

C. If Jackie and her brother want to be sure they have enough money for the grapes, whose estimate would be better to use? Why do you think so?

7. Michael's father travels 36 miles to work every day.

A. About how many miles does he travel to and from work in one week (5 days)? Solve this problem in your head. Then, explain how you solved it. Be sure to tell what convenient numbers you used.

B. Share your method with a classmate. What convenient numbers did your classmate choose?

Estimating Mileage

Jerome and his family are thinking about taking a vacation. Jerome found a mileage chart.

	Chicago	Indianapolis	Louisville	St. Louis
Chicago	×	179	294	302
Indianapolis	179	×	112	257
Louisville	294	112	×	275
St. Louis	302	257	275	×

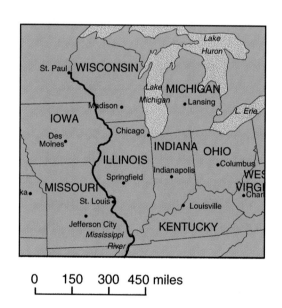

0   150   300   450 miles

8. **A.** How far is it from Chicago to Indianapolis?

B. Give two possible convenient numbers for this distance.

9. About how many miles will they travel if Jerome's family drives from Chicago to Indianapolis, and then back home to Chicago?

10. **A.** Which drive is longer: the drive from Chicago to Indianapolis or the drive from Indianapolis to St. Louis?

B. About how much longer?

11. First, Jerome's family plans on taking the following trip: Chicago to Louisville, Louisville to St. Louis, and St. Louis back home to Chicago. About how many miles is this trip?

12. Jerome's family changes plans. They decide on the following trip: Chicago to Indianapolis, Indianapolis to Louisville, and Louisville back home to Chicago. About how many miles will they drive altogether?

13. Their car goes about 21 miles on one gallon of gasoline. At the start of the trip, their gas tank has about 12 gallons of gas.

    A. About how many miles can they travel on 12 gallons of gas?

    B. Will they have to get more gas before they reach Indianapolis? Before they reach Louisville?

14. At the time they were leaving, gasoline cost about $1.69 per gallon in Chicago. They estimated that they would need about 28 gallons of gas in all to make the trip. If gas costs about the same in other cities as in Chicago, about how much money will they spend for gas on the trip?

15. Jerome's parents averaged 48 miles per hour on the entire trip. By the time they got back to Chicago, did the family drive for more or less than 8 hours? How did you decide?

Homework

Estimate answers to these problems. Be ready to tell how you used convenient numbers.

1. Ana found 12 tomatoes on one tomato plant. Ana has 11 tomato plants. If all the plants have about the same number of tomatoes, about how many tomatoes do the plants have altogether?

2. A box of crackers weighs 269 grams. About how much do 5 boxes of crackers weigh together?

3. If a pizza costs $3.75, a bag of apples $2.50, and a quart of milk $.80, about how much money is needed to buy one of each?

4. If a pizza costs $3.75, about how much will 3 pizzas cost?

5. Jacob's brother works at a fast-food restaurant and earns $5.15 an hour. If he worked 20 hours one week, about how much money did he earn?

6. Tanya earned $5.45 baby-sitting on Monday and $8.70 on Tuesday. She spent $6.65 of this money on Wednesday. About how much money does she have left?

7. Mount McKinley in Alaska is the highest mountain in the United States. It is 20,320 feet above sea level. The highest mountain in the 48 contiguous states (all the states except Alaska and Hawaii) is Mount Whitney in California. Mount Whitney is 14,494 feet above sea level. About how much higher is Mount McKinley than Mount Whitney?

Use the map below to answer Questions 8–13.

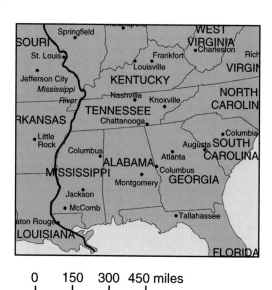

	Montgomery	Atlanta	Nashville	Jackson
Montgomery	×	163	286	247
Atlanta	163	×	250	381
Nashville	286	250	×	416
Jackson	247	381	416	×

0   150   300   450 miles

8. **A.** How far is it from Montgomery, Alabama, to Jackson, Mississippi?

   B. What is a convenient number to use in place of this number?

9. **A.** How far is it from Nashville, Tennessee, to Montgomery, Alabama?

   B. What is a convenient number to use in place of this number?

10. About how many miles is a drive from Nashville, Tennessee, to Montgomery, Alabama, and back home to Nashville?

11. **A.** Which drive is longer: a drive from Montgomery to Nashville or a drive from Montgomery to Jackson?

   B. About how much longer?

12. About how long is the following trip: from Jackson to Montgomery, from Montgomery to Nashville, and then Nashville back home to Jackson?

13. About how long is the following trip: from Atlanta to Montgomery, Montgomery to Jackson, and Jackson back home to Atlanta?

Multiplying Round Numbers

The Beautiful Blooms Garden Store sells many trays of flowers. A tray of flowers has 6 rows. There are 8 flowers in each row.

1. How many flowers are in each tray?

Ana and Grace went to the Beautiful Blooms Garden Store. They noticed that the trays of flowers were stored on a shelf. Ana counted 28 trays on a shelf.

Ana said, "I wonder how many flowers are on one of these shelves."

Grace replied, "We can estimate the number of flowers on a shelf: 48 flowers is about 50 and 28 trays is about 30 trays. So what is 50 × 30?"

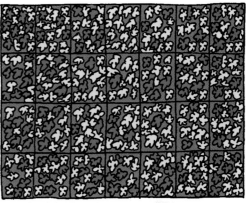

28 trays of flowers on a shelf

2. Ana learned that patterns often help us multiply. Find the following products using a calculator if needed. Describe any patterns you see.

   A. 5 × 3 =

   B. 5 × 30 =

   C. 50 × 3 =

   D. 50 × 30 =

   E. 50 × 300 =

   F. 500 × 30 =

   G. 500 × 300 =

3. About how many flowers did Ana and Grace see on a shelf?

4. Discuss other ways to compute 50 × 30.

---

5. Find the following pairs of products in your head. Check your work on a calculator if needed.

    A. 80   80   **B.** 20   20   **C.** 50   50
        ×2 ×20   ×4 ×40   ×7 ×70

    D. 90   90   **E.** 70   70   **F.** 30   30
        ×7 ×70   ×1 ×10   ×6 ×60

    G. $90 \times 20 =$ **H.** $40 \times 50 =$ **I.** $60 \times 40 =$

6. **A.** Ana and Grace counted 10 shelves of marigolds. If there are 28 trays on each shelf, about how many trays of marigolds are there?

    Grace said, "Wow, there's a lot of marigolds here. There are 10 shelves and about 30 trays on each shelf. Since $10 \times 30 = 300$, I estimated 300 trays of marigolds."

    B. Ana said, "If each tray has about 50 flowers and there are about 300 trays, that means there are $50 \times 300 = 15,000$ marigolds. That's amazing!"

28 trays on each of 10 shelves is about 10×30 or 300 trays.

300 trays with about 50 flowers on each is 50×300 or 15,000 marigolds.

What is another way to estimate the total number of flowers?

Find the following products with your calculator. Look for patterns.

7. $4 \times 7 =$
   $40 \times 7 =$
   $4 \times 70 =$
   $40 \times 70 =$
   $400 \times 70 =$
   $40 \times 700 =$
   $400 \times 700 =$

8. $6 \times 7 =$
   $60 \times 7 =$
   $6 \times 70 =$
   $60 \times 70 =$
   $600 \times 70 =$
   $60 \times 700 =$
   $600 \times 700 =$

9. $8 \times 5 =$
   $80 \times 5 =$
   $8 \times 50 =$
   $80 \times 50 =$
   $800 \times 50 =$
   $80 \times 500 =$
   $800 \times 500 =$

10. Ana says she can multiply 40×40 in her head easily. What method do you think Ana is using? What is 40×40?

11. Ana saw that for every zero in the factors, there is a zero in the product. Do you agree? Explain.

12. Grace says multiplying 400×50 is tricky. What is 400×50? Why is it tricky?

In Question 6, Ana and Grace used convenient numbers to estimate the number of flowers they saw.

For Questions 13–18, complete steps A and B.

   A. Estimate the following products in your head by finding convenient numbers. Be prepared to share your strategies.

   B. Use a calculator to compute the product. Then, use your estimate to see if your answer is reasonable.

13. $32 \times 6 =$ 14. $4 \times 67 =$ 15. $8 \times 99 =$

16. $30 \times 41 =$ 17. $40 \times 49 =$ 18. $300 \times 24 =$

19. Describe a way to compute the exact product in your head in Question 15 without using a calculator or pencil and paper.

Homework

Find the products using mental computation.

1.	40	2.	60	3.	500	4.	800	5.	300
	$\times 70$		$\times 60$		$\times 60$		$\times 30$		$\times 30$

6.	100	7.	600	8.	400	9.	2000	10.	6000
	$\times 100$		$\times 40$		$\times 200$		$\times 800$		$\times 700$

11. Explain how to multiply two numbers that end in zeros.

For Questions 12–24, estimate the products using convenient numbers.

12.	42	13.	76	14.	69
	$\times 8$		$\times 4$		$\times 7$

15. Describe a way to compute the exact product in Question 14 using mental math.

16. $60 \times 34 =$ **17.** $50 \times 79 =$ **18.** $320 \times 70 =$ **19.** $496 \times 90 =$

The Bessie Coleman Parent Teacher Committee (PTC) decided to plant a garden by the school.

20. If there are about 38 daisies in a flat and 23 families each donate a flat of daisies to the garden, about how many daisy plants were donated?

21. The PTC bought 32 trays of assorted flowers. Each tray contains 48 flowers. About how many plants did the PTC buy?

22. A rose bush costs $6.89. The PTC bought 18 bushes. About how much did the PTC spend on rose bushes?

23. The PTC bought 35 bags of top soil. Each bag weighs 40 pounds. About how many pounds of top soil did they buy?

24. The PTC held a fun fair to help with the cost of the garden. Adult tickets cost $5.75 and children's tickets cost $2.25. The PTC sold 89 adult tickets and 112 children's tickets. About how much money did they make?

A Camping Trip

Estimate, then solve each problem. Use your estimate to check whether your solution is reasonable.

Ana and her family are going camping at the Potawatomi (POD-A-WAD-TO-MI) State Park in Wisconsin. The fee to camp in the park is $12.00 a night for families who live in Wisconsin and $16.00 a night for people who do not live in Wisconsin.

1. Ana's family is arriving on Tuesday and staying until Sunday afternoon. Ana's family lives in Illinois. How much does Ana's family have to pay?

2. Nadia, a fourth grader from Milwaukee, Wisconsin, is also camping from Tuesday until Sunday. How much does Nadia's family pay to stay at the park?

3. How much more does Ana's family pay than Nadia's?

A campground is a big area where many people can pitch their tents. A campground is divided into campsites. Each family that camps at the park gets a campsite.

4. There are 4 campgrounds in the park. Each campground has 120 campsites. How many families can stay at the park at one time?

5. Ana, who is 10 years old, her 12-year-old brother Felipe, and Dalia, her 5-year-old sister, want to explore the park. Their father and mother ask them to help put up the tent. Dalia looked at her watch when they began. It was 2:06. They finished setting up the tent at 2:52. How long did it take them to set up the tent?

6. One evening, Ana's family ate dinner at a restaurant in a nearby town. The restaurant had an "all-you-can-eat" fish dinner. The cost is $7.00 for adults, $5.00 for children ages 6–11, and $2.50 for children ages 3–5. If the whole family orders the fish dinner, how much will the total bill be?

Ana's 11-year-old cousin Roberto, his mother, and his little sister Angela come to the park on Friday. They set up their tent at a nearby campsite. The families decide to go canoeing together. It costs $8.00 to rent a canoe for 1 hour. Each canoe holds 3 people.

7. Every person who is in a boat needs a life jacket. How many adult life jackets do they need? (Adults are ages 12 and up.) How many children's life jackets do they need?

8. How many canoes will they need to rent? There must be at least one adult in every canoe. (Adults are ages 12 and up.) Draw a picture of how Ana's and Roberto's families can seat themselves in the canoes.

9. How much will they have to pay if they canoe for 1 hour?

10. How much will they have to pay if they canoe for 2 hours?

11. **A.** After canoeing, Ana's and Roberto's families decide to stop for frozen yogurt at the snack shop. A single-dip cone is 69¢. The price includes tax. Estimate how much money is needed to buy a cone for every person in both families.

    B. Ana gives the cashier $10.00 to pay for all the cones. About how much change will she get back?

12. The families decide to go on a long hike Saturday morning. Ana's father brought ingredients to make gorp. Gorp is a high-energy snack that is easy to take on a hike. Here is his recipe for 4 servings of gorp:

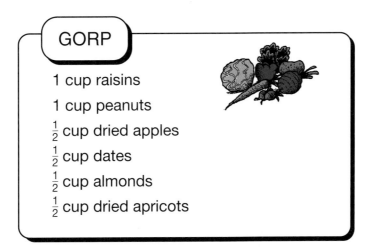

GORP

1 cup raisins

1 cup peanuts

$\frac{1}{2}$ cup dried apples

$\frac{1}{2}$ cup dates

$\frac{1}{2}$ cup almonds

$\frac{1}{2}$ cup dried apricots

    Ana's father wants to make a serving of gorp for everybody who went camping. How many servings of gorp does he need to make?

13. How many cups of peanuts should he use?

14. How many cups of dried apricots should he use?

15. Driving home from their vacation, Roberto's mother says they will travel about 50 miles in 1 hour. It takes them about 6 hours to get home. About how far is the park from their home?

16. Make up a story for the multiplication problems below and solve the problem. Your story can be about camping or anything else.

$$\begin{array}{r} 12 \\ \times 8 \\ \hline \end{array} \qquad \begin{array}{r} 8 \\ \times 6 \\ \hline \end{array} \qquad \begin{array}{r} \$1.75 \\ \times 8 \\ \hline \end{array}$$

Unit 8

Measuring Up: An Assessment Unit

	Student Guide	Discovery Assignment Book	Adventure Book	Unit Resource Guide*
Lesson 1				
Volume	◎	◎		
Lesson 2				
Fill It First	◎	◎		
Lesson 3				
Volume vs. Number	◎	◎		
Lesson 4				
Review Problems	◎			
Lesson 5				
Hour Walk				◎
Lesson 6				
Midyear Test				◎
Lesson 7				
Midyear Experiment and Portfolio Review	◎	◎		
Lesson 8				
Facts I Know: Multiplication and Division Facts	◎	◎		◎

*Unit Resource Guide pages are from the teacher materials.

Volume

The Crow and the Pitcher

This is a very old story of a very thirsty crow. The crow, ready to die of thirst, flew with joy to a pitcher which he saw some distance away. When he came to the pitcher, he found water in it, but so near the bottom that he was not able to drink. Then, he tried to knock over the pitcher so he might at least get a little of the water. But, he did not have enough strength for this. At last, seeing some pebbles nearby, he dropped them one by one into the pitcher, so little by little, he raised the water to the very brim and satisfied his thirst.

1. Why did the water in the pitcher rise?

2. Do you think the water in the pitcher rose the same amount each time a pebble was dropped in? Why or why not?

The **volume** of a rock is the amount of space it takes up. The volume of the pitcher is the amount of space inside it.

We measure volume in cubic units. A **cubic centimeter** (cc) is the amount of space taken up by a cube that is one centimeter long on each side.

1 cubic centimeter

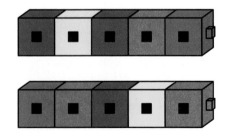

What is the total volume of these centimeter connecting cubes?

We can also measure the volume of an object using a graduated cylinder. This method is called **measuring volume by displacement** because you find out how much water the object displaces or pushes away.

3. Look carefully at the scale of the graduated cylinder before the cubes are added.

    A. How much water is in this graduated cylinder?

    B. How much water did the cubes displace or push away?

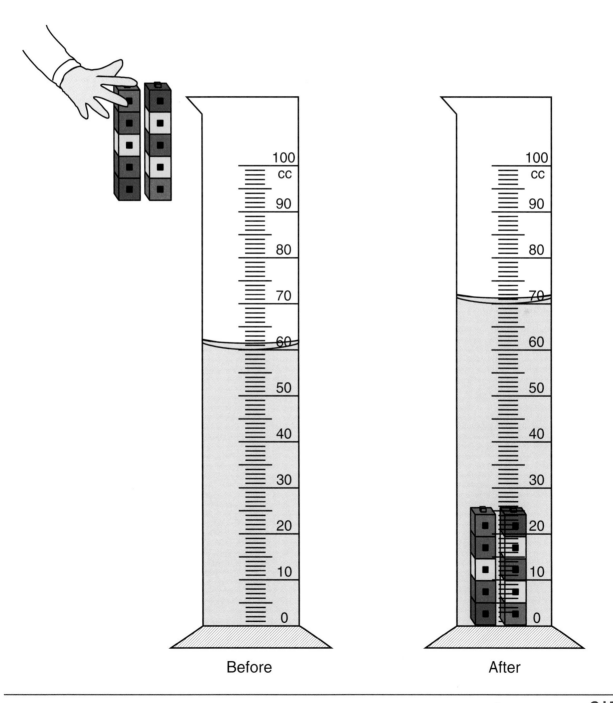

Before   After

4. We can estimate the volume of a rock by making a model of the rock using centimeter connecting cubes and counting the cubes. Estimate the volume of the rock using the picture of the cubes.

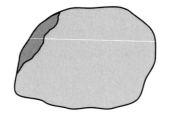
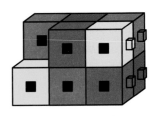

We can find a more exact measure of the volume of the rock by putting it into a graduated cylinder. The volume of the rock is the amount of water it displaces or pushes away.

5. A. Look carefully at the scale of the graduated cylinder before the rock is added. How much water is in the graduated cylinder?

   B. Look at the scale after the rock has been added. What is the volume of the rock?

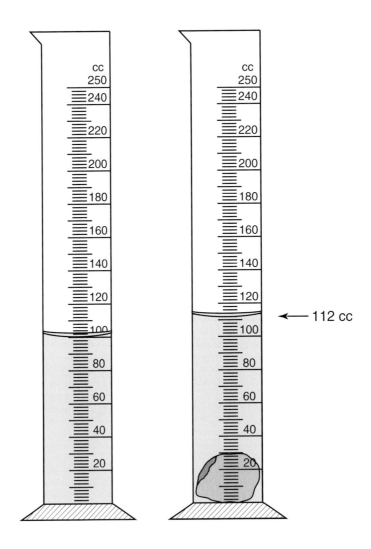

← 112 cc

Units of Volume

We can find the volume of a pitcher using a graduated cylinder, too. We sometimes measure liquid volume in **milliliters (ml)** or **liters (l).**

One milliliter is the same as one cubic centimeter.

1 cc = 1 ml

One liter is 1000 milliliters.

Jackie put water in a graduated cylinder until it reached the 250-cc mark. She emptied the cylinder into a pitcher. She did this four times until the pitcher was full.

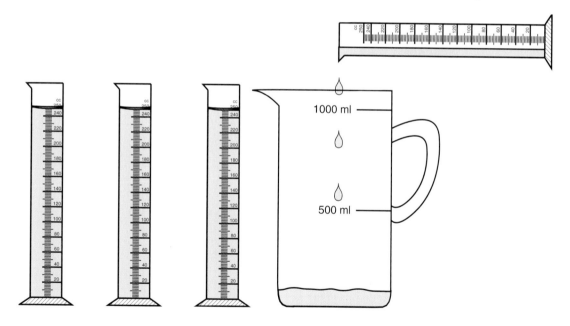

6. What is the volume of the pitcher? Give your answer in cubic centimeters.

7. How many milliliters does the pitcher hold?

8. Give the volume of the pitcher in liters.

9. A cubic foot is the amount of space taken up by a cube that is one foot long on each side. The volume of a 12-pack of soda is about half a cubic foot. What is the largest number of 12-packs of soda that will fit into a refrigerator that can hold 15 cubic feet?

Fill It First

In this game, teams predict the rise in water level as marbles are added to a graduated cylinder. The winner is the team with the highest score after each team has added a total of 20 cc of marbles.

You will need two teams of two students to play.

Rules

1. Fill your graduated cylinder with water to the 50-cc mark.
   - Add water to the cylinder until it almost reaches the 50-cc mark.
   - Use an eyedropper to add the last few drops carefully.
   - To read the water level correctly, put your eyes at the level of the water.
   - When water creeps up the sides of a cylinder, it forms a **meniscus** which makes it look as though there are two lines. Read the lower line of the meniscus.

2. Each team makes a score sheet like the one shown here:

Fill It First Score Sheet

Predicted Volume in cc	Actual Volume in cc	Points

3. Team 1 spins the spinner to find out whether to add one, two, three, or four marbles to the water in their graduated cylinder.

4. Before adding the marbles, Team 1 predicts the volume of the marbles and records the prediction on the score sheet.

5. Team 1 carefully slides the marble(s) into the water and calculates the volume of the marbles. If their prediction is correct, the team scores one point for each marble added. Both teams must agree on the actual volume of the marbles. Then, Team 2 takes a turn.

6. When it is Team 1's turn again, they spin to find the number of marbles they will add to their cylinder. Before adding the marbles, team members predict the **total** volume of all the marbles in the cylinder after the new marbles are added. Then, they slide the marbles into the cylinder. If they predicted correctly, they earn a point for each new marble added.

7. The first team to have a total of 20 cc of marbles in their cylinder scores an extra three points. The team then waits for the other team to have a total of 20 cc of marbles.

8. The team with the highest score wins.

Homework

Order of Operations Review

Solve the problems. Remember to use the correct order of operations. First, do all the multiplications and divisions, working from left to right. Then, do all the additions and subtractions, working from left to right.

If you are using a calculator from home, check to see if it follows the correct order of operations. Try the first example. If the answer in the display is 10, then the calculator follows the order of operations. If the calculator gives an answer of 1, then it does not follow the order of operations.

Here are two examples:

A. $6 \times 2 - 8 \div 4 = ?$ (First, multiply 6 times 2. Also, divide 8 by 4.)
$12 - 2 = ?$ (Then, subtract 2 from 12.)
$12 - 2 = 10$

B. $8 + 4 \times 6 - 1 = ?$ (First, multiply: $4 \times 6 = 24$.)
$8 + 24 - 1 = ?$ (Then, add and subtract from left to right.)
$32 - 1 = 31$

1. $6 \times 4 \div 8 + 1 = ?$

2. $6 \times 4 \div 1 + 8 = ?$

3. $6 \times 4 \div 8 \times 1 = ?$

4. $8 + 16 \div 4 = ?$

Fill It First

Operation Target

Operation Target is a game that can be played many ways. One set of rules for the game is in Unit 7 Lesson 1. Here is another way to play:

- Use the four digits 1, 4, 6, and 8 and four operations (+, −, ×, and ÷).
- You must use each of the four digits exactly once.
- You can use each operation more than once or not at all.
- You can make two-digit numbers by putting two digits together. For example, you can use the numbers 14 or 68.
- No operation should give you a fraction, a decimal, or a negative number.

5. Here is a way to make the number 1:
    4 − 18 ÷ 6 = ? (First, divide: 18 ÷ 6 = 3)
    4 − 3 = 1 (Then, subtract 3 from 4.)

    Find another way to make the number 1 following the new rules.

6. Make at least five numbers using these rules.

7. What is the largest number you can make?

8. What is the smallest number you can make?

Challenge: Make all the numbers from 0 to 9.

Volume vs. Number

Planning the Experiment

Mrs. Dewey's class is playing the game *Fill It First* using marbles. Frank and Nicholas are on one team and Jackie and Maya are on the other team. Jackie and Maya are winning because they have been able to predict correctly the volume of the marbles more often than Frank and Nicholas.

"We lost again. They sure are lucky!" said Frank. "Their predictions are right almost every time."

"It may not be luck," said Nicholas. "They may have a way to figure out what the volume will be."

"How do they do it?" asked Frank.

"I don't know," said Nicholas. "Maybe they are following a pattern."

"I sure can't see a pattern on our score sheet. The numbers jump around too much," said Frank. "Before we play again, let's make a table that can help us make better predictions. We can find the volume of different numbers of marbles and look for a pattern that can help us."

"Won't that be cheating?" asked Nicholas.

Frank and Nicholas's Score Sheet

Predicted Volume in cc	Actual Volume in cc	Points
10 cc	6 cc	0
12 cc	11 cc	3
15 cc	13 cc	0

"Not if we figure it out for ourselves," said Frank. "We need to do something. Mrs. Dewey said that the next time we play the game, we are going to use a different-size marble. We'll have to think about the numbers of marbles, volume, and which size of marble we're using. We'll never be able to keep all that straight."

"Okay. Let's figure something out and ask Mrs. Dewey if we can work on it before we play the game again," said Nicholas. "Whatever we do, we'll have to do two experiments, one for each size of marble."

Here are Frank and Nicholas's data tables:

Small Marbles

N Number of Marbles	V Volume in cc
2	
4	
8	

Large Marbles

N Number of Marbles	V Volume in cc

Mrs. Dewey thought Frank and Nicholas had such a good idea that she encouraged all the teams to design experiments to help them make predictions: "If you use the TIMS Laboratory Method, it will help you organize your thinking."

You are going to do the experiments Mrs. Dewey's class is working on. The results of the experiments should help you make predictions when you play the game *Fill It First*. Here are some things to think about as you plan your experiments:

Discuss

1. What are the two main variables in the experiments?

2. A. Which of the two main variables is the manipulated variable? Justify your answer.
   B. Which is the responding variable? Justify your answer.
   C. What letters will you use to stand for the two main variables?

3. The boys want to look for patterns in the data to help them make predictions about the volume of the marbles when they know the number of marbles. What important variable should be held fixed in each experiment so that they can do this?

4. A. What values for the number of small marbles did Frank and Nicholas choose?

   B. How will these values help them see patterns?

   C. What values will you choose?

Conducting the Experiment

You will collect and organize data that will help you make predictions about the volume of marbles when you know the number of marbles. You will investigate two sizes of marbles, so you will need to do two experiments.

Make a plan for your experiments. Draw a picture of your plan. Be sure to identify the variables in your picture. Label the main variables with letters.

- Label the columns of each of the *Two-column Data Tables* with the variables. Include units where needed.
- Your teacher will help you choose at least three values for the manipulated variable. The largest value will be no more than 8 marbles.

Volume vs. Number Data Tables

Experiment 1 Small Marbles		Experiment 2 Large Marbles	

- Use a 250-cc graduated cylinder to measure the volume of the marbles.

- Choose a convenient amount of water to use in your cylinder. Use at least 140 cc.
- Collect the data.

Graph

Graph your data on a piece of *Centimeter Graph Paper.*

- Label each axis and write in the units.
- The scale on the horizontal axis should go to 15 or more.
- The scale on the vertical axis should go to 40 or more.

5. Plot your data points for both sizes of marbles on a single piece of graph paper.

6. When the number of marbles equals 0, what is the volume of the marbles? Add this point to your graph for both sets of data.

7. **A.** If your points for the small marbles lie close to a line, use a ruler to draw a best-fit line.

   B. If your points for the large marbles lie close to a line, use a ruler to draw a best-fit line.

Explore

8. Why does the water level rise when you add marbles to the graduated cylinder?

9. Compare the line for the larger marble to the line for the smaller marble. How are they alike? How are they different?

10. **A.** Use your graph to estimate the volume of 7 small marbles. Show your work on your graph. Record your estimate.

    B. Did you use interpolation or extrapolation to find your answer?

    C. Check your estimate. Measure the volume of 7 small marbles. Record the volume.

D. How close is your estimate to the measured volume? Is it within 1 or 2 cc?

E. If your estimate was not close, you may need to correct your data on your graph before answering any more questions. Your teacher can help you decide.

11. A. Predict the volume of 15 small marbles using your graph. Show how you made your prediction. Record your prediction.

B. Did you use interpolation or extrapolation to find your answer?

C. Check your prediction by measuring the volume of 15 small marbles. Record the measured volume.

D. How close is your prediction to the measured volume? Is it within 3 cc?

12. A. Estimate the volume of 24 small marbles. Explain how you made your prediction and record it.

B. Check your prediction by measuring the volume of 24 small marbles. Record the measured volume.

C. How close is your prediction to the measured volume? Is it within 4 cc or 5 cc?

13. Irma and Jessie are playing *Fill It First* with the same large marbles you used. When they add the marbles for their turn, they will have a total of 9 marbles. Help them predict the volume of the 9 marbles. Show how you made your prediction.

14. Irma and Jessie have 150 cc of water in their graduated cylinder. They have added large marbles until the water level is 168 cc. How many large marbles are in the cylinder? Explain how you know.

15. Two students brought marbles from home. Keenya did the experiment with her marbles and Jacob did the experiment with his. They graphed their data on the same graph. Which line (A or B) did Keenya draw? Explain.

Keenya's Marbles

Jacob's Marbles

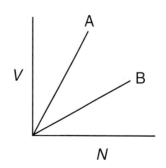

Review Problems

You will need a ruler and a calculator to complete the problems.

1. Make a factor tree to find the prime factors for the following numbers.

   A. 28   B. 124   C. 125

2. Solve the following problems in Question 2 without a calculator.

   A.   1267   B.   17,146   C.   3000
       +1499   −   459   ×9

   D.   49   E.   500   F.   70
       ×7   ×8   ×60

3. Write the following numbers using base-ten shorthand.

   A. 467   B. 7615   C. 1042

4. Tell what the circled digit stands for in each of the following problems. The circled digit in the example stands for 30 or 3 tens.

   Example:

       1③2
      +7 9

   A. 2 0 , 0 0 4   B.   4 2 3 6   C.   ①
              × 7   +2④9   1 2 7 8
       ─────────   +5 0 5 3
           2⑧   ─────────
                                                  1

5. Find the median for this set of numbers: 12, 15, 17, 13, 9, 25, 12, 17. Then, use a calculator to find the mean.

6. Write each of the following numbers in words.

   A. 1214   B. 77,589   C. 134,121

7. Write the following as numbers.

   A. two thousand twenty-four

   B. forty-four thousand, three hundred sixty-nine

   C. two hundred sixty-five thousand, three hundred twenty-eight

8. Label the following angles as acute, right, or obtuse.

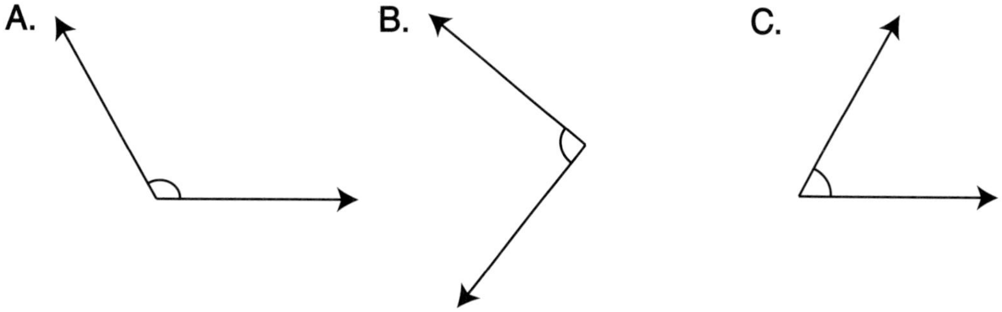

A.

B.

C.

9. Find the area of the following shape in square inches.

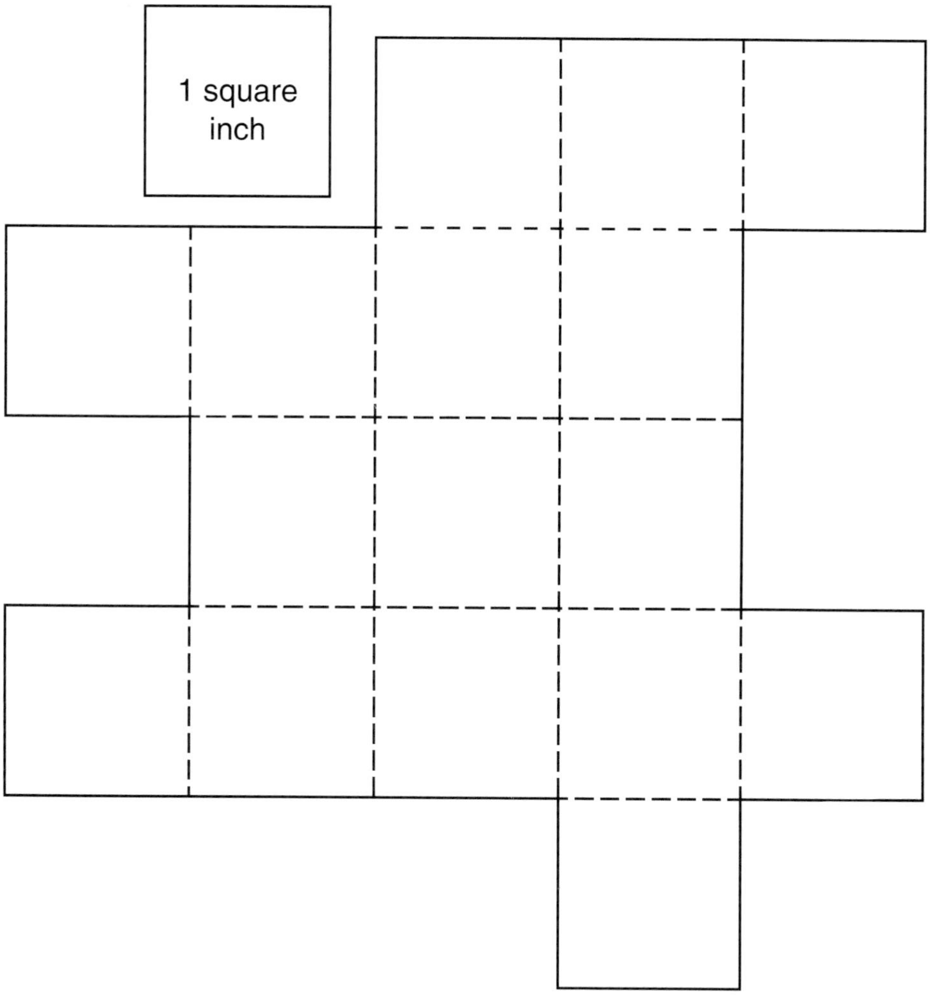

1 square inch

10. Find the perimeter of the shape.

11. Solve the given fact. Then write all the other number sentences in the same fact family.

A. $28 \div 4 =$

B. $7 \times 7 =$

Midyear Experiment and Portfolio Review

This is a good time to review your portfolio. Reviewing the work in your portfolio can help you see how much you have improved in math since the beginning of the year.

Experiment Review

The students in Mrs. Dewey's room were looking back through the labs in their collection folders. Ming found the survey he completed in the beginning of the school year that studied the main interests of his classmates. He decided to compare this work with other labs he had completed during the first half of the year. He organized his work on an *Experiment Review Chart* in the *Discovery Assignment Book.*

Reviewing the labs that you did this year is a good way to help you choose work for your portfolio.

I. Look through your *Student Guide* and your collection folder to help your class make a list of the labs you have completed so far this year.

2. Use the following questions as you review a lab. Record your work on the *Experiment Review Chart.*

   A. What variables did you study in this lab?

   B. Did you have to keep any variables fixed, so that the experiment would be fair? If so, which ones?

   C. Did you measure anything? If so, what did you measure? What units did you use?

D. How many trials did you do?

E. Describe the shape of your graph.

F. What were the most important problems you solved using your data and your graph?

Portfolio Review

3. If you have not done so recently, choose items from your collection folder to add to your portfolio.

4. Your *Experiment Review Chart* is a good choice for your portfolio.

5. Choose one or two pieces of work from this unit to include in your portfolio. Select pieces that are like other pieces of work that you put in your portfolio earlier in the year. For example, if you already have a lab in your portfolio, add the lab *Volume vs. Number*. Or, if you included a written solution to a problem like *Helipads for Antopolis* from Unit 2 or *Professor Peabody Invents a Ball* from Unit 5, then add *Hour Walk* to your portfolio now. Your teacher may help you make your choices.

6. Add to your Table of Contents. The Table of Contents should include the name of each piece of work, a short description of the work, and the date it was finished.

7. Write a paragraph comparing two pieces of work in your portfolio that are alike in some way. For example, you can compare two labs or your solutions to two problems you have solved. One piece should be new and one should be from earlier in the year. Here are some questions for you to think about as you write your paragraph:

   - Which two pieces did you choose to compare?
   - How are they alike? How are they different?
   - Do you see any improvement in the newest piece of work as compared to the older work? Explain.
   - If you could redo the older piece of work, how would you improve it?
   - How could you improve the newer piece of work?

8. Write about your favorite piece of work in your portfolio. Tell why you liked it. Explain what you learned from it.

Facts I Know: Multiplication and Division Facts

Picturing Fact Families

1. The picture below represents the following problem: If a rectangle has a total of 20 squares in 4 rows, how many squares are in each row?

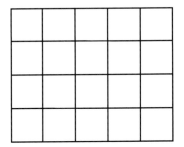

   What division sentence describes this problem?

2. The picture below represents the following problem: If a rectangle has a total of 20 squares in 5 rows, how many squares are in each row?

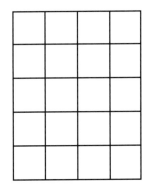

   A. What division sentence describes this problem?

   B. These two division sentences are members of the same **fact family.** What are the other number sentences that are in this same fact family?

3. Solve the given fact. Then name other facts in the same fact family.
   A. $9 \times 7 = ?$ **B.** $6 \times 4 = ?$ **C.** $7 \times 8 = ?$

Division Facts and *Triangle Flash Cards*

4. The directions that follow tell you how to use your *Triangle Flash Cards* to practice the division facts. Work with a partner. Use your *Triangle Flash Cards: 5s* and *10s*.

Facts I Know

A. One partner covers the number in the square. This number will be the answer to a division problem. The answer to a division problem is called the **quotient.** The number in the circle is the **divisor.** The divisor is the number that divides the largest number on the flash card. The second person solves a division fact with the two uncovered numbers as shown below.

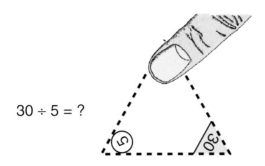

$30 \div 5 = ?$

B. Place each flash card in one of three piles: those facts you know well and can answer quickly, those that you can figure out with a strategy, and those that you need to learn.

C. Begin your *Division Facts I Know* chart. Circle the facts you know well and can answer quickly.

For example, Jacob knew $30 \div 5 = 6$. 5 is the divisor, so Jacob circled the 30 in the row for a divisor of 5.

Division Facts I Know

×	0	1	2	3	4	5	6	7	8	9	10
0	0	0	0	0	0	0	0	0	0	0	0
1	0	1	2	3	4	5	6	7	8	9	10
2	0	2	4	6	8	10	12	14	16	18	20
3	0	3	6	9	12	15	18	21	24	27	30
4	0	4	8	12	16	20	24	28	32	36	40
5	0	5	10	15	20	25	(30)	35	40	45	50
6	0	6	12	18	24	30	36	42	48	54	60
7	0	7	14	21	28	35	42	49	56	63	70
8	0	8	16	24	32	40	48	56	64	72	80
9	0	9	18	27	36	45	54	63	72	81	90
10	0	10	20	30	40	50	60	70	80	90	100

Divisor

Recording $30 \div 5 = 6$ as a Fact I Know.

D. Sort the 5s and 10s flashcards again. This time your partner covers the number in the circle. The number in the square is now the **divisor** and the covered number in the circle is the answer to the division problem, the **quotient.** If we use the same example, 6 is now the **divisor.** Jacob knew this division problem also, 30 ÷ 6 = 5, so he drew a circle around the 30 in the row for a divisor of 6 on his *Division Facts I Know* chart. He circled 30 twice on his chart.

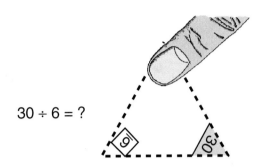

30 ÷ 6 = ?

E. Update your *Division Facts I Know* chart each time you go through the set of *Triangle Flash Cards.* Circle the facts you know well and can answer quickly.

F. Discuss how you can figure out facts you do not recall right away. Share your strategies with your partner.

G. Practice the last two piles at home for homework—the facts you can figure out with a strategy and those you need to learn. Make a list of these facts.

5. As you practice the division facts and update your *Division Facts I Know* chart, compare it to your *Multiplication Facts I Know* chart. Look for facts in the same fact family. Do you know any complete fact families? Which family or families? Explain.

You will continue to use *Triangle Flash Cards* to study all the groups of division facts, in the units to come. You will update your *Division Facts I Know* chart each time you go through the cards. If you know one or two of the facts in a fact family, use those facts to help you learn the others.

Unit 9

Shapes and Solids

	Student Guide	Discovery Assignment Book	Adventure Book	Unit Resource Guide*
Lesson 1				
Lines	◎			
Lesson 2				
What's Your Angle?	◎	◎		
Lesson 3				
Symmetry	◎	◎		
Lesson 4				
Journey to Flatopia			◎	
Lesson 5				
Prisms	◎	◎		
Lesson 6				
Finding the Volume of a Prism	◎			
Lesson 7				
Building an Octahedron		◎		
Lesson 8				
Constructing a Prism				◎

Unit Resource Guide pages are from the teacher materials.

Lines

TIMSville

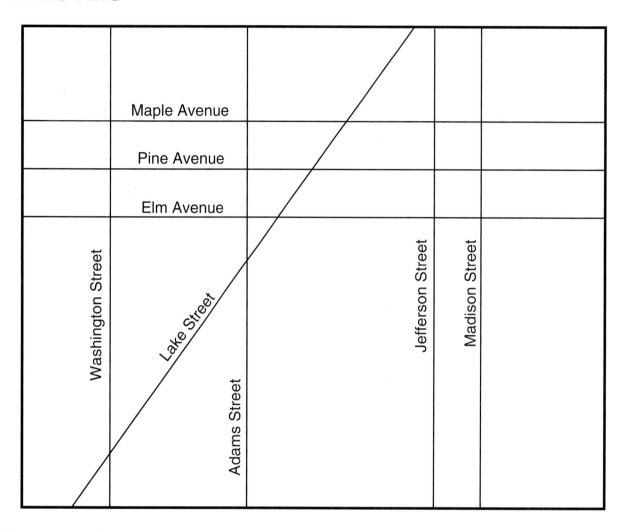

The map of TIMSville shows that Maple Avenue and Pine Avenue go in the same direction. We say Maple Avenue and Pine Avenue are **parallel.** These streets always stay the same distance apart. They will never **intersect** (meet) even if they went on, in the same direction, forever.

Lake Street and Madison Street are not parallel. If you continued them still going straight, they would intersect.

Pine Avenue and Jefferson Street are **perpendicular.** This means they form right angles where they intersect.

Washington Street and Lake Street intersect. However, they are not perpendicular.

1. Name a street parallel to Elm Avenue.

2. Name a street parallel to Madison Street.

3. Name a street perpendicular to Maple Avenue.

4. Name a street perpendicular to Washington Street.

5. Name two streets that Lake Street intersects.

On our map of TIMSville, we have drawn straight lines for each street. In mathematics we often just say "**line**" instead of "straight line." For the rest of this unit we will always mean straight line when we say line.

Streets always have a beginning and an end. In mathematics, a line goes on forever in both directions. It has no beginning or end. What we have drawn on our maps are called line segments. A **line segment** has two endpoints. To draw a picture of a line, we draw a line segment and put arrows at the ends to show that it keeps going on infinitely (forever).

Lines are often named by two points on the line. This is line AC.

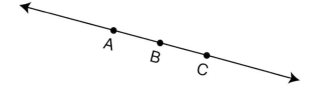

We write $\overleftrightarrow{AC}$. We can also call it $\overleftrightarrow{AB}$ or $\overleftrightarrow{BC}$.

The line segment AB is the part of the line that starts at A and ends at B. We write $\overline{AB}$ to show that we mean this segment.

6. Name two other line segments that are part of $\overleftrightarrow{AC}$.

7. This is line RT. ($\overleftrightarrow{RT}$)

    A. What are two other names for this line?
    B. Name at least 2 line segments that are part of $\overleftrightarrow{RT}$.

Rays are similar to lines, but they go on forever in only one direction. A ray has one endpoint.

8. This is ray XY. We can write ray XY like this: $\overrightarrow{XY}$. A ray is named by its endpoint first, followed by another point on the ray. What is another name for this ray?

9. Name the two rays you see here that make up ∠R.

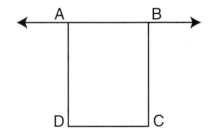
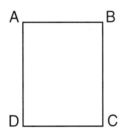

Talking about Shapes

ABCD is a rectangle. A rectangle has 4 line segments. Each line segment is part of a line. $\overline{AB}$ is part of $\overleftrightarrow{AB}$.

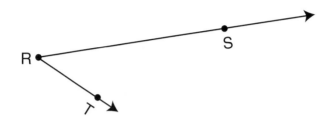

10. **A.** Name the 4 line segments that make up rectangle ABCD.
    B. $\overline{AD}$ is part of what line?
    C. $\overline{DC}$ is part of what line?
    D. There appear to be two pairs of parallel line segments. Name them.
    E. The angles of a rectangle are right angles. Name a line segment that is perpendicular to $\overline{AB}$.
    F. Name a line segment that is perpendicular to $\overline{CD}$.
    G. Name all the pairs of parallel lines.
    H. Name a line perpendicular to $\overleftrightarrow{AB}$.

11. Quadrilateral HIJK is a special quadrilateral called a **parallelogram.** A parallelogram is a quadrilateral with two pairs of opposite sides that are parallel.

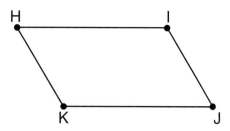

    A. Name two pairs of parallel line segments.

    B. Name two pairs of parallel lines.

    C. Measure all the line segments. What do you notice?

12. Is quadrilateral LMNO a parallelogram? Explain.

An **equilateral triangle** is a triangle that has three sides of equal length. All the triangles in this picture are equilateral triangles.

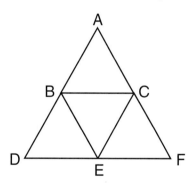

13. **A.** Name all the equilateral triangles you see in the figure.

    B. Name all the segments that appear to be parallel in the figure.

1. Name the line segments that form the sides of the parallelogram.

2. Name three points on the line segment NO.

3. Name the parallel line segments.

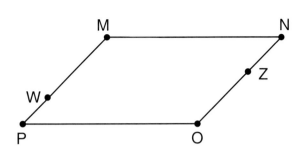

The figure below shows many lines, line segments, and rays.

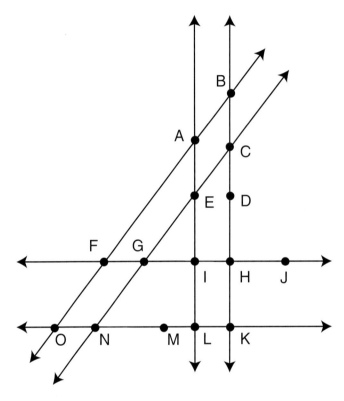

4. One triangle in this figure is triangle GEI. Name at least three other triangles in the figure.

5. Name three pairs of lines that appear to be parallel.

6. Name a pair of lines that appear to be perpendicular.

7. Name three shapes that appear to be parallelograms.

8. Which of the following pairs intersect (meet)?

   A. $\overrightarrow{LN}$ and $\overrightarrow{EC}$

   B. $\overrightarrow{AF}$ and $\overrightarrow{HI}$

   C. $\overline{IH}$ and $\overline{EC}$

   D. $\overleftrightarrow{LK}$ and $\overleftrightarrow{AB}$

What's Your Angle?

Looking at Angles

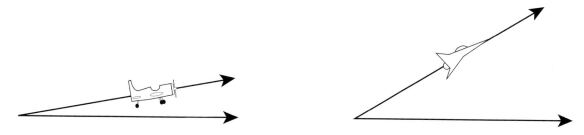

1. If both airplanes fly at the same speed, which airplane will be higher after 40 seconds? Why?

The paths of the two airplanes in the picture form angles with the ground. Different planes take off at different angles. A small plane has a climbing angle of about 10°. A jet can climb at a 30° angle. When a pilot is taking off, he or she needs to think about the climbing angle. Angles are also very important for drawing, building, and finding direction.

Recall that the sides of the angle meet at a point called the **vertex** of the angle. The sides of an angle are rays that have the same endpoint. Points are usually named with capital letters. We can call the angle here angle A and write ∠A as shorthand. We can also use 3 letters to name an angle. The angle here can be called ∠DAB or ∠BAD.

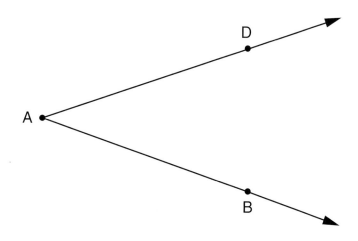

Measuring Angles

We measure the opening between the two sides of the angle in degrees. Protractors are used to measure angles. The measure of the angle shown here lies between 70° and 80°. Angle Z measures 73°. We write ∠Z = 73°. Notice where the vertex of the angle is placed.

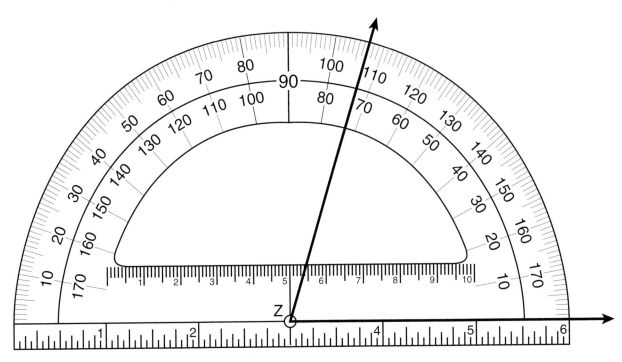

2. Is the angle shown above an acute or an obtuse angle?

3. A. Is the measure of this angle less than or greater than 90°?

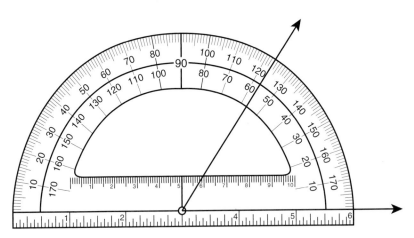

   B. Between which two numbers on the protractor does the measure of this angle lie?

   C. What is the measure of the angle?

4. **A.** Is the measure of this angle less than or greater than 90°?

   B. Between which two numbers on the protractor does the measure of the angle lie?

   C. Which scale do you use, the inside scale on the protractor or the outside scale to read this angle measure?

   D. What is the measure of the angle?

Using Angles

5. How many acute angles do you see in the drawing? How could you name them?

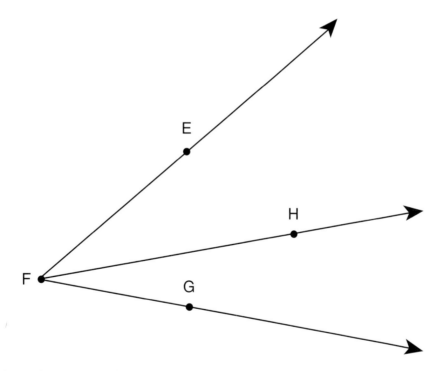

In the drawing there are three angles that could be called ∠F. In order not to confuse them, we use three letters to name each angle. Find the measure of each of the angles.

6. ∠EFH =

7. ∠HFG =

8. ∠EFG =

The park district for the town of TIMSville has decided to build a new playground. One of the features will be a sandbox for little children. The town is asking for designs for the sandbox. A design for the sandbox must have all straight sides. The sandbox will be located between two sidewalks that meet at a 50° angle. So, one of the angles of the sandbox must be 50°.

Here is the design Ana submitted. She used the scale 1 cm = 1 foot.

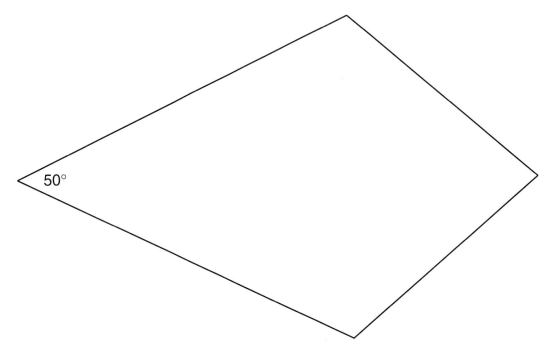

9. Design a sandbox for TIMSville's new playground. Your sandbox can have a different number of sides.

10. Design a different sandbox for the playground.

Shapes like the one Ana designed for the playground are called polygons. A **polygon** is a figure whose sides are line segments that are all connected. Every endpoint of a side meets the endpoint of exactly one other side and no sides overlap. The word *polygon* comes from the prefix *poly* (many) and suffix *gon* (angles). So, a polygon has many angles (or you could say many sides).

These shapes are polygons:

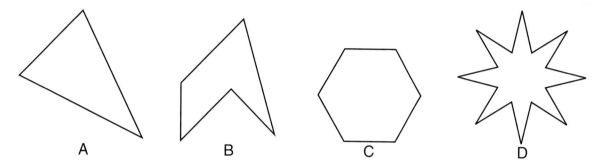

These shapes are not polygons:

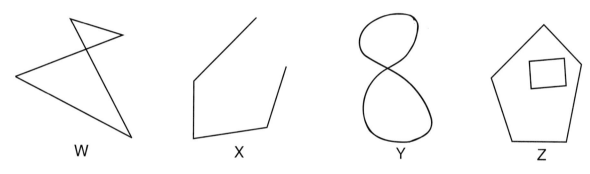

11. Explain why each of the shapes above is not a polygon.

We often name polygons with letters. When we say the name, we go around the shape. For example, the shape Ana drew is a quadrilateral. A **quadrilateral** is a polygon with 4 sides (or we can say 4 angles).

There are many ways we can say the name of this quadrilateral. Three ways are: ABCD, CBAD, or DABC.

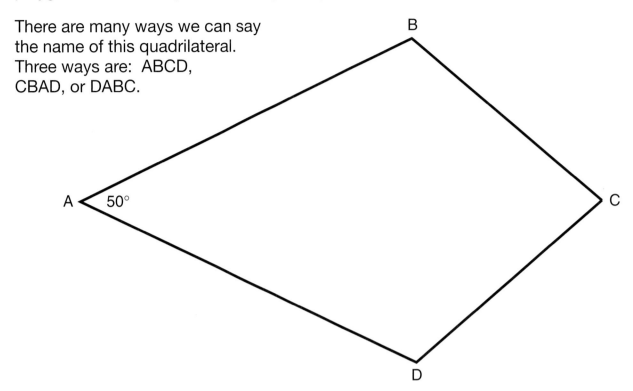

12. Find measures of all the angles in Ana's quadrilateral. Use a ruler to trace the design on another sheet of paper first.

   A. ∠A =   **B.** ∠B =   **C.** ∠C =   **D.** ∠D =

Homework

You will need a protractor to complete this homework.

1. Nila made a design for a sandbox. Her design is shown here. She labeled the angles A, B, C, D, and E. The sandbox needed to have a 130° angle.

   A. Which angle do you think is 130°?

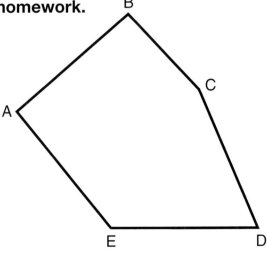

B. Trace the design on another paper, extend the sides with the edge of your protractor, and measure the angles of Nila's design.

∠A =

∠B =

∠C =

∠D =

∠E =

C. List 5 ways to name Nila's design.

2. Design a 3-sided sandbox for a playground. All the sides must be straight and there must be a 45° angle in the design.

3. Design a 6-sided sandbox for a playground. All the sides must be straight and there must be a 90° angle in the design.

4. **A.** Use a ruler to trace this figure first. Then, find the measure of the angles.

∠RST = ?

∠TSU = ?

∠RSU = ?

B. What is the sum of the measures of ∠RST and ∠TSU? How does the sum compare to the measure of ∠RSU?

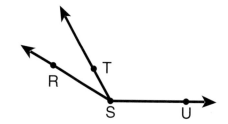

5. James works for the Sparkling Clean Window Washing company. His boss told him that when using a ladder to clean windows, the ladder must make an angle with the ground between 65° and 75° in order to be safe to climb. The picture here shows a ladder leaning against a building.

A. What is the measure of the angle between the ladder and the ground?

B. Will this ladder be safe to climb?

C. What is the measure of the angle between the ladder and the building (the top angle)?

D. What is the measure of the angle between the house and the ground?

What's Your Angle?

6. The picture below shows many angles. Describe 5 angles you see in the picture.

7. Here is a side view of a playground slide. Measure the angles.

∠A =
∠B =
∠C =
∠D =

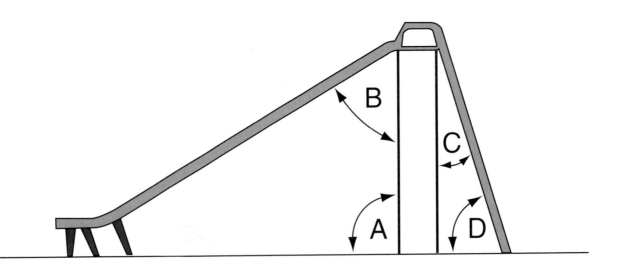

Symmetry

Turn and Line Symmetry

The picture shown below has a pattern that repeats as you turn it about the point in the center. This picture has **turn symmetry.** The **center of turning** is the point in the middle. The picture has $\frac{1}{6}$-**turn symmetry** because if you turn it $\frac{1}{6}$ of a full 360° turn, it lines back up with itself.

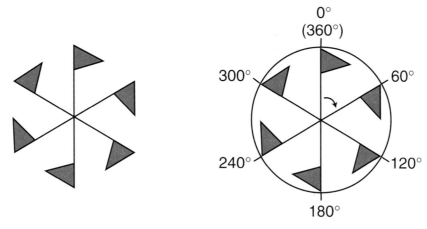

The heart shown here does not have turn symmetry. The heart has a different kind of symmetry called **line symmetry.** The heart has one line of symmetry. If you folded the heart along the line of symmetry, the two pieces fit exactly on top of one another.

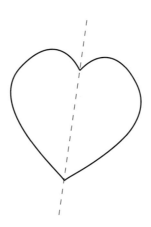

The square below has both turn and line symmetry.

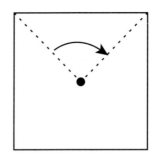

If you traced the figure, marked the center, and turned the square $\frac{1}{4}$ of a turn (90°) about the center, the traced figure would lie on the original. The square could be turned 4 times like this before it made a complete circle. The square has $\frac{1}{4}$-turn symmetry.

The square also has 4 lines of symmetry. You can fold the square on those lines and the halves of the square will match exactly.

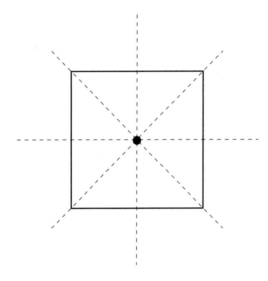

1. Look at each of the shapes below. Answer the following questions for each. You can use the shapes on the *Pattern Block Shapes* Activity Page in the *Discovery Assignment Book* to help you.

- Does the shape have turn symmetry?
- If the shape has turn symmetry, tell what kind of turn symmetry.
- Does the shape have line symmetry?
- If the shape has line symmetry, tell how many lines of symmetry.

A.

B.

C.

D.

E.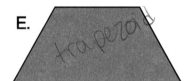

F.

G.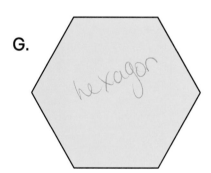

2. Many cultures use symmetry in their designs. Describe the symmetries you see in the following designs.

A. A design from ancient Pompeii (Roman Empire)

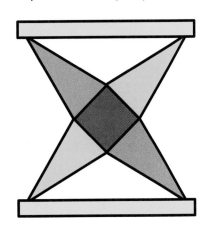

B. An Arabian design

C. An Apache design

D. A Latvian design

Making Spinners

The idea of turn symmetry is seen in many places; for example, in spinners used for games.

The workers at the TIMS Toy Company are designing spinners for board games. Here is a spinner they designed for a game that is divided into 3 equal pieces. When children play the game, there is an equal chance of the spinner landing on any of the 3 areas.

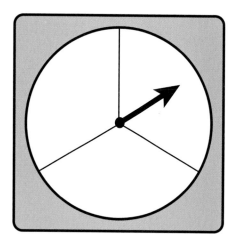

For Questions 3 and 4, you will need the *Blank Spinners* Activity Page in the *Discovery Assignment Book,* a protractor, and a calculator. Answer these questions after creating your spinners:

- **How big is the angle in each part of the spinner? Use your protractor to measure.**
- **What is the sum of all the angles? Does this make sense? Explain.**

3. Design a spinner that is divided into 4 equal pieces. Explain your work.

4. Design a spinner that is divided into 5 equal pieces. Explain your work.

Prisms

Mrs. Dewey's class is studying three-dimensional shapes. Another name for a three-dimensional shape is a **solid.** The class is thinking of ways of describing and recording their shapes. Linda has a cereal box.

The sides of the box are called **faces.**

   I. How many faces does Linda's cereal box have?

Two faces intersect in an **edge.**

   2. How many edges does Linda's cereal box have?

The corners are called **vertices.**

   3. How many vertices does Linda's cereal box have?

Linda wanted to draw her box. First she drew a rectangle for the front face.

Linda then drew parallel line segments, all the same length.

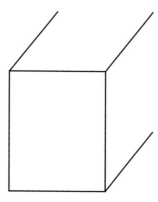

Then, Linda added two more edges:

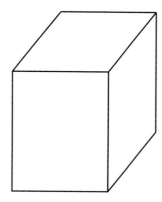

Grace showed Linda how to draw the edges that cannot be seen so that they are dotted. This helps us remember which edges are in the back, from our point of view.

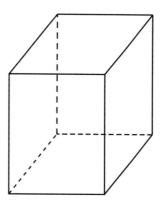

4. Do you know another way to draw a box? If you do, draw a box using your method. Otherwise, use Linda's method to draw a box. You may wish to look at a box as you draw.

Making Nets from Boxes

Linda was interested in the way boxes are made. She decided to flatten out her box. Linda decided to cut along three of the top edges and four of the vertical edges. This is what she got.

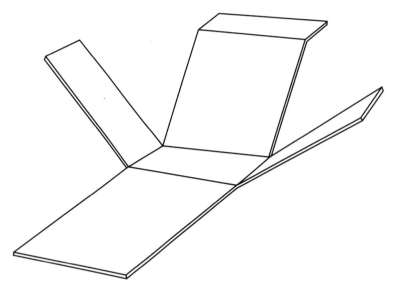

Linda flattened her box and turned it over. This is what it looked like:

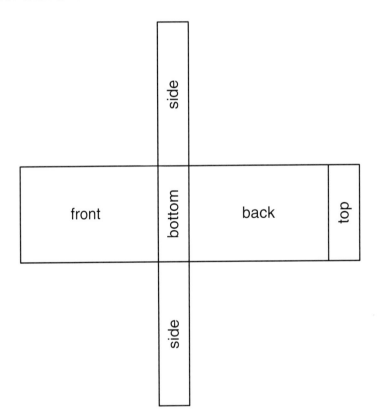

This is what we call a **net** for the box.

5. There are other ways to flatten a box. Work with your group to make as many different nets of a box as you can. Each person in the group should have a box to cut. Make one net at a time. Discuss before you cut so that you do not repeat a net.

6. Draw a picture of your nets. Label the rectangles that were the bottom, top, and sides of the box.

Different Kinds of Prisms

Boxes are examples of special kinds of three-dimensional shapes. These shapes are prisms.

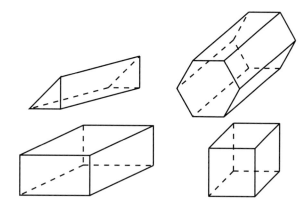

These shapes are not prisms.

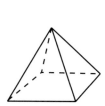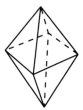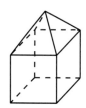

A **prism** is a three-dimensional shape. Prisms have two identical faces called bases. The bases are parallel to each other. The other faces are parallelograms.

One way to sketch a prism is to draw the two bases and then connect the matching vertices. You may want to trace the bases from a picture, a pattern block, or some other object. Here is a way to draw a pentagonal prism:

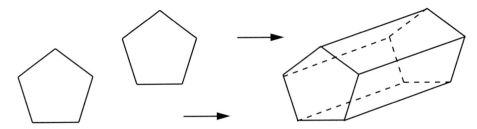

You may wish to dot the lines that show the edges that are in the back of the figure. Prisms can be drawn with or without the dotted lines. Compare the drawing of the following pentagonal prism with the one above. Which one seems clearer to you?

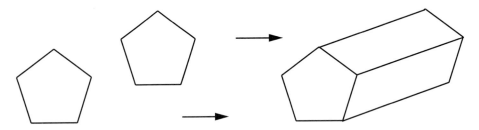

7. How many faces does a pentagonal prism have? How many edges? How many vertices?

Homework

Boxes

1. Find a box at home. Make a sketch of the box showing its length, width, and height. You can measure using centimeters or inches.

For Questions 2–5, decide whether the figure is a net of a cube. You may need to trace the figures on a separate sheet of paper and cut them out.

2.

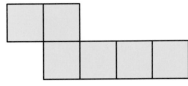

3.

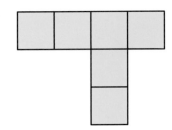

4.

5.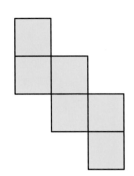

For Questions 6–12:

- Decide whether the shape is a prism.
- If the shape is a prism, describe the bases.
- How many faces does the shape have?

6.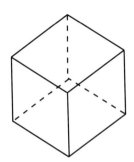

7.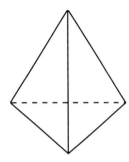

8.

9.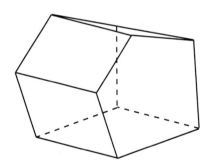

10.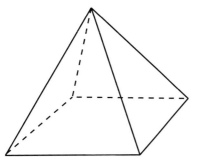

11.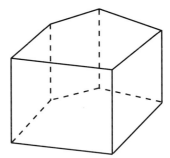

12.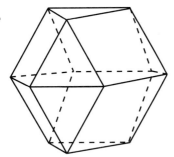

Finding the Volume of a Prism

Volumes of Prisms

1. Use centimeter connecting cubes to build the prism shown in the picture at the right.

    A. How many centimeters tall is the prism? This is the prism's height.

    B. How many square centimeters cover the base of the prism? This is the area of the base.

    C. Count the number of cubic centimeters in the prism. This is the prism's volume.

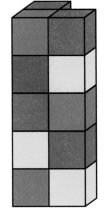

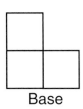

Base

2. Build each of the three prisms shown below.

A.

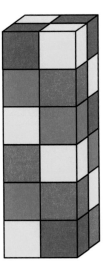

B.

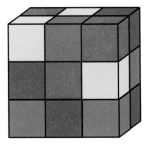

C.

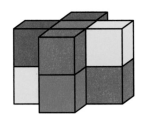

---

3. Copy the data table on a piece of paper. Find the area of the base, the height, and the volume of each of the prisms in Question 2. Complete the table.

Prism	Area of Base in sq cm	Height in cm	Volume in cc
A			
B			
C			

4. **A.** Look at the information in the table. Describe any patterns you see.

   B. Describe a method for finding the volume of a prism without counting cubes.

   C. Check your method. Use it to find the volume of the prism in Question 1. Did you find the same volume using your new method as you did when you counted cubes?

One way to think about volume is to ask how many cubes (or parts of cubes) fit into the object.

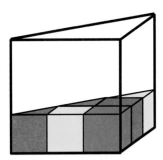

5. Jackie got a box of chocolates for her birthday. The box is a triangular prism.

A. Jackie traced the base of the box on a piece of *Centimeter Grid Paper* as shown here. What is the area of the base?

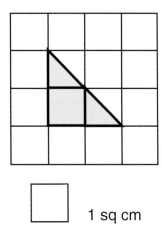

☐ 1 sq cm

B. The height (or length) of the box is 10 cm. Use your method for finding the volume of a prism to find the volume of Jackie's box.

Juice Box Volume

6. About how much is a ml of juice? A cupful, a spoonful, or less than a spoonful? (Remember, 1 ml = 1 cc.)

7. Is your juice box a prism?

8. Find the volume of your juice box. Explain the steps you used. Give the volume of your juice box in ml.

9. Look at the label of your juice box. Was the volume you calculated close to the volume printed on the box? Explain.

Volumes of other prisms can be found using the same method: Find the area of the base and then multiply by the height.

10. Find the volume of the right triangular prism you built in Lesson 5.

11. **A.** What is the area of the base of the prism shown in the picture below?

    B. What is the volume of the prism?

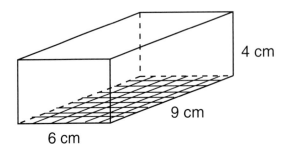

Homework

For Questions 1–4, a picture of a box is shown for each problem. Find the volume of the box. You can use a calculator to help you multiply.

1.

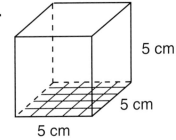

2.

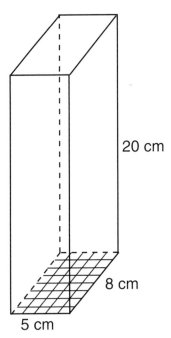

Finding the Volume of a Prism

3. The area of the triangular base of this prism is 15 sq cm.

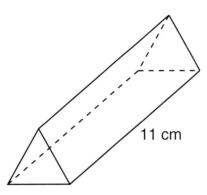

11 cm

4. The area of the hexagonal base of this prism is about 26 sq cm.

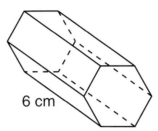

6 cm

5. Ana found that the area of the bottom (the base) of her purse is 90 sq cm. To find the volume, she measured the height of her purse. It is 15 cm tall. What is the volume of Ana's purse?

Unit 10
Using Decimals

	Student Guide	Discovery Assignment Book	Adventure Book	Unit Resource Guide*
Lesson 1				
m, dm, cm, mm	◎	◎		
Lesson 2				
Tenths	◎	◎		
Lesson 3				
Hundredths	◎	◎		◎
Lesson 4				
Downhill Racer	◎			◎
Lesson 5				
Decimal Hex		◎		
Lesson 6				
Alberto in TenthsLand			◎	

Unit Resource Guide pages are from the teacher materials.

m, dm, cm, mm

Meters (m)

Your teacher has made marks 1 and 2 **meters** above the floor. Use these marks to help you answer the questions below.

1. Are you more than 1 meter tall?

2. Are you more than 2 meters tall?

3. Are you closer to 1 meter or 2 meters?

4. As a class, measure objects around the classroom to the nearest whole meter. The symbol for meter is **m.** Keep track of the data on the *Class Measurement Tables* in the *Discovery Assignment Book.*

Class Measurement Table

Object	Measurement (nearest m)
Height of door	
Width of classroom	
Length of classroom	
Width of chalkboard	
Length of paper clip	
Length of pencil	

5. Jackie measured her calculator to the nearest meter and found it to be 0 meters long. What does this measurement (0 m) tell you? What unit would give you a better measurement for this length?

6. Sometimes it is good enough to measure to the nearest whole meter. Sometimes it is not. Usually, it does not make sense to measure a calculator to the nearest meter. List two things that probably should not be measured to the nearest meter.

7. List two things that you would measure to the nearest meter.

Decimeters (dm)

8. How many skinnies can you line up on a meterstick? Line them up along a meterstick to find out.

9. The length of one skinny is a **deci**meter. The symbol for decimeter is **dm.** How many dm are in 1 meter? How many dm are in $\frac{1}{2}$ meter?

10. A decimeter is $\frac{1}{10}$ of a meter. What do you think **deci-** means?

11. As a class, measure the objects in the table from Question 4 again, but this time to the nearest whole decimeter. Make a new table for this data like the one shown below.

Class Measurement Table

Object	Measurement (nearest dm)
Height of door	
Width of classroom	
Length of classroom	

---

12. John measured a paper clip to the nearest decimeter and found it to be 0 decimeters long. What information does this measurement tell you? What unit would give you a better measurement for a paper clip?

13. Sometimes it is good enough to measure to the nearest whole decimeter. Sometimes it is not. List two things that should be measured to the nearest decimeter.

Centimeters (cm)

A **cent**ury is 100 years; a **cent**ennial is a 100-year anniversary; a **cent**ipede is said to have 100 legs. What do you think **cent-** means?

A **cent**imeter is $\frac{1}{100}$ of a meter and a **cent** is $\frac{1}{100}$ of a dollar. In other words, there are 100 centimeters in a meter and 100 cents in a dollar.

14. How many bits can you line up along a meterstick? How did you decide?

15. How long is a bit?

16. As a class, measure the objects from Question 4 again, but this time measure to the nearest whole centimeter. Make a new table for this data like the one shown below.

17. List two things it makes sense to measure to the nearest whole centimeter. List two things it does not make sense to measure in centimeters.

18. Find an object that measures less than 1 centimeter.

Class Measurement Table

Object	Measurement (nearest cm)
Height of door	
Width of classroom	
Length of classroom	

Millimeters (mm)

If you look at a meterstick very carefully, you will see little spaces between short lines. Each one of these spaces is a millimeter.

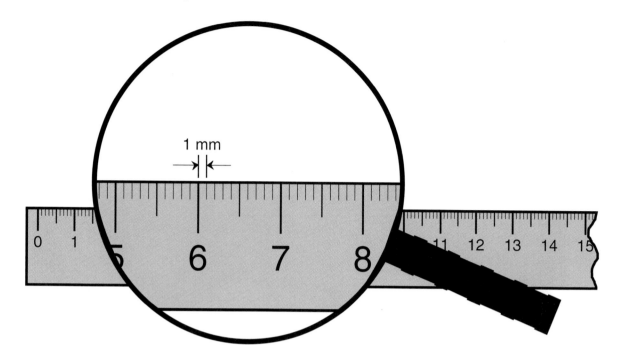

19. There are 1000 **millimeters** in a meter. What do you think **milli-** means?

20. How many millimeters are in a centimeter?

21. How many millimeters are in a decimeter? How did you decide?

22. People generally use millimeters to measure very short lengths. Give an example of when it would make sense to measure in millimeters.

Measuring with Metersticks, Skinnies, and Bits

John measured the length of the chalkboard in his classroom. First, he used two metersticks. He saw that less than half of a third meterstick would fit. John said, "To the nearest whole meter, this length is 2 meters."

---

m, dm, cm, mm

Next John put down four skinnies. John said, "Each meterstick is ten decimeters, and each skinny is one decimeter long. I have two metersticks and four skinnies. So, to the nearest decimeter, this length is 24 whole decimeters."

John still had a little space left. He put down one bit. One bit is one centimeter long.

Mrs. Dewey complimented John's work: "John, you have done a terrific job. You have found the length of the chalkboard using the fewest pieces. You can write down this measurement using decimals. How many metersticks did you use?" "Two," said John.

Mrs. Dewey wrote "2." on the board. "Each decimeter is one-tenth of a meter. How many skinnies did you use?" "Four," said John.

Mrs. Dewey wrote "2.4" on the board. "Each centimeter is one-hundredth of a meter. How many bits did you use?" "One," said John.

Mrs. Dewey wrote "2.41" on the board. "This number is read two and forty-one hundredths." John showed 2.41 m with two metersticks, four skinnies, and 1 bit.

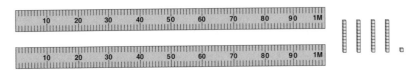

John continued to measure objects around the room to the nearest hundredth of a meter. For example, Mrs. Dewey had a life-size poster of a professional basketball player on the wall. John decided to measure the height of this player. He used 1 meterstick, 9 skinnies, and 8 bits. John wrote "1.98 meters" for this measurement. That told him the player's height was 1 meter, 9 decimeters, and 8 centimeters.

23. John wrote the following measurements on his paper. He used the fewest pieces for each measurement. How many metersticks, skinnies, and bits did John use for each measurement?

   A. 3.45 m
   B. 0.59 m
   C. 2.70 m
   D. 2.07 m

Homework

Even though we often use customary units of measure (inches, pints, pounds, and so on) in everyday life, there are many times we use metric units of measure (centimeters, liters, grams, and so on).

1. Look for metric units in the newspaper, on labels, and around the house. Make a list showing what the unit is and what is being measured. If you can, bring in the paper with the measurement on it.

2. **A.** Cut a piece of string 1 meter long.

    B. Carry your meter string with you all the time for one week.

    C. Estimate the length of various objects to the nearest meter. Then, use your meter string to measure the objects to the nearest meter. Make a table showing the objects, your estimates, and your measurements.

3. Go on a measure hunt in your home. Look for objects that are between the specified lengths. Complete a data table like this one. (*Hint*: Half of your string is 0.5 m.)

Rule	Object
Between 1 and 2 m	
Between 1 and 1.5 m	
Between 0.5 and 1 m	

---

m, dm, cm, mm

Tenths

A New Rule for Base-Ten Pieces

In the last lesson, Lee Yah used skinnies to measure to the nearest decimeter. She lined up skinnies along a meterstick. She learned that a skinny is one decimeter long and that a decimeter is one tenth of a meter.

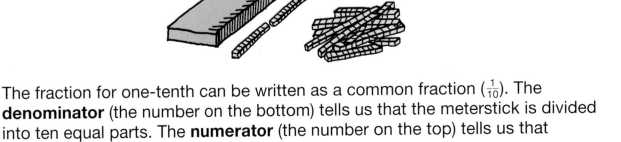

1. A. How many skinnies can you lay along the edge of your meterstick?

    B. The length of one skinny is what fraction of a meterstick?

The fraction for one-tenth can be written as a common fraction ($\frac{1}{10}$). The **denominator** (the number on the bottom) tells us that the meterstick is divided into ten equal parts. The **numerator** (the number on the top) tells us that a skinny is one of these parts.

The fraction for one-tenth can also be written as a decimal fraction (0.1). The decimal point tells us that the numbers to the right of the decimal point are smaller than 1.

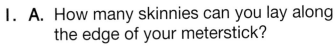

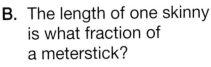

$\frac{1}{10}$ – numerator
$\;\;$ – denominator

$\quad$ 0.1
$\quad$ ↑
decimal point

2. Place 3 skinnies along the edge of the meterstick.

    A. The length of 3 skinnies is what fraction of a meter?

    B. Write this fraction as a common fraction and as a decimal fraction.

3. Place 5 skinnies along the edge of the meterstick.

    A. The length of 5 skinnies is what fraction of a meter?

    B. Write this fraction as a decimal fraction.

    C. Write this fraction as a common fraction in two different ways.

Doing mathematics is sometimes like playing a game. Just as you cannot play a game without rules, you cannot do mathematics without rules. But, just as people sometimes change game rules, we sometimes change rules in mathematics. And, just as we can still play a game if everyone agrees to the new rules, we can still do mathematics if everyone agrees to the new rules.

Now we are going to change a rule for base-ten pieces. When you worked with base-ten pieces before, usually a bit was one whole. When a bit is the unit, then a skinny is 10 units, a flat is 100 units, and a pack is 1000 units. Now we are going to change which piece is the whole. **For now, a flat will be one whole.**

4. Use skinnies to cover a flat.

    A. How many skinnies did you use?

    B. If a flat is 1 unit, then what fraction is a skinny?

5. **A.** Place 6 skinnies on your flat. Skip count by tenths as you place each skinny. Start like this: one-tenth, two-tenths, three-tenths. . . .

    B. What fraction of the flat is 6 skinnies?

    C. Write this fraction as a common fraction and a decimal fraction.

6. **A.** Nicholas placed 4 skinnies on his flat. Put 4 skinnies on your flat. Skip count by tenths as you place each skinny.

   B. What fraction of the flat is 4 skinnies?

   C. Write this fraction as a common fraction and a decimal fraction.

7. **A.** Linda placed 10 skinnies on her flat. Put 10 skinnies on your flat. Skip count by tenths as you place each skinny.

   B. How many tenths is 10 skinnies?

   C. Linda noticed that 10 skinnies covered one whole. She recorded this 3 ways: $\frac{10}{10}$, 1, and 1.0. Explain how each of these represents the same number.

You can use the *Tenths Helper* to show how many tenths are in one whole and two wholes.

8. **A.** Cover your *Tenths Helper* with flats. How many flats did you use?

   B. What number does this represent?

9. **A.** Place 10 skinnies on your *Tenths Helper*. Count by tenths as you place each skinny on the chart.

   B. When you are skip counting by tenths, what number comes after 9 tenths? (*Hint:* There is more than one answer to this question.)

   C. Continue placing skinnies on your chart. What number will you say as you place the eleventh skinny on the chart? (*Hint:* There is more than one answer to this question.)

   D. How many skinnies does it take to fill the *Tenths Helper*?

   E. How many tenths are in two wholes?

Keenya uses a *Tenths Helper* to show tenths. First she places 12 skinnies on the chart. She counts by tenths as she places each skinny. Then, she records the value of 12 skinnies on the chart.

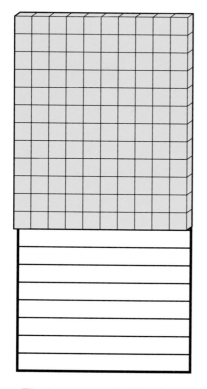

First, place 12 skinnies on your chart.

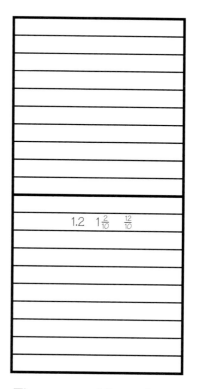

$1.2 \quad 1\frac{2}{10} \quad \frac{12}{10}$

Then, record the value in more than one way.

Use the *Tenths Helper* to complete Questions 10–11. Use the skinnies to show each number, then record its value on the chart in more than one way.

10. **A.** 17 skinnies

    B. 4 skinnies

    C. 15 skinnies

    D. 9 skinnies

    E. 1 skinny

    F. 13 skinnies

    G. 18 skinnies

11. Fill in all of the values in your *Tenths Helper.* If needed, use skinnies to build each number.

Tenths

More Tenths

12. Romesh used base-ten pieces to make the following number. If a flat is one whole, what number did Romesh make?

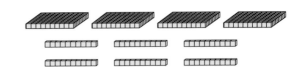

13. If a flat is one whole, then what is the value of a pack? (*Hint*: How many flats does it take to make 1 pack?)

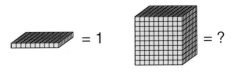

If a flat is 1, the pieces below show a number a little more than 21.

If a flat is 1, then these pieces are twenty-one and three-tenths. This can be written either 21.3 or $21\frac{3}{10}$. We can record this using base-ten shorthand.

$21\frac{3}{10}$ or 21.3

Explore

14. Use base-ten pieces to make these numbers. Then, use base-ten shorthand to show what pieces you used. (Remember: The flat is one whole.)

   A. 1.7   **B.** 3.4   **C.** 0.6   **D.** 13.2   **E.** 10.1

15. Give decimals and common fractions for the base-ten shorthand below:

   A.

   B.

   C.

   D.

---

16. Use base-ten pieces to make a number between 2 and 3. Use base-ten shorthand to show the pieces you used. Then, write your number.

17. Use base-ten pieces to make a number between 2.5 and 3. Use base-ten shorthand to show the pieces you used. Then, write your number.

The Fewest Pieces Rule

The Fewest Pieces Rule says that you should trade ten base-ten pieces for the next size up whenever you can. Ten skinnies should be traded for a flat and ten flats should be traded for a pack. For example, if you had these base-ten pieces:

Using the Fewest Pieces Rule, you should trade ten skinnies for a flat. You would then have these pieces:

For Questions 18–20, the flat is one whole. Follow these directions:

    A. **Use base-ten shorthand to show how to make the number using the fewest base-ten pieces.**

    B. **Then, write a decimal for the number.**

Make each number first with base-ten pieces. Then, trade to get the fewest pieces. Finally, write the number.

18. ||||| |||||

19. ▢▢ ||||| ||||| ||||| ||

20. ▢▢ ||||| ||||| ||||| |||

Showing Numbers in Several Ways

Numbers can be shown in more than one way using base-ten pieces. Suppose a flat is one whole. Then, 2.3 can be shown in these three ways:

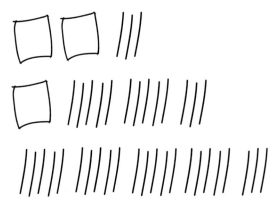

21. Use base-ten pieces to make 3.2 in several ways. Use base-ten shorthand to show each way you find. Circle the solution that uses the fewest pieces.

22. Work with a partner to practice making numbers with base-ten pieces and writing them using decimals and common fractions. One person should lay out packs, flats, and skinnies. The other person should write numbers for the pieces. Keep track of your work in a table like this:

Tenths Data Table

Base-Ten Shorthand	Fraction of a Flat	
	Common	Decimal

Hundredths

Exploring Hundredths

Jackie is counting the pennies in her penny bank to see how many dollars she has. She puts the pennies into piles of 100 since she knows that 100 pennies equals 1 dollar. Jackie knows that 1 penny is one-hundredth of a dollar. You can write the fraction for one-hundredth as a common fraction or as a decimal fraction:

$\frac{1}{100}$
common fraction

0.01
decimal fraction

I. A. What does the denominator mean in the fraction $\frac{1}{100}$?

B. What does the numerator mean in the fraction $\frac{1}{100}$?

C. In the decimal fraction 0.01 what do the zeros mean?

After Jackie finished putting her pennies into piles of 100, she found that she had 28 pennies (28¢) left over. These 28 pennies are a fraction of a dollar. We can write it as a common fraction ($\frac{28}{100}$) or a decimal fraction (0.28). We say: twenty-eight hundredths.

2. A. Jackie found 14 pennies in the bottom of her desk drawer. What fraction of a dollar does this represent?

B. Write this fraction as both a decimal fraction and as a common fraction.

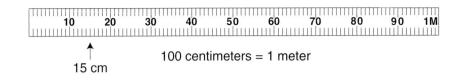

100 centimeters = 1 meter

15 cm

3. **A.** Frank knows that there are 100 centimeters in a meter. That means that the length of one centimeter is 0.01 or $\frac{1}{100}$ of a meter. Frank's pencil is 15 cm long. What fraction of a meter is the length of the pencil?

   B. Write this fraction as both a decimal fraction and as a common fraction.

Irma wanted to use base-ten pieces to show hundredths. She learned in the last lesson that if a flat is 1 whole, then a skinny is 0.1 and a pack is 10.

= 10   = 1   = 0.1

4. Which base-ten piece should Irma use to show one-hundredth? Explain why you chose the piece you did.

5. **A.** How many hundredths does a skinny represent? Write this number as a common and as a decimal fraction.

   B. How many hundredths does a flat represent? Write this number as a common fraction and as a decimal fraction.

Nicholas used the following base-ten pieces to show a number. If a flat is one whole, then what number do these pieces represent?

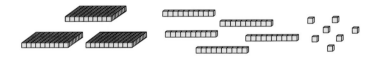

These pieces show 3 wholes, 5 tenths, and 7 hundredths. We can write $3\frac{57}{100}$ or 3.57 for this number. We read both $3\frac{57}{100}$ and 3.57 as "Three and fifty-seven hundredths."

6. **A.** Irma placed the following base-ten pieces on her desk. If a flat is one whole, then what number do these pieces represent?

   B. Write this number as a common fraction and as a decimal fraction.

7. Mrs. Dewey showed the following base-ten pieces to the class. She asked each student to record the number for these pieces.

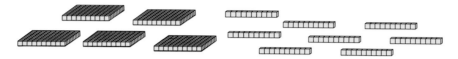

Romesh recorded 5.80 and Jessie recorded 5.8. Explain why both students are correct.

8. Get a handful of mixed skinnies and bits and count them by hundredths. Count the skinnies first (ten-hundredths, twenty-hundredths, thirty-hundredths, . . .) and then count on for the bits. When you finish, write the number for your handful.

Tanya used the following base-ten pieces to show the number 3.67.

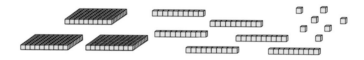

She recorded her work using base-ten shorthand.

9. Use base-ten pieces to make these numbers. Then, use base-ten shorthand to show what pieces you used. A flat is one whole.

    A. 2.34   **B.** 0.08   **C.** 0.15   **D.** 13.42   **E.** 3.04

10. Give a decimal number and a common fraction for the base-ten shorthand below:

    A.

    B.

    C.

    D.

11. A. Use base-ten pieces to make 0.1 and 0.2.

   B. Use base-ten pieces to make a number more than 0.1 but less than 0.2. Use base-ten shorthand to show the pieces you used. Then, write your number.

12. A. Use base-ten pieces to make 2.5 and 2.6.

   B. Use base-ten pieces to make a number more than 2.5 but less than 2.6. Use base-ten shorthand to show the pieces you used. Then, write your number.

For Questions 13–15, use base-ten shorthand to show how to make the number using the fewest base-ten pieces. Then, write a decimal for the number.

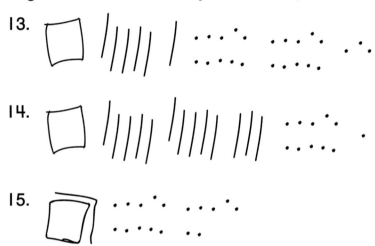

13.

14.

15.

16. If you do not follow the fewest base-ten pieces rule, then the same number can be shown in several ways. Use base-ten pieces to make 0.42 in several ways. Use base-ten shorthand to show each way you find.

Homework

Playing *Hundredths, Hundredths, Hundredths*

Complete these questions after playing *Hundredths, Hundredths, Hundredths*.

1. Lee Yah and Jerome were playing *Hundredths, Hundredths, Hundredths*. Jerome tried to trick Lee Yah by making this number:

For her fractions Lee Yah wrote $\frac{23}{100}$ and 0.023 and said, "Twenty-three hundredths." Lee Yah said she should earn 3 points.

Jerome thought that Lee Yah was wrong, but he couldn't explain why. What do you think?

2. Luis and Ana were playing *Hundredths, Hundredths, Hundredths.* Ana made the following number.

Write the common fraction and the decimal fraction for Ana's number.

3. When it was his turn, Luis made the following number.

Write the common fraction and the decimal fraction for Luis's number.

4. Jessie and Roberto were playing *Hundredths, Hundredths, Hundredths.* Roberto made the following number.

Write the common fraction and the decimal fraction for Roberto's number.

5. When it was Jessie's turn, she wanted to make 6.48. Use base-ten shorthand to show Jessie's number.

6. Roberto wanted to build the number 9.06. Use base-ten shorthand to show what pieces he should use.

7. Jessie wrote nine and six-hundredths like this: 9.6. Explain why this is incorrect.

Downhill Racer

Jackie and her brother Derrick want to play with their toy cars. They set up a ramp using the steps in front of their apartment building and a piece of thick plywood.

Jackie suggested using a meterstick to find how far each car traveled. Derrick wondered, "Will the cars roll different distances if we put the ramp on different steps?"

I think the cars will roll farther with the ramp on a higher step.

1. Do you think a car will roll farther when the ramp is set up on a higher step? Explain why you think so.

Jackie and Derrick did an experiment to find out how far each car rolled when the ramp was put on steps of different heights. First, they talked about how to be sure that the experiment was fair. Derrick suggested that the starting line on the ramp should stay the same.

2. What other variables should not change during the experiment? Why?

3. Jackie and Derrick decided to run three trials for each different height. Why was this a good idea?

Use the TIMS Laboratory Method to do an experiment like Jackie and Derrick's. Use a car and a ramp to study the relationship between the height of the ramp (*H*) and the distance your car will roll on the ground (*D*).

Use blocks or books to change the height of the ramp. The height (*H*) is the height of the blocks (or books). The blocks should touch the ramp at the same place for the entire experiment. The distance (*D*) should be measured from the bottom of the ramp to the back wheels of the car.

4. What is the manipulated variable?

5. What is the responding variable?

Draw a picture of the lab. Be sure to show the two main variables, Height (*H*) and Distance (*D*). Also show the length of your ramp and where your starting line is.

6. Later, you will make and check predictions about how far your car rolls. Unless you are careful now, you may not be able to check your predictions later. Write a paragraph that describes exactly how you set up your lab, so that later you can set it up again in exactly the same way. (*Hint:* Look at your answer to Question 2.)

7. **A.** Work with your group to do the experiment.

- Discuss what values for the height (*H*) you will use.
- Measure the height in centimeters.
- Measure the distance (*D*) the car rolls to the nearest hundredth of a meter. Use decimals to record your measurements of this distance.
- Do three trials for each height. Average the three distances for each height by finding the median distance.
- Keep track of your data in a table like this one:

H Ramp Height (in cm)	*D* Distance Rolled (in m)			
	Trial 1	Trial 2	Trial 3	Average

B. Why is it a good idea to find the average distance?

8. **A.** Plot your data points on *Centimeter Graph Paper.* Put the manipulated variable on the horizontal axis and the responding variable on the vertical axis. Remember to title your graph, label axes, and record units. Before you scale your axes, discuss with your group how much room you need on your graph for extrapolation. (*Hint:* Look at Questions 9–12.)

B. Look at your points on the graph. Do the points lie close to a straight line? If so, use a ruler to fit a line to the points. Extend the line in both directions.

Answer the following questions using your graph:

9. If the height of the ramp were 10 cm,
   A. How far would your car roll? $H = 10$ cm; Predicted $D = ?$
   B. Did you interpolate or extrapolate?
   C. Check your prediction. $H = 10$ cm; Actual $D = ?$
   D. Was your predicted distance close to the actual distance?

10. If the height of the ramp were 16 cm,
    A. How far would your car roll? $H = 16$ cm; Predicted $D = ?$
    B. Did you interpolate or extrapolate?
    C. Check your prediction. $H = 16$ cm; Actual $D = ?$
    D. Was your predicted distance close to the actual distance?

11. A. Predict how high the ramp should be if you want the car to roll 1.5 m. Explain how you found your answer.
    B. Check your prediction. How close did your car roll to 1.5 m?

12. Imagine doing the experiment again, this time letting the car go from a lower starting point on the ramp. Would your new line look like Line A or Line B? Explain why you think so.

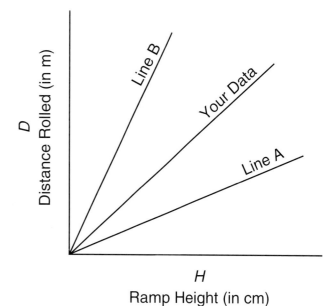

13. Sometimes knowing one variable helps in predicting another.
    A. Does knowing the height of the ramp (H) help you predict what the distance rolled (D) will be?
    B. Does knowing the distance rolled (D) help you predict what the height of the ramp (H) was?
    C. As the height of the ramp (H) increases, how does the distance (D) change?

Downhill Racer

You will need a calculator, a ruler, and a piece of graph paper to answer Questions 14–19.

14. After Mrs. Dewey's class finished the experiment *Downhill Racer*, they did another experiment using ramps. In the new experiment, each group kept the height of the ramp the same and used the same car all the time. They chose three distances from the end of the ramp for starting points. Then, they rolled the cars down the ramp from each starting point and measured the distance the car rolled in centimeters. Here is one group's picture of the experiment.

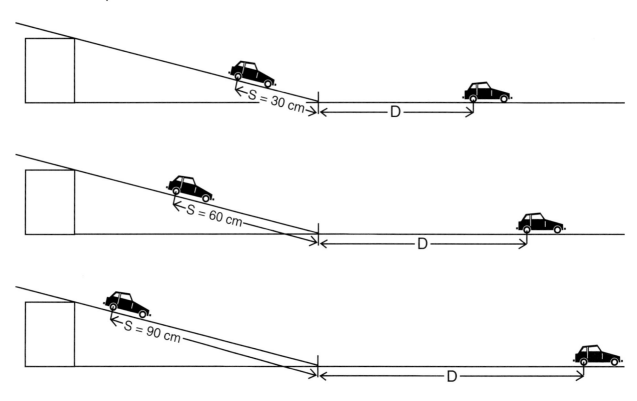

    A. What is the manipulated variable in this experiment?

    B. What is the responding variable in this experiment?

    C. Give one fixed variable.

    D. Is the manipulated variable numerical or categorical?

15. John's group rolled its car down the ramp three times from the starting point that was 60 cm from the end of the ramp. Here are the distances the car rolled for three trials: 83 cm, 84 cm, and 89 cm.

   A. Find the mean distance for these trials. Give your answer to the nearest centimeter.

   B. Find the median distance.

16. Nila's group chose to do four trials. Here are the distances the car rolled from a starting point that was 120 cm from the end of the ramp: 189 cm, 177 cm, 186 cm, and 188 cm.

   A. Find the mean distance for these trials.

   B. Find the median distance. Give your answer to the nearest centimeter.

17. Here is Shannon's data. Make a graph of the data.

Shannon's Data

H Starting Distance From End of Ramp (in cm)	D Distance Rolled (in cm)			
	Trial 1	Trial 2	Trial 3	Average
30	48	47	47	47
60	87	84	86	86
90	144	142	145	144

18. **A.** Use your graph to predict the distance the car will roll if Shannon uses the same lab setup and she starts to roll the car down the ramp 45 cm from the end of the ramp.

    B. Did you use interpolation or extrapolation to find your answer?

19. **A.** Use your graph to predict the distance the car will roll if Shannon uses the same lab setup and she starts to roll the car down the ramp 120 cm from the end of the ramp.

    B. Did you use interpolation or extrapolation to find your answer?

Miss Take made the following graph for Roberto's data. She has made many mistakes. How many can you find? Write a letter to Miss Take explaining as many errors as you can find.

Name: _Miss Take_

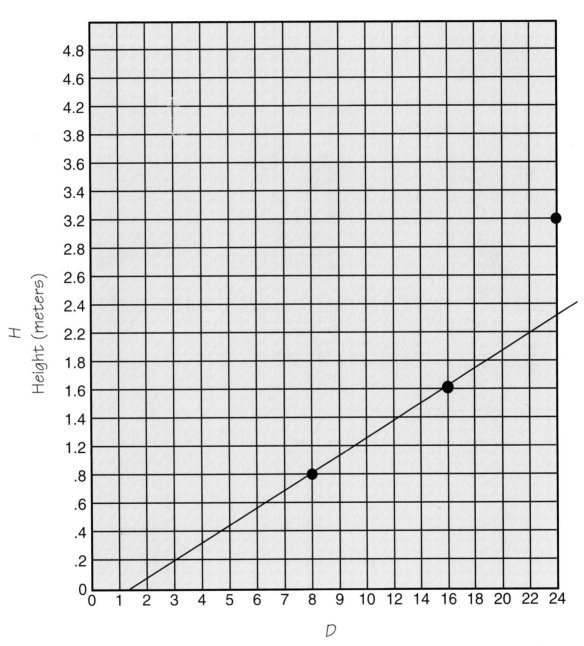

Unit 11

Multiplication

	Student Guide	Discovery Assignment Book	Adventure Book	Unit Resource Guide*
Lesson 1				
Modeling Multiplication	@			
Lesson 2				
More Multiplication	@			
Lesson 3				
Compact Multiplication	@			
Lesson 4				
All-Partials Revisited	@			@
Lesson 5				
More Compact Multiplication	@			
Lesson 6				
Phil and Howard's Excellent Egyptian Adventure			@	
Lesson 7				
Visiting Egypt	@			

Unit Resource Guide pages are from the teacher materials.

Modeling Multiplication

Break-Apart Products

There are many different ways of modeling multiplication problems. One way is to use an array. Another way is to use base-ten pieces. In this lesson and the other lessons in this unit, a bit has a value of 1 whole. Both pictures below model 3×12.

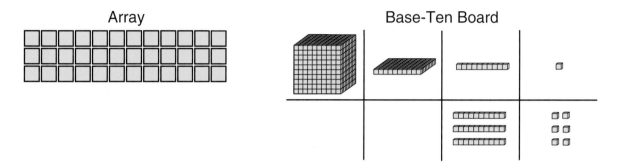

For Questions 1–4, give a multiplication sentence for each picture.

1.

Base-Ten Board

2.

Array

3. **4.**

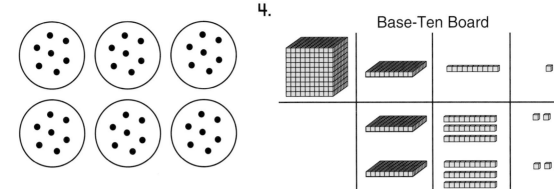

Base-Ten Board

For Questions 5 and 6, model the multiplication problem by drawing a picture.

5. 4×21

6. 5×32

For Questions 7 and 8, complete the break-apart number sentences.

7. $4 \times 45 = ? \times 40 + ? \times 5$
$\quad\quad = ? + ?$
$\quad\quad = ?$

8. $7 \times 28 = 7 \times ? + ? \times 8$
$\quad\quad = ? + ?$
$\quad\quad = ?$

9. When we multiply 6×34 using the all-partials method, we can think about the base-ten pieces.

$$
\begin{array}{r}
34 \\
\times\ 6 \\
\hline
24 \\
180 \\
\hline
204
\end{array}
$$

$24 \longleftarrow 6 \times 4$: 6 groups of 4 bits
$180 \longleftarrow 6 \times 30$: 6 groups of 3 skinnies

Write a break-apart number sentence for 6×34.

10. When we multiply 7×27 using the all-partials method, we can think about the base-ten pieces.

$$
\begin{array}{r}
27 \\
\times\ 7 \\
\hline
49 \\
140 \\
\hline
189
\end{array}
$$

$49 \longleftarrow 7 \times 7$: 7 groups of 7 bits
$140 \longleftarrow 7 \times 20$: 7 groups of 2 skinnies

Write a break-apart number sentence for 7×27.

Multiplying on the Base-Ten Board

11. This shows 23 in base-ten shorthand.

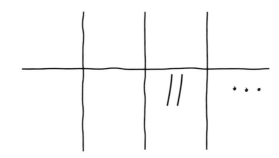

A. There are 2 ——?—— and 3 ——?——.

This shows the answer when you multiply 10 × 23 = 230 in base-ten shorthand.

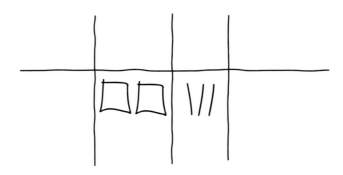

B. There are 2 ——?—— and 3 ——?——.

C. Describe how the base-ten pieces change when you multiply a number by 10.

12. This shows 23 in base-ten shorthand.

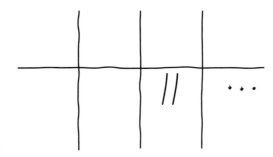

Modeling Multiplication

This shows the answer when you multiply $100 \times 23 = 2300$ in base-ten shorthand.

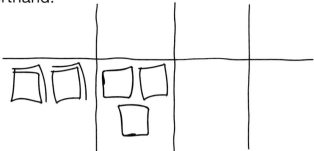

Explain how the base-ten pieces change when you multiply a number by 100.

Show just the answers to the following multiplication problems in base-ten shorthand. Draw in the column markings to help you.

13. **A.** 2×23

    B. 20×23

    C. Compare the shorthand for parts A and B. What is an easy way to think about 20×23?

14. **A.** 3×45

    B. 30×45

    C. Compare the shorthand for parts A and B. What is an easy way to think about 30×45?

15. **A.** 4×17

    B. 40×17

    C. 400×17

    D. Compare the shorthand for parts A, B, and C. What is an easy way of thinking about 40×17 and 400×17?

Do the following groups of problems and watch for patterns. Use a calculator when needed to check your work.

16.	17.	18.
2×3	4×8	5×4
2×30	4×80	5×40
20×3	40×8	50×4
20×30	40×80	50×40
20×300	40×800	50×400
200×3000	400×8000	500×4000

19. Explain how you can quickly compute products that end in zeros.

Compute the following sets of problems. Watch for patterns.

20. **A.** $\begin{array}{r} 31 \\ \times 3 \\ \hline \end{array}$
    B. $\begin{array}{r} 310 \\ \times 3 \\ \hline \end{array}$
    C. $\begin{array}{r} 3100 \\ \times 3 \\ \hline \end{array}$
    D. $\begin{array}{r} 31,000 \\ \times 3 \\ \hline \end{array}$

21. **A.** 70×14
    B. 70×140
    C. 70×1400
    D. $70 \times 14,000$

22. **A.** 4×25
    B. 4×250
    C. 4×2500
    D. $4 \times 25,000$

Homework

For Questions 1–6, solve each problem two ways:

   A. Write a break-apart number sentence using multiples of 10 if possible.

   B. Use the all-partials method or facts you know to solve the problem.

   1. $6 \times 8 =$
   2. $7 \times 6 =$
   3. $8 \times 7 =$
   4. $5 \times 24 =$
   5. $6 \times 12 =$
   6. $36 \times 4 =$

Find the following products.

   7. $15 \times 5 =$
   8. $40 \times 6 =$
   9. $8 \times 22 =$
   10. $10 \times 5 =$
   11. $7 \times 100 =$
   12. $40 \times 10 =$
   13. $21 \times 3 =$
   14. $5 \times 30 =$
   15. $60 \times 40 =$
   16. $42 \times 10 =$
   17. $12 \times 20 =$
   18. $30 \times 50 =$
   19. $17 \times 20 =$

20. Nila and her sister put together 5 jigsaw puzzles. If each puzzle has 32 pieces, how many pieces do the 5 jigsaw puzzles have?

Modeling Multiplication

21. Jerome practices piano for 30 minutes every day after school. He has two weeks to practice before the recital. How many minutes will he practice on school nights from now until the recital? How many hours?

22. Shannon is in a bowling league after school on Wednesday. This week she bowled an 86 in each game of a three-game series. What was her total score for the series?

23. After school for a week, Jesse sold Chocos for the Little League fund-raiser. One hundred twenty families each bought $5 worth of Chocos. How much money did Jesse raise?

24. Lee Yah watched 45 minutes of TV each day for 4 days. How many minutes did she watch in all?

For Questions 25–32, find the missing numbers. There may be more than one answer for some of the problems.

25. $8 \times 60 = n$

26. $7 \times n = 140$

27. $50 \times n = 10,000$

28. $70 \times n = 490,000$

29. $n \times 200 = 4200$

30. $n \times 12 = 360,000$

31. $n \times m = 80$

32. $n \times m = 240,000$

Solve Questions 33–38 using either paper and pencil or mental math. You may use the all-partials method, base-ten pieces, or base-ten shorthand. Estimate to make sure your answer is reasonable.

33. $\begin{array}{r} 57 \\ \times 5 \\ \hline \end{array}$

34. $\begin{array}{r} 96 \\ \times 6 \\ \hline \end{array}$

35. $\begin{array}{r} 75 \\ \times 7 \\ \hline \end{array}$

36. $\begin{array}{r} 43 \\ \times 5 \\ \hline \end{array}$

37. $\begin{array}{r} 62 \\ \times 4 \\ \hline \end{array}$

38. $\begin{array}{r} 81 \\ \times 9 \\ \hline \end{array}$

More Multiplication

1. Pilot Jones flies her airplane about 324 minutes each week. Estimate the number of minutes Pilot Jones flies in a month. Assume there are 4 weeks in a month.

2. Use any method you wish to calculate the exact number of minutes Pilot Jones flies in a month. Explain your work with numbers, words, pictures, or base-ten pieces.

You can find the total number of minutes by modeling 4×324 using the base-ten pieces.

Base-Ten Board

Another way of solving the problem is to use the all-partials method of multiplication.

$$
\begin{array}{r}
324 \\
\times\,4 \\
\hline
16 \\
80 \\
\underline{1200} \\
1296
\end{array}
$$

3. Explain where the partial product 80 came from.

4. Which base-ten pieces model 80?

5. Explain where the partial product 1200 came from.

6. Which base-ten pieces model 1200?

Do the following problems using the all-partials method.

7. $\begin{array}{r} 132 \\ \times\,3 \\ \hline \end{array}$
  8. $\begin{array}{r} 3624 \\ \times\,2 \\ \hline \end{array}$
  9. $\begin{array}{r} 1205 \\ \times\,4 \\ \hline \end{array}$

10. Grace notices that many of the partial products end in zeros. Circle the zeros in the partial products in Questions 7–9.

11. Explain where the zeros came from in Questions 7–9.

12. Professor Peabody always leaves out digits when he uses the all-partials method to multiply. Copy the problems and find the missing digits as you find the products. Be careful to line up the columns.

A. $\begin{array}{r} 24 \\ \times\,3 \\ \hline 12 \\ 6\square \\ \hline \end{array}$
  B. $\begin{array}{r} 734 \\ \times\,8 \\ \hline 32 \\ 24\square \\ 56\square\square \\ \hline \end{array}$
  C. $\begin{array}{r} 4251 \\ \times\,7 \\ \hline 7 \\ 35\square \\ 14\square\square \\ 28\square\square\square \\ \hline \end{array}$

13. Explain patterns you see in Question 12.

14. Does leaving out the missing digits in Question 12 affect the answer to the multiplication problems? Why or why not?

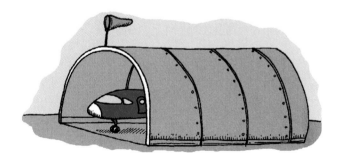

More Multiplication

15. Grace computed 3×306 like this:

$$
\begin{array}{r}
306 \\
\times\,3 \\
\hline
18 \\
900 \\
\hline
918
\end{array}
$$

    A. Is Grace correct?

    B. Why are there only two partial products in this problem?

Homework

Do the following pairs of problems. Use the answer from the first problem to help solve the second problem in each pair without computing.

1. **A.**
   $$
   \begin{array}{r} 32 \\ \times\,6 \\ \hline \end{array}
   \qquad
   \begin{array}{r} 320 \\ \times\,6 \\ \hline \end{array}
   $$

   B.
   $$
   \begin{array}{r} 403 \\ \times\,9 \\ \hline \end{array}
   \qquad
   \begin{array}{r} 4030 \\ \times\,9 \\ \hline \end{array}
   $$

   C.
   $$
   \begin{array}{r} 275 \\ \times\,3 \\ \hline \end{array}
   \qquad
   \begin{array}{r} 2{,}750{,}000 \\ \times\,3 \\ \hline \end{array}
   $$

Do the following problems. First make a mental estimate of the answer. Then do the problem. Compare your estimate with the answer.

2. Remember, there are 24 hours in a day. How many hours are there in a week?

3. One type of airplane can carry 229 passengers. North-South Airlines flies its airplane from Minneapolis to Ft. Lauderdale five times a week. How many people can travel every week from Minneapolis to Ft. Lauderdale on North-South Airlines?

4. An airplane has a cruising speed of about 558 miles per hour. How far can the aircraft travel in 3 hours?

5. Another airplane has a cruising speed of 1336 miles per hour. How far can this aircraft travel in 3 hours?

Practice Problems

Estimate your answer before solving the following problems.

6. 6×45 **7.** 8×32 **8.** 5×3049

9. 6×421 **10.** 30×312 **11.** 6×7213

12. 40×2301 **13.** 3×3008 **14.** 60×4250

15. 8×3453 **16.** 7×3024 **17.** 38×100

18. 124×200 **19.** 300×47 **20.** 94×400

21. 329×500 **22.** 417×60 **23.** 30×865

24. Explain your estimation strategy for Question 9.

25. Explain a mental math strategy for solving Question 13.

Did You Know?

Mrs. Dewey's classroom, Room 204, is in Bessie Coleman School. Bessie Coleman was the world's first African-American female aviator.

When Bessie's brother returned to America after World War I, he told Bessie that French women could fly airplanes. At that time, Bessie worked as a manicurist in a Chicago barber shop. Hearing this news, Bessie decided she too could learn to fly. She went to school to learn French. Then, she went to France. In 1921 she earned her pilot's license from the Federation Aeronautique Internationale. When she returned to Chicago, her home, she became an air circus performer. A street and a library in Chicago are named after Bessie Coleman.

Compact Multiplication

Kris enjoys looking at travel brochures and dreams about seeing all 50 states and other parts of the world as well. Kris thinks it would be great to be a travel agent.

Travel agents need to think about transporting large groups of people. If an airplane holds 123 passengers, how many people will 4 flights of that airplane carry?

Jacob showed Kris his method for solving the problem. He first estimated the product. Since 123 is about 100 and $4 \times 100 = 400$, Jacob knows the product will be over 400. Since 23 is about 25 and $4 \times 25 = 100$, Jacob thinks the product will be about 500 since $400 + 100 = 500$.

Compact Multiplication

Jacob solved the problem by using the all-partials method of multiplication. Nicholas said he had a shortcut way of computing the product. Compare Jacob's method and Nicholas's method.

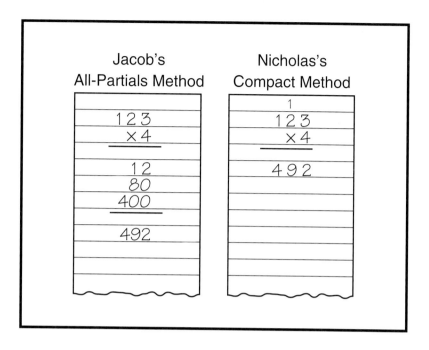

Review Jacob's method. Can you see how he found his answer?

Nicholas began by multiplying $3 \times 4 = 12$. Nicholas knows this is 1 ten and 2 ones.

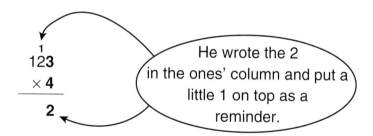

He wrote the 2 in the ones' column and put a little 1 on top as a reminder.

The 1 Nicholas wrote above the problem as a reminder is called a **carry.** Nicholas then multiplied 4×2 tens = 8 tens and he then added the extra ten to get 9 tens.

He put the 9 in the tens' column.

Last, Nicholas multiplied 4 × 1 hundred = 4 hundreds.

1. Which method do you prefer: Jacob's method or Nicholas's method? Why?

He put the 4 in the hundreds' column.

$$\begin{array}{r} {\scriptstyle 1} \\ 123 \\ \times\, 4 \\ \hline 492 \end{array}$$

One type of airplane can carry up to 376 passengers. How many people can 4 flights of the aircraft carry?

Nicholas did the problem using the compact method:

$$\begin{array}{r} {\scriptstyle 3\;2} \\ 376 \\ \times\, 4 \\ \hline 1504 \end{array}$$

2. Why did Nicholas place a 2 above the problem? What does this 2 mean?

3. How did Nicholas get the 0 in the tens' column of the answer?

4. Why did Nicholas place a 3 above the problem? What does this 3 mean?

5. How did Nicholas get the 5 in the hundreds' column of the answer?

6. How did Nicholas get the 1 in the thousands' column of the answer?

Homework

1. Jerome wanted to check his answer to the problem 227 × 4. He knew 908 was a reasonable answer. However, he wasn't sure about the 0 in the tens' place. He laid down the base-ten pieces as shown.

Base-Ten Board

$$\begin{array}{r} {\scriptstyle 1\;2} \\ 227 \\ \times\, 4 \\ \hline 908 \end{array}$$

A. How many bits are there?

B. How did Jerome record these bits using the compact method?

C. There are 8 skinnies shown on the base-ten board. Was Jerome correct in placing a 0 in the tens' column instead of an 8? Why or why not?

D. Would the answer 808 make sense? How did Jerome get the 9 in the hundreds' place?

Compute the following products. Try to use the compact method or mental math. Estimate your product first. Use your estimate to make sure your answer is reasonable.

2. 52
   ×3

3. 325
   ×2

4. 280
   ×5

5. 307
   ×3

6. 49
   ×2

7. 43
   ×5

8. 416
   ×6

9. 401
   ×8

10. 3210
    ×5

11. 4200
    ×6

12. 8007
    ×9

13. 6018
    ×7

14. Grace went to the airport to meet her grandmother who was coming to Chicago from Rochester, New York. On the way home in the car, Grace's grandmother commented on the trip.

    A. On the flight to Chicago, there were 139 passengers. They were served twice during the flight. If each passenger drank a total of two cans of juice or soda, how many cans would the flight attendants need?

    B. Is this more or less than 20 twelve-packs?

15. Grace's grandmother told her that the plane she took to Chicago seemed small compared to the one she took to Hawaii. The main cabin of the larger plane was split into two parts. One part had 14 rows of 9 seats. The other part had 11 rows of 9 seats. The flight to Hawaii was filled to capacity.

    A. How many seats did the flight to Hawaii have?

    B. How many more passengers were on the flight to Hawaii than on the flight to Chicago?

16. Grace's grandmother met Pilot Johnson. He told her that he has flown round trip from Rochester to Chicago nine times in the past week. It is 528 miles one way from Rochester to Chicago. How many miles has Pilot Johnson traveled in all on the Rochester-Chicago route?

17. When they were picking up Grandma's luggage, an announcement was made for the returning flight to Rochester. Passengers could check in 3 bags and carry on 2 bags. If the returning flight to Rochester has 148 passengers, what is the largest number of pieces of luggage the airline will allow for this flight?

18. Nila gave the answer of 1000 for the following problem. Explain why Nila is wrong. Tell how to find the correct answer.

$$500 \times 20 =$$

19. $650 \times 100 =$

20. $760 \times 50 =$

21. $1350 \times 20 =$

All-Partials Revisited

TIMSville built a new school. The new school has 14 classrooms. Each classroom has 24 desks. How many desks are in the new school?

I. **A.** Estimate the number of desks in the new school. Then, compare your estimate to Ana's solution.

Ana decided to model this multiplication problem using base-ten shorthand. She split the 14 classrooms into a group of 10 classrooms and a group of 4 classrooms.

10 classrooms with
24 desks in each

4 classrooms with
24 desks in each

There are 14 classrooms with
24 desks in each.

Ana computed the product using the all-partials method:

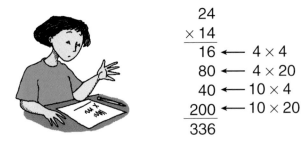

$$
\begin{array}{r}
24 \\
\times\ 14 \\
\hline
16 \quad\longleftarrow\ 4 \times 4 \\
80 \quad\longleftarrow\ 4 \times 20 \\
40 \quad\longleftarrow\ 10 \times 4 \\
200 \quad\longleftarrow\ 10 \times 20 \\
\hline
336
\end{array}
$$

She multiplied $4 \times 4 = 16$ and $4 \times 20 = 80$. Then, she multiplied $10 \times 4 = 40$ and $10 \times 20 = 200$. Her total is 336 so there are enough desks for 336 students.

B. Match the partial products with the base-ten shorthand.

2. Jessie also used the all-partials method. She multiplied 10×20 first.

$$
\begin{array}{r}
24 \\
\times\ 14 \\
\hline
200 \quad\longleftarrow\ 10 \times 20 \\
40 \quad\longleftarrow\ 10 \times 4 \\
80 \quad\longleftarrow\ 4 \times 20 \\
16 \quad\longleftarrow\ 4 \times 4 \\
\hline
336
\end{array}
$$

She liked this method because the first product she found was the most important. Why might Jessie think her first product was the most important?

3. The new school has an auditorium with 32 rows of seats. Each row has 18 seats.

A. Estimate the number of seats in the auditorium.

B. Ana found the exact number of seats by using the all-partials method. Copy the problem and fill in the missing numbers.

$$
\begin{array}{r}
32 \\
\times\ 18 \\
\hline
?? \\
240 \\
?? \\
300 \\
\hline
???
\end{array}
$$

C. How did Ana get the partial product 240?

D. How did Ana get the partial product 300?

4. Compute 43×27 by using the all-partials method.

1. Irma used the all-partials method to do the problem 87×32. Copy the problem and fill in the missing numbers in her work and complete the problem.

$$
\begin{array}{r}
32 \\
\times\, 87 \\
\hline
?? \\
2?? \\
?6? \\
?40? \\
\hline
\end{array}
$$

2. Roberto solved the problem 47×52 using the all-partials method.

$$
\begin{array}{r}
47 \\
\times\, 52 \\
\hline
14 \\
80 \\
35 \\
200 \\
\hline
\cancel{329} \\
\end{array}
$$

   A. Is Roberto's answer of 329 reasonable? Explain why or why not.

   B. What did Roberto do wrong?

   C. Find the correct answer.

For Questions 3–7, decide whether the estimate is a "could be" or "crazy" estimate. If the estimate seems appropriate, record your answer as "could be." If the estimate is too high or too low, record your answer as "crazy." Explain how you decided.

3. Tanya said, "76×42 is close to 280."

4. Romesh said, "35×35 is between 900 and 1600. 1200 is my estimate."

5. Luis said, "The answer to 17×34 is less than 400."

6. Jessie said, "57×26 is less than 1000."

7. Shannon said, "A good estimate for 11×55 is 550."

For Questions 8–15, find the products using the all-partials method. Remember to estimate to see if your answer is reasonable. Choose two problems and explain your estimation strategies for them.

8. 14×15

9. 45×12

10. 37×23

11. 64×78

12. 56×18

13. 93×44

14. 81×29

15. 62×65

16. Jacob's older sister Cara uses a graphing calculator. Her classroom has a set of 25. If one calculator costs $97, how much did the classroom set cost?

17. Smackin Good Apple Company shipped 14 small boxes of apples to Martha's Market. Each small box has 48 apples in it. How many apples did Martha's Market receive?

18. Grace is starring in the school play. Her parents purchased tickets in advance. They got seat numbers 211 and 212. Grace looks for her parents from the stage. She knows there are 18 seats in a row. She also knows seat number 1 is in the first row. Where should Grace look to find her parents? About which row? (*Hint:* Use the picture to help you.)

19. The auditorium at Bessie Coleman School has 18 seats in each row and 33 rows. The movie theater has 28 seats in each row and 28 rows. Which has more seats? How many more?

More Compact Multiplication

A grocer received a shipment of eggs. The box contained 24 cartons of eggs. Each carton contained 12 eggs. How many eggs did the grocer receive?

1. Estimate the number of eggs by thinking about the base-ten pieces.

Jacob and Nicholas solved the problem using their paper-and-pencil methods.

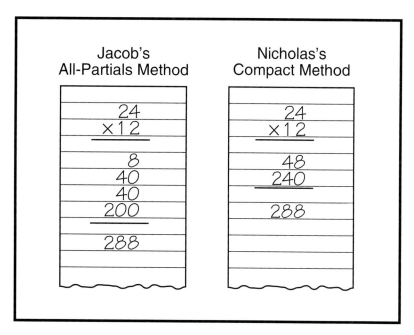

2. Identify the base-ten pieces which match each of the partial products in Jacob's method.

Nicholas showed how to do 12×24 using the compact method. He first multiplied 2×24. To do this, he multiplied 2×4 to get 8 and wrote the 8 in the ones' column. He then multiplied 2×20 to get 40 and wrote 4 in the tens' column.

$$
\begin{array}{r}
24 \\
\times\ 12 \\
\hline
\mathbf{48}
\end{array}
$$

For the next part of the problem, Nicholas multiplied 10×24. He first multiplied 10×4 to get 40.

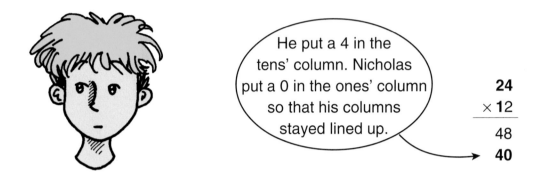

He put a 4 in the tens' column. Nicholas put a 0 in the ones' column so that his columns stayed lined up.

$$
\begin{array}{r}
24 \\
\times\ 12 \\
\hline
48 \\
\mathbf{40}
\end{array}
$$

Then, he multiplied 10×20 to get 200.

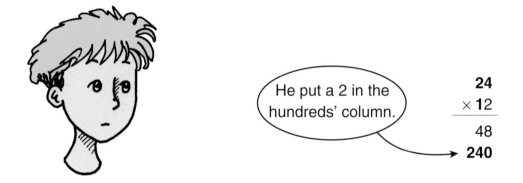

He put a 2 in the hundreds' column.

$$
\begin{array}{r}
24 \\
\times\ 12 \\
\hline
48 \\
\mathbf{240}
\end{array}
$$

Nicholas then added to get 288.

$$
\begin{array}{r}
24 \\
\times\ 12 \\
\hline
48 \\
240 \\
\hline
288
\end{array}
$$

3. Compute 74×23 using the all-partials method.

To compute 74×23 using the compact method, Nicholas first multiplied $4 \times 3 = 12$. He put a 2 in the ones' column and a 1 above the problem as a reminder. He then multiplied $4 \times 20 = 80$. He now has 8 tens and the extra 1 ten, so he has 9 tens altogether. Nicholas wrote a 9 in the tens' column.

$$
\begin{array}{r}
1 \\
23 \\
\times\,74 \\
\hline
92
\end{array}
$$

Nicholas then multiplied $70 \times 3 = 210$. He put a 0 in the ones' column and a 1 in the tens' column. He put a 2 above the problem as a reminder. He crossed out the 1 above the problem since he had taken care of it.

$$
\begin{array}{r}
2 \\
\cancel{1} \\
23 \\
\times\,74 \\
\hline
92 \\
10
\end{array}
$$

Nicholas then multiplied $70 \times 20 = 1400$. This means he has 4 hundreds and the 2 extra hundreds, or 6 hundreds total. Nicholas put a 6 in the hundreds' column and a 1 in the thousands' column. He didn't have to carry the 1 because he had no more partial products to compute.

$$
\begin{array}{r}
2 \\
\cancel{1} \\
23 \\
\times\,74 \\
\hline
92 \\
1610 \\
\hline
1702
\end{array}
$$

Nicholas found the product $74 \times 23 = 1702$.

Here is another problem that Nicholas did using the compact method.

$$
\begin{array}{r}
\overset{5}{\cancel{8}} \\
49 \\
\times\, 64 \\
\hline
196 \\
2940 \\
\hline
3136
\end{array}
$$

4. Why did Nicholas put a 3 above the problem?

5. How did Nicholas get a 9 in the tens' column of the first partial product?

6. How did Nicholas get the 4 in the tens' column and the 0 in the ones' column of the second partial product?

7. Why did Nicholas put a 5 above the problem?

8. How did Nicholas get a 9 in the hundreds' column in the second partial product?

Compute the problems using the compact method.

9. 34×79 10. 27×82 11. 42×28

Homework

1. Jackie solved the problem 47×52 using the all-partials method. Then, she tried using the compact method.

$$
\begin{array}{r}
54 \\
\times\, 47 \\
\hline
28 \\
350 \\
160 \\
2000 \\
\hline
2538
\end{array}
\qquad
\begin{array}{r}
\overset{1}{\cancel{2}} \\
54 \\
\times\, 47 \\
\hline
378 \\
2160 \\
\hline
2538
\end{array}
$$

A. Why did Jackie place a 1 above the problem in the compact method?

B. How did Jackie get a 6 in the tens' place in the second partial product in the compact method?

C. Where is Jackie's record of multiplying 7×50 in the compact method?

D. How did Jackie get 2160 when using the compact method?

2. Which of the following are the four partial products which make up the problem below using the all-partials method?

$$\begin{array}{r} 27 \\ \times\, 69 \\ \hline \end{array}$$

6×20 60×7 2×90 9×7

60×20 90×20 20×9 9×20

Find the following products.

3. $25 \times 15 =$ 4. $46 \times 34 =$ 5. $58 \times 76 =$ 6. $95 \times 64 =$

7. $70 \times 23 =$ 8. $68 \times 90 =$ 9. $52 \times 55 =$ 10. $76 \times 33 =$

11. The Victory Videos store was selling *Math and the Music Factory* videos for $14. Mrs. Dewey bought a dozen of these videos for the school library. How much did the videos cost in all?

12. On Monday night, only 17 movies were rented. On Saturday night, 16 times as many movies were rented. How many movies were rented on Saturday night?

13. A newly released movie was available for sale. Last weekend alone, Victory Videos sold 98 copies of this movie. If one copy costs $24, how much money did Victory Videos receive for this movie?

14. Victory Videos has about 36 different sections. Each section has 6 shelves. Each shelf has about 10 movies on it. About how many videos can fill the video store?

15. Victory's ad in the paper reads, "We have 5 times as many videos as Urban Video." Urban Video has about 6000 videos. About how many videos does Victory Videos have?

16. There are 28 Victory Videos stores throughout the city. On average, each store has 28 employees. How many people work for Victory Videos?

Visiting Egypt

Solve the following problems about a fictional king in Egypt. Use paper and pencil or mental math. Estimate to be sure your answer is reasonable.

1. King Omar has eight stables full of camels. Each stable has 25 camels. How many camels does King Omar have?

2. Each camel has three riders. How many camel riders does King Omar have?

3. The camels can each carry back five bundles of dates to King Omar. How many bundles of dates can they bring back to the king?

4. Half of King Omar's camels became ill and could only carry back two bundles of dates instead of five bundles each. How many bundles came back to the king?

5. One night, 25 camels ran away.
   A. How many camels are left?
   B. How many bundles of dates can the remaining camels bring back to King Omar if none are ill?

6. King Omar sent 30 groups of laborers to build a pyramid. Each group has 50 laborers. How many laborers did King Omar send?

7. Each group of laborers can build one small pyramid every year. How many small pyramids can King Omar have built each year?

8. How many small pyramids can be built in 15 years?

9. How many small pyramids can be built in 25 years?

10. **A.** $37 \times 45 =$

 B. $2340 \times 9 =$

 C. $80 \times 53 =$

 D. $93 \times 70 =$

 E. $79 \times 46 =$

 F. $50 \times 600 =$

 G. $25 \times 40 =$

 H. $44 \times 44 =$

 I. $307 \times 7 =$

11. Explain your estimation strategy for Question 10H.

12. Describe a mental math strategy for Question 10I.

Unit 12
Exploring Fractions

	Student Guide	Discovery Assignment Book	Adventure Book	Unit Resource Guide*
Lesson 1				
Fraction Strips	◉	◉		
Lesson 2				
Adding and Subtracting with Fraction Strips	◉			
Lesson 3				
Comparing Fractions	◉			
Lesson 4				
Frabble Game and Bubble Sort	◉	◉		
Lesson 5				
Equivalent Fractions	◉			
Lesson 6				
Pattern Block Fractions	◉			◉
Lesson 7				
Solving Problems with Pattern Blocks	◉			
Lesson 8				
Fraction Puzzles	◉			◉
Lesson 9				
Midterm Test				◉

Unit Resource Guide pages are from the teacher materials.

Fraction Strips

Lee Yah demonstrated folding fourths for her class.

"First, I folded my strip into two equal pieces. I folded my strip by matching the edges and then making a crease in the middle. Next, I kept it folded and then I folded it in half again. When I unfold the strip, it is divided into 4 equal pieces. Since the 4 parts are all the same size, each piece is $\frac{1}{4}$ of the strip."

She showed three of the pieces to show $\frac{3}{4}$ of the strip.

In a fraction, the bottom number is the **denominator.** This number tells us how many equal pieces the whole is divided into. The top number, the **numerator,** tells us how many of the pieces we are concerned with.

$$\frac{3}{4} \quad \begin{array}{l} \longleftarrow \text{ numerator} \\ \longleftarrow \text{ denominator} \end{array}$$

1. In the fraction $\frac{3}{4}$, what information does the denominator give us?

2. What information does the numerator give us in the fraction $\frac{3}{4}$?

3. What happens to the size of the fractional parts as the denominator gets bigger?

Halves, Fourths, and Eighths

1. Tanya showed the following fraction using her fraction strips. What fraction is she showing?

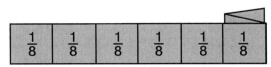

2. Luis showed the following fraction using his fraction strips. What fraction is he showing?

3. Ming showed the following fraction using his fraction strips. What fraction is he showing?

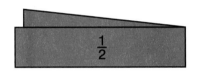

4. Write a fraction for each fraction strip.

A.

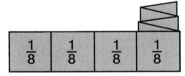

B.

C.

D.

5. Roberto has 8 buttons. Three of the buttons are red, three of the buttons are green, and two of the buttons are blue.

  A. What fraction of the buttons are red?

  B. What fraction of the buttons are green?

  C. What fraction of the buttons are red or blue?

6. Jessie, Nila, Irma, and Tanya are standing together.

  A. What fraction of the girls are wearing red?

  B. What fraction of the girls are wearing glasses?

7. Linda folded her eighths strip to show $\frac{3}{8}$.

  A. In the fraction $\frac{3}{8}$ what information does the denominator give us?

  B. In the fraction $\frac{3}{8}$ what information does the numerator give us?

Thirds, Sixths, Ninths, and Twelfths

8. Romesh made the following fraction using his fraction strips. What fraction did he make?

9. Jessie made the following fraction using her fraction strips. What fraction did she make?

10. Nicholas made the following fraction using his fraction strips. What fraction did he make?

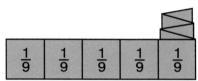

11. Write a fraction for each fraction strip.

A.

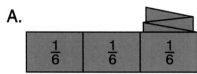

B.

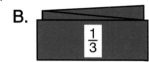

C.

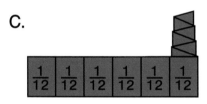

D.

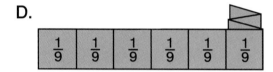

E.

12. Use the strips below to write two fractions equal to $\frac{4}{6}$.

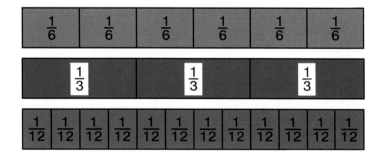

13. Use the strips below to find two fractions equal to $\frac{4}{12}$.

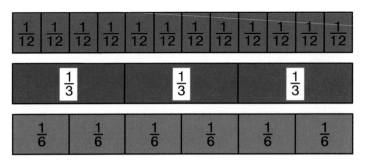

| $\frac{1}{12}$ | $\frac{1}{12}$ | $\frac{1}{12}$ | $\frac{1}{12}$ | $\frac{1}{12}$ | $\frac{1}{12}$ | $\frac{1}{12}$ | $\frac{1}{12}$ | $\frac{1}{12}$ | $\frac{1}{12}$ | $\frac{1}{12}$ | $\frac{1}{12}$ |

| $\frac{1}{3}$ | $\frac{1}{3}$ | $\frac{1}{3}$ |

| $\frac{1}{6}$ | $\frac{1}{6}$ | $\frac{1}{6}$ | $\frac{1}{6}$ | $\frac{1}{6}$ | $\frac{1}{6}$ |

Fifths and Tenths

14. Michael showed the following fraction with his fraction strips. What fraction did he show?

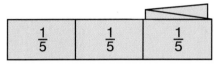

15. Roberto showed the following fraction with his fraction strip. What fraction did he show?

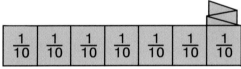

16. Lee Yah showed the following fraction with her fraction strip. What fraction did she show?

---

17. Write a fraction for each fraction strip.

A.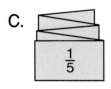

$\frac{1}{10}$ $\frac{1}{10}$ $\frac{1}{10}$ $\frac{1}{10}$

B.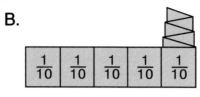

$\frac{1}{10}$ $\frac{1}{10}$ $\frac{1}{10}$ $\frac{1}{10}$ $\frac{1}{10}$

C.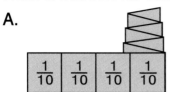

$\frac{1}{5}$

D.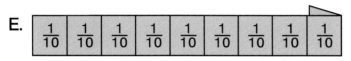

$\frac{1}{5}$ $\frac{1}{5}$ $\frac{1}{5}$ $\frac{1}{5}$ $\frac{1}{5}$

E.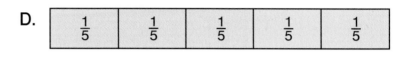

$\frac{1}{10}$ $\frac{1}{10}$ $\frac{1}{10}$ $\frac{1}{10}$ $\frac{1}{10}$ $\frac{1}{10}$ $\frac{1}{10}$ $\frac{1}{10}$ $\frac{1}{10}$

18. Use the fraction strips below to find a fraction equal to $\frac{4}{5}$.

| $\frac{1}{5}$ | $\frac{1}{5}$ | $\frac{1}{5}$ | $\frac{1}{5}$ | $\frac{1}{5}$ |

$\frac{1}{10}$ $\frac{1}{10}$ $\frac{1}{10}$ $\frac{1}{10}$ $\frac{1}{10}$ $\frac{1}{10}$ $\frac{1}{10}$ $\frac{1}{10}$ $\frac{1}{10}$ $\frac{1}{10}$

19. Use the fraction strips below to find five fractions equal to $\frac{1}{2}$. What do you notice about each of the denominators?

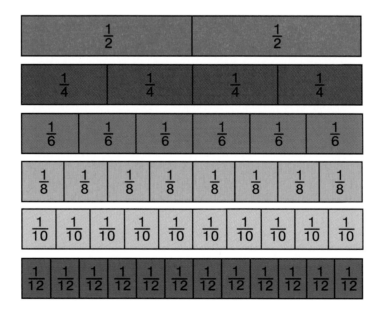

20. Use the fraction strips below to find three fractions equal to $\frac{2}{3}$.

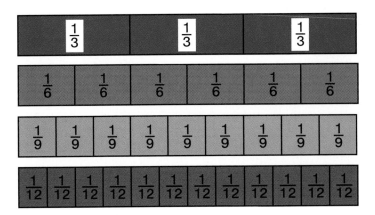

    A. What do you notice about each of the denominators?

    B. What do you notice about each of the numerators?

21. Use the fraction strips below to find two fractions equal to $\frac{3}{4}$.

    A. What do you notice about each of the numerators?

    B. What do you notice about each of the denominators?

Discuss

Mrs. Dewey asked her class to use their fraction strips to add $\frac{1}{4}$ and $\frac{2}{4}$. Keenya explained her solution to the class:

"First, I folded my strip that shows fourths so that 1 piece or $\frac{1}{4}$ of the strip was showing. Then, I added $\frac{2}{4}$ of the strip by unfolding 2 more pieces. I ended up with $\frac{3}{4}$ of my strip showing. So, $\frac{1}{4} + \frac{2}{4} = \frac{3}{4}$."

Next, Mrs. Dewey asked the class to use their fraction strips to subtract $\frac{3}{8}$ from $\frac{7}{8}$.

Jacob explained his solution to the class:

"I started with my strip that is divided into eighths. I folded it so that $\frac{7}{8}$ of the strip was showing. Then, I folded $\frac{3}{8}$ of the strip or 3 more pieces of the strip back since I was subtracting. This left me with $\frac{4}{8}$ of the strip showing, so $\frac{7}{8} - \frac{3}{8} = \frac{4}{8}$."

Adding and Subtracting with Fraction Strips

Work with a partner to solve the following problems. You will need to use two sets of fraction strips. Write a number sentence for each problem.

1. Maya has $\frac{5}{8}$ of a yard of fabric. She needs $\frac{3}{8}$ of a yard of fabric for a craft project. How much fabric will she have left over after she completes her project?

2. Frank is baking a cake. The recipe calls for $\frac{1}{4}$ cup of oil and $\frac{3}{4}$ cup of water. How much liquid will Frank add to the cake mix?

3. Jessie used $\frac{5}{12}$ of a board for a sign. What fraction of the board is left for another project?

4. There was $\frac{5}{6}$ of a pie on the counter when Luis got home from school.
   A. Luis ate $\frac{2}{6}$ of the pie. How much of the pie is left?
   B. Luis's sister ate another $\frac{1}{6}$ of the pie. Now how much of the pie is left?
   C. Use your fraction strips to find another fraction that is equal to your answer to Question 4B.

5. Ming rode his bike $\frac{8}{10}$ mile to Frank's house. He then rode $\frac{8}{10}$ mile back home again. How far did Ming ride altogether?

6. Irma must finish her homework and practice piano before she can go outside to play. It takes her $\frac{3}{4}$ hour to do her homework and she practices piano for $\frac{2}{4}$ hour. How long does she have to wait before going outside to play?

7. Use your fraction strips to complete the following number sentences.
   A. $\frac{3}{8} + \frac{2}{8} =$ B. $\frac{7}{10} + \frac{5}{10} =$ C. $\frac{3}{6} + \frac{3}{6} =$
   D. $\frac{11}{12} - \frac{4}{12} =$ E. $\frac{3}{5} - \frac{1}{5} =$ F. $\frac{7}{8} - \frac{3}{8} =$

Homework

Use your fraction strips to complete the following problems. Write a number sentence for each problem.

1. Grace needed $\frac{5}{8}$ of a yard of ribbon to decorate the outside edge of a picture frame. She needed another $\frac{3}{8}$ of a yard of ribbon to decorate the inside edge of her frame. How much ribbon did she need to finish the frame?

2. **A.** On Monday, John ate $\frac{1}{5}$ of a box of cookies. On Tuesday, he ate another $\frac{2}{5}$ of the cookies. What fraction of the cookies did he eat altogether?

   B. What fraction of the cookies is left?

3. **A.** Jerome lives $\frac{7}{10}$ of a mile from school. If he has already walked $\frac{3}{10}$ of a mile, how much farther does he have to go before he gets to school?

   B. Use your fraction strips to find another fraction that is equal to your answer.

4. Tanya and Nila used their fraction strips to add fractions. Look at their work. Write a number sentence to show what they did.

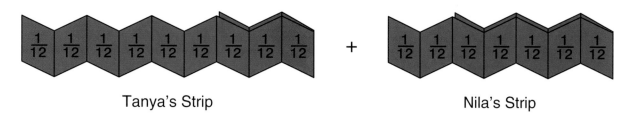

Tanya's Strip   Nila's Strip

5. Use your fraction strips to complete the following number sentences.

   A. $\frac{1}{12} + \frac{4}{12} =$ **B.** $\frac{7}{10} - \frac{5}{10} =$ **C.** $\frac{5}{8} + \frac{3}{8} =$

6. Maya and Jerome used their fraction strips to show the following addition problem. Write a number sentence for their work.

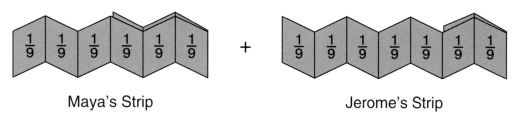

Maya's Strip   Jerome's Strip

7. Michael and his brother shared a pizza.

   A. Michael ate $\frac{2}{8}$ of a whole pizza. How much pizza was left?

   B. His brother ate another $\frac{3}{8}$ of the whole pizza. How much pizza was left?

   C. How much pizza did Michael and his brother eat altogether?

Comparing Fractions

Fraction Chart

Whole											

$\frac{1}{2}$	$\frac{1}{2}$

$\frac{1}{3}$	$\frac{1}{3}$	$\frac{1}{3}$

$\frac{1}{4}$	$\frac{1}{4}$	$\frac{1}{4}$	$\frac{1}{4}$

$\frac{1}{5}$	$\frac{1}{5}$	$\frac{1}{5}$	$\frac{1}{5}$	$\frac{1}{5}$

$\frac{1}{6}$	$\frac{1}{6}$	$\frac{1}{6}$	$\frac{1}{6}$	$\frac{1}{6}$	$\frac{1}{6}$

$\frac{1}{8}$	$\frac{1}{8}$	$\frac{1}{8}$	$\frac{1}{8}$	$\frac{1}{8}$	$\frac{1}{8}$	$\frac{1}{8}$	$\frac{1}{8}$

$\frac{1}{9}$	$\frac{1}{9}$	$\frac{1}{9}$	$\frac{1}{9}$	$\frac{1}{9}$	$\frac{1}{9}$	$\frac{1}{9}$	$\frac{1}{9}$	$\frac{1}{9}$

$\frac{1}{10}$	$\frac{1}{10}$	$\frac{1}{10}$	$\frac{1}{10}$	$\frac{1}{10}$	$\frac{1}{10}$	$\frac{1}{10}$	$\frac{1}{10}$	$\frac{1}{10}$	$\frac{1}{10}$

$\frac{1}{12}$	$\frac{1}{12}$	$\frac{1}{12}$	$\frac{1}{12}$	$\frac{1}{12}$	$\frac{1}{12}$	$\frac{1}{12}$	$\frac{1}{12}$	$\frac{1}{12}$	$\frac{1}{12}$	$\frac{1}{12}$	$\frac{1}{12}$

Explore

Use your fraction strip chart to complete the following questions.

1. Grace and her little sister each ordered a personal pizza for dinner. Grace ate $\frac{3}{4}$ of her pizza. Her little sister ate $\frac{1}{2}$ of her pizza. Who ate more pizza?

2. Roberto walks $\frac{7}{10}$ of a mile to get to school. Keenya walks $\frac{2}{3}$ of a mile to get to school. Who lives closer to the school, Keenya or Roberto?

3. Use your chart to find the fractions that are equal to $\frac{1}{2}$ on the chart. Make a list of these fractions.

4. Use your fraction chart to compare the following pairs of fractions. Write number sentences using <, >, or =. For example, $\frac{1}{2} > \frac{1}{3}$.

    A. $\frac{1}{4}, \frac{1}{2}$ B. $\frac{2}{3}, \frac{1}{2}$ C. $\frac{1}{2}, \frac{2}{5}$

    D. $\frac{1}{2}, \frac{3}{6}$ E. $\frac{5}{12}, \frac{1}{2}$ F. $\frac{6}{9}, \frac{1}{2}$

5. Use $\frac{1}{2}$ as a benchmark or your fraction chart to compare the following pairs of fractions. Write number sentences using <, >, or =.

    A. $\frac{3}{4}, \frac{1}{3}$ B. $\frac{2}{5}, \frac{7}{10}$ C. $\frac{5}{8}, \frac{5}{12}$

    D. $\frac{2}{4}, \frac{6}{12}$ E. $\frac{3}{9}, \frac{2}{3}$ F. $\frac{3}{5}, \frac{1}{4}$

6. Use your fraction chart to put the following fractions in order from smallest to largest.

    A. $\frac{1}{3}, \frac{1}{6}, \frac{1}{2}$ B. $\frac{3}{5}, \frac{3}{4}, \frac{3}{12}$ C. $\frac{2}{10}, \frac{2}{4}, \frac{2}{9}$

7. Look at your answers for Question 6. Use them to help you answer this question: If two or more fractions have the same numerator, how can you tell which one is smallest?

8. Put the following fractions in order from smallest to largest.

    A. $\frac{4}{6}, \frac{1}{3}, \frac{1}{2}$ B. $\frac{7}{9}, \frac{4}{10}, \frac{3}{4}$ C. $\frac{3}{5}, \frac{5}{6}, \frac{1}{4}$ D. $\frac{5}{6}, \frac{5}{12}, \frac{5}{8}$

9. Explain your strategies for Questions 8A and 8D.

Homework

Complete the following questions. You may use your fraction chart to help you.

1. Find all the fractions equal to $\frac{1}{4}$ on your chart. Make a list of these fractions.

2. Jackie needs $\frac{5}{8}$ of a yard of fabric for a pillow. Luis needs $\frac{3}{4}$ of a yard of fabric for a banner. Who needs more fabric, Jackie or Luis?

3. Jessie's mom brought a pie to the potluck dinner. It was cut into 6 pieces. Romesh's dad also brought a pie, but it was cut into 12 pieces. At the end of the night $\frac{1}{6}$ of Jessie's pie was left and $\frac{3}{12}$ of Romesh's pie was left. If the pies were the same size, who had more left-over pie, Jessie's mom or Romesh's dad?

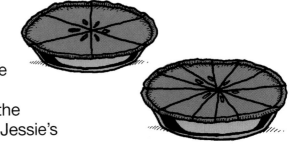

4. Nila practiced her flute for $\frac{1}{2}$ hour on Monday, $\frac{3}{4}$ hour on Tuesday, and $\frac{1}{3}$ hour on Wednesday.

   A. On which day did she practice the longest period of time?

   B. On which day did she practice the shortest period of time?

5. Use your fraction chart to compare the following pairs of fractions. Write a number sentence for each one using <, >, or =.

   A. $\frac{3}{10}, \frac{1}{2}$ **B.** $\frac{4}{8}, \frac{1}{2}$ **C.** $\frac{1}{2}, \frac{2}{12}$

6. Use $\frac{1}{2}$ as a benchmark or your fraction chart to compare the following pairs of fractions. Write a number sentence for each one using <, >, or =.

   A. $1, \frac{1}{10}$ **B.** $\frac{6}{9}, \frac{5}{12}$ **C.** $\frac{3}{8}, \frac{3}{5}$

7. Use your fraction chart to put the following fractions in order from smallest to largest.

   A. $\frac{4}{8}, \frac{4}{6}, \frac{4}{10}$ **B.** $\frac{3}{5}, \frac{3}{10}, \frac{3}{8}$ **C.** $\frac{4}{8}, \frac{4}{12}, \frac{4}{6}$

   D. If two fractions have the same numerator, how can you tell which one is smaller?

8. Put the following fractions in order from smallest to largest. Be prepared to explain your strategies.

   A. $\frac{7}{12}, \frac{1}{3}, \frac{3}{8}$ **B.** $\frac{3}{5}, \frac{5}{12}, \frac{1}{2}$ **C.** $\frac{2}{3}, \frac{3}{4}, \frac{1}{6}$

   D. $\frac{1}{5}, \frac{1}{4}, \frac{1}{6}$ **E.** $\frac{7}{12}, \frac{1}{12}, \frac{5}{12}$ **F.** $\frac{1}{2}, \frac{3}{4}, \frac{2}{9}$

Frabble Game and Bubble Sort

This game can be played by two, three, or four players.

Materials

One Fraction Chart from Lesson 3 for each student
One deck of *Standard Frabble Cards* (24 cards)
    for each group
Two wild cards for each player
Pencil and paper for scoring

Playing Frabble

1. Shuffle the *Standard Frabble Cards* and divide them evenly among all players.

2. Give each player two wild cards.

3. Players place all their cards face up in front of them.

4. The player with the Start card begins the game by placing this card in the center of the playing area.

5. The player to the left of the starting player takes the next turn by adding one card to the game following these rules.

   • Cards with smaller fractions are placed to the left.

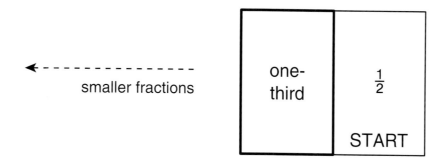

   • Cards with larger fractions are placed to the right.

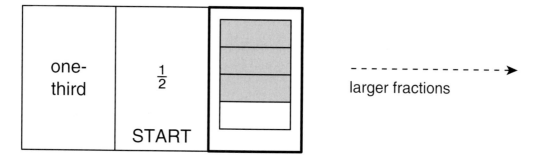

- Cards with equal fractions are placed above or below.

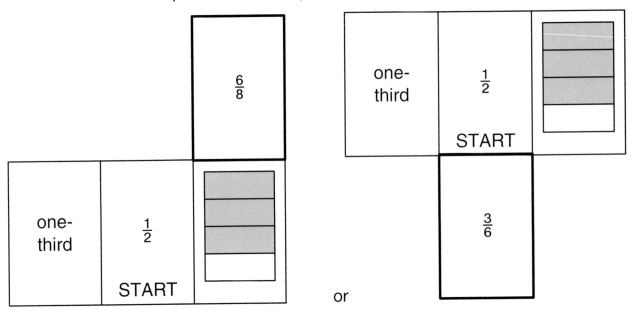

or

- You can place a wild card at any time. To place a wild card, you must give the card a name that is not already on the board. For example, a wild card named $\frac{2}{6}$ can be placed below the one-third card.

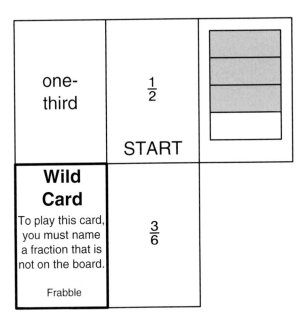

- You may not move any card that has already been played. For example, you may not move the $\frac{3}{4}$ card over in order to place a $\frac{2}{3}$ card between the $\frac{1}{2}$ and the $\frac{3}{4}$ card in the example shown above.

6. If you do not have a card that can be placed on the board, you lose a turn. The game ends when no player can take a turn. The player with the most points wins the game.

Scoring

One player is chosen to write down each person's points at the end of each turn. Points are scored by these rules:

- The player who places the "Start" card earns one point for placing one card on the board.
- Each player earns:
  1 point for each card played
  1 point for each card connected to the new card in the row
  1 point for each card on the board that has a fraction equal to the card played

Example 1: The player who places the "one" card earns four points. The player gets one point for playing the card and three points for the three cards connected to the new card in the same row.

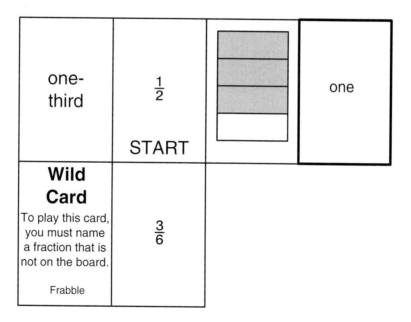

Example 2: The player who adds the $\frac{1}{1}$ card earns two points: One point for playing the card ($\frac{1}{1}$) and one point for the equal fraction (one).

one-third	$\frac{1}{2}$ START		one
Wild Card To play this card, you must name a fraction that is not on the board. Frabble	$\frac{3}{6}$		$\frac{1}{1}$

Example 3: The player who adds the $\frac{6}{8}$ card earns a total of five points: One point for the card added ($\frac{6}{8}$); three points for the cards connected in the row (wild card, $\frac{3}{6}$, and $\frac{1}{1}$); and one point for the equal fraction (picture of $\frac{3}{4}$).

one-third	$\frac{1}{2}$ START		one
Wild Card To play this card, you must name a fraction that is not on the board. Frabble	$\frac{3}{6}$	$\frac{6}{8}$	$\frac{1}{1}$

Equivalent Fractions

Irma wants to bake some cookies. Her recipe calls for $\frac{3}{4}$ cup sugar. Irma can only find a $\frac{1}{8}$-cup measure. She needs to know how many eighths of a cup of sugar is the same as $\frac{3}{4}$ cup. She knows that two $\frac{1}{8}$-cup measures hold the same amount of sugar as a $\frac{1}{4}$-cup measure. She knows that she needs enough

sugar to fill three $\frac{1}{4}$-cup measures because she needs $\frac{3}{4}$ cup. She reasons that she must fill the $\frac{1}{8}$ cup twice as many times, or six times. Irma also remembers what she learned in math class: If you multiply (or divide) the numerator and the denominator of a fraction by the same number, you will get an equal or equivalent fraction. **Equivalent fractions** are fractions that have the same value.

To solve this problem Irma can use this number sentence: $\frac{3}{4} = \frac{?}{8}$.

1. **A.** Help Irma solve this problem. Think of a strategy she can use.

   B. Irma knows that $4 \times 2 = 8$. Since she multiplied 4 times 2 to find the new denominator, she also must multiply 3 times 2 in order to find the missing numerator. Complete this number sentence for Irma: $\frac{3}{4} = \frac{?}{8}$.

2. Romesh is helping his father pack a box of key chains for a fundraiser. The box holds $\frac{1}{2}$ pound of merchandise. Each key chain weighs $\frac{1}{16}$ of a pound. Romesh must decide how many key chains he can fit in the box.

   A. Help Romesh by completing this number sentence: $\frac{1}{2} = \frac{?}{16}$.

   B. How many key chains can Romesh pack in the box?

Equivalent Fractions

3. **A.** Use your fraction chart to find three fractions that are equivalent to $\frac{3}{9}$. Write number sentences to record the equivalent fractions.

   B. Find three other fractions that are equivalent to $\frac{3}{9}$. Write number sentences to record the equivalent fractions.

   C. Explain the strategy you used to find the equivalent fractions.

4. Complete the number sentence: $\frac{4}{8} = \frac{?}{12}$. Explain how you know.

5. **A.** Use your fraction chart to find a fraction that is equivalent to $\frac{3}{5}$. Write a number sentence to record the equivalent fractions.

   B. Find three other fractions that are equivalent to $\frac{3}{5}$. Write number sentences to record the equivalent fractions.

   C. Explain the strategy you used to find the equivalent fractions.

6. Complete the number sentences below. Use your fraction chart.

   A. $\frac{3}{4} = \frac{?}{8}$ **B.** $\frac{1}{2} = \frac{?}{10}$ **C.** $\frac{2}{3} = \frac{?}{9}$ **D.** $\frac{6}{9} = \frac{?}{12}$

   E. $\frac{1}{2} = \frac{4}{?}$ **F.** $\frac{6}{10} = \frac{?}{5}$ **G.** $\frac{8}{12} = \frac{2}{?}$ **H.** $\frac{3}{12} = \frac{?}{8}$

Homework

1. Maya wrote number sentences to show fractions that are equivalent to $\frac{1}{2}$. She forgot to write in some of the numerators and denominators. Write Maya's number sentences filling in the missing numbers to make each fraction equivalent to $\frac{1}{2}$.

   A. $\frac{1}{2} = \frac{3}{?}$ **B.** $\frac{1}{2} = \frac{?}{18}$ **C.** $\frac{1}{2} = \frac{12}{?}$

   D. $\frac{1}{2} = \frac{?}{60}$ **E.** $\frac{1}{2} = \frac{50}{?}$ **F.** $\frac{1}{2} = \frac{?}{?}$

2. Write 5 fractions equivalent to $\frac{2}{3}$.

3. Romesh is packing a box filled with plastic cars for his father. The box holds $\frac{3}{4}$ pound of merchandise. Each plastic car weighs $\frac{1}{16}$ pound.

   A. Complete this number sentence to help Romesh decide how many sixteenths of a pound is equivalent to $\frac{3}{4}$ pound. $\frac{3}{4} = \frac{?}{16}$.

   B. How many plastic cars can Romesh pack in the box?

   C. What is another name for $\frac{1}{16}$ of a pound?

4. Write 5 fractions equivalent to $\frac{2}{5}$.

5. Shannon wants to purchase $\frac{1}{3}$ yard of ribbon. There are 36 inches in a yard.

    A. Complete the following number sentence to help the clerk decide how many inches of ribbon she must cut: $\frac{1}{3} = \frac{?}{36}$.

    B. How many inches of ribbon should she cut?

6. Use the Fraction Chart to complete the number sentence: $\frac{6}{8} = \frac{?}{12}$.

Complete the following number sentences.

7. $\frac{1}{2} = \frac{?}{12}$

8. $\frac{3}{4} = \frac{?}{16}$

9. $\frac{4}{6} = \frac{?}{9}$

10. $\frac{3}{5} = \frac{?}{20}$

11. $\frac{10}{16} = \frac{?}{8}$

12. $\frac{8}{24} = \frac{?}{3}$

13. $\frac{10}{15} = \frac{?}{3}$

14. $\frac{1}{5} = \frac{?}{100}$

15. $\frac{1}{5} = \frac{?}{20}$

16. $\frac{75}{100} = \frac{?}{4}$

17. $\frac{2}{4} = \frac{?}{6}$

18. $\frac{20}{24} = \frac{5}{?}$

Use <, >, or = to write number sentences to compare the following pairs of numbers.

19. $\frac{5}{9}, \frac{1}{2}$

20. $\frac{3}{4}, \frac{30}{40}$

21. $\frac{72}{100}, \frac{7}{10}$

Pattern Block Fractions

When Are Halves Different?

When Jacob and Jerome looked at their data for the *Bouncing Ball* lab, they wondered what would happen if they dropped a tennis ball from a tall building. Jacob said, "Every time we dropped a ball during the lab, it bounced back about half of the drop height. Think how high a ball would bounce if we dropped it from the top of the Sears Tower in Chicago. That's one of the tallest buildings in the world."

Jerome said, "The CN Tower in Toronto is even taller. If we dropped the ball from the top of it, the ball would bounce even higher!"

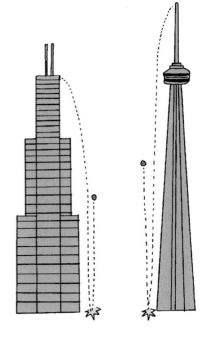

1. If each ball bounces one-half the distance of the drop height, will the bounce heights be the same? Why or why not?

2. When are halves different?

Jerome and Jacob used fractions to estimate the bounce height. In this activity, you will study fractions using pattern blocks.

Exploring Pattern Blocks

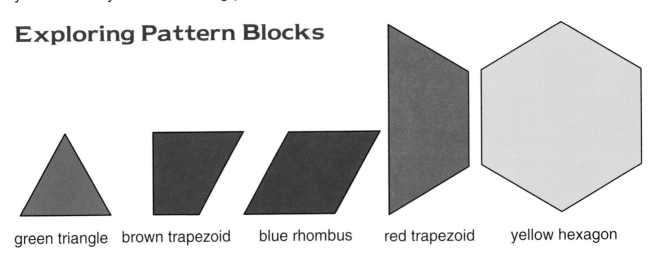

green triangle brown trapezoid blue rhombus red trapezoid yellow hexagon

---

Pattern Block Fractions

Use the blocks to help you answer the following questions:

3. How many brown trapezoids equal one yellow hexagon?

4. How many brown trapezoids equal one red trapezoid?

5. How many red trapezoids equal one yellow hexagon?

6. One brown trapezoid is (less than, greater than, or equal to) one red trapezoid.

7. How many brown trapezoids equal three red trapezoids?

8. One brown trapezoid is (less than, greater than, or equal to) one green triangle.

9. How many green triangles equal one yellow hexagon?

10. One yellow hexagon equals two brown trapezoids plus how many green triangles?

11. How many green triangles equal two brown trapezoids?

12. How many green triangles equal two blue rhombuses?

13. Two blue rhombuses are (less than, greater than, or equal to) one brown trapezoid.

Exploring Pattern Block Fractions

14. Each of these figures shows thirds using pattern blocks. Build these figures with pattern blocks. Place three blue rhombuses on a yellow hexagon. Place three green triangles on a red trapezoid.

   A. If the red trapezoid is one whole, which block shows $\frac{1}{3}$?

   B. If the blue rhombus is $\frac{1}{3}$, which block shows one whole?

   C. If the red trapezoid is one whole, show $\frac{2}{3}$.

---

15. **A.** Show halves using pattern blocks in as many ways as you can.

B. If the yellow hexagon is one whole, which block shows $\frac{1}{2}$?

C. If the green triangle is $\frac{1}{2}$, which block is one whole?

D. If the brown trapezoid is $\frac{1}{2}$, which block is one whole?

16. **A.** If the yellow hexagon is one whole, which block shows $\frac{1}{4}$?

B. If the yellow hexagon is one whole, show $\frac{3}{4}$.

C. If the yellow hexagon is one whole, show $\frac{5}{4}$.

17. **A.** If the green triangle is $\frac{1}{6}$, which block is one whole?

B. If the yellow hexagon is one whole, show $\frac{3}{6}$.

C. If the yellow hexagon is one whole, show $\frac{5}{6}$.

18. If the red trapezoid is one whole, name each of the following fractions:

A. one green triangle

B. two green triangles

C. one blue rhombus

D. one brown trapezoid

E. three brown trapezoids

F. five green triangles

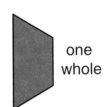

one whole

19. If the yellow hexagon is one whole, name each of the following fractions:

A. one red trapezoid

B. one brown trapezoid

C. two brown trapezoids

D. one blue rhombus

E. two green triangles

F. two blue rhombuses

G. three red trapezoids

one whole

Fraction Sentences

For Questions 20–26, the yellow hexagon is one whole. The red trapezoid is $\frac{1}{2}$. We can show $\frac{1}{2}$ using brown blocks. Since 1 red trapezoid equals 2 brown trapezoids, then $\frac{1}{2} = \frac{2}{4}$ or $\frac{1}{2} = \frac{1}{4} + \frac{1}{4}$.

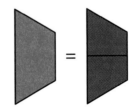

$$\frac{1}{2} = \frac{2}{4}$$
or
$$\frac{1}{2} = \frac{1}{4} + \frac{1}{4}$$

20. Show $\frac{1}{2}$ using green blocks. (Cover a red trapezoid with green blocks.) Write a number sentence to represent this figure.

21. The blue rhombus is $\frac{1}{3}$. Show $\frac{1}{3}$ using green blocks and write a number sentence to represent this figure.

We can show 1 whole with two or more colors and write a number sentence to represent the figure.

$$1 = \frac{2}{4} + \frac{1}{6} + \frac{1}{3}$$

22. Show 1 whole another way using two or more colors. Write a number sentence for your figure.

For Questions 23–26, show each fraction using two or more colors. Write a number sentence for each figure.

23. Show $\frac{1}{2}$.

24. Show $\frac{3}{4}$.

25. Show $\frac{2}{3}$.

26. Show $\frac{3}{2}$.

Homework

Use your fraction chart, the Fraction Chart in Lesson 3, or imagine pattern blocks to help you solve these problems.

1. Michael used $\frac{1}{2}$ yard of ribbon to decorate a gift for his mother. Irma used $\frac{2}{3}$ yard for her mother's present. Who used more ribbon?

2. Lee Yah drank $\frac{1}{3}$ cup of juice and Roberto drank $\frac{1}{2}$ cup. Who drank more juice?

3. Put these fractions in order from smallest to largest: $\frac{5}{6}, \frac{1}{4}, \frac{1}{2}$.

4. Put these fractions in order from smallest to largest: $\frac{1}{2}, \frac{1}{3}, \frac{3}{4}$.

5. Put these fractions in order from smallest to largest: $\frac{2}{3}, \frac{1}{2}, \frac{1}{6}$. Explain your strategy.

6. Add or subtract.

   A. $\frac{2}{6} + \frac{3}{6} =$

   B. $\frac{1}{4} + \frac{2}{4} =$

   C. $\frac{1}{3} + \frac{2}{3} =$

   D. $\frac{3}{4} - \frac{1}{4} =$

   E. $\frac{5}{6} - \frac{2}{6} =$

   F. $\frac{3}{3} - \frac{1}{3} =$

7. Write three equivalent fractions for $\frac{3}{4}$.

Solving Problems with Pattern Blocks

You may use pattern blocks or your fraction chart to help you solve these problems.

1. Wednesday is pizza day at Bessie Coleman School. Each table in the lunchroom gets one pizza to share fairly among the students at the table. There are three students at Table A and four students at Table B.

   A. What fraction of the pizza will each student at Table A eat?

   B. What fraction of the pizza will each student at Table B eat?

   C. Who gets to eat more pizza, the students at Table A or the students at Table B?

   D. Which fraction is larger, $\frac{1}{3}$ or $\frac{1}{4}$? Explain how you know.

2. The cook made three small fruit pies that are all the same size. She divided the apple pie into 12 pieces, the cherry pie into six pieces, and the peach pie into four pieces. John ate two pieces of apple pie, Shannon ate two pieces of cherry pie, and Brandon ate two pieces of peach pie.

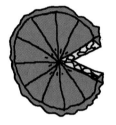  

   A. What fraction of the apple pie did John eat?

   B. What fraction of the cherry pie did Shannon eat?

   C. What fraction of the peach pie did Brandon eat?

   D. Who ate the most pie? Tell how you know.

   E. Who ate the least pie?

3. One whole is divided into eight zax. Each zax is the same size. The same size whole is divided into ten snarks. Each snark is the same size.

   A. What fraction of the whole is one zax?

   B. What fraction of the whole is one snark?

   C. Which is larger, one zax or one snark? Explain.

4. Put each group of fractions in order from smallest to largest.

A. $\frac{1}{2}, \frac{1}{6}, \frac{1}{3}, \frac{1}{4}, \frac{1}{12}$

B. $\frac{2}{6}, \frac{2}{3}, \frac{2}{4}, \frac{2}{12}$

C. $\frac{1}{10}, \frac{1}{8}, \frac{1}{5}$

D. $\frac{3}{10}, \frac{3}{8}, \frac{3}{5}$

5. Describe a strategy for ordering fractions if the numerators are the same.

To solve the problems in Questions 6–8, you may use any tools such as pattern blocks, the Fraction Chart in Lesson 3, or pictures. Write number sentences to record your solutions.

6. Each of the following pairs of students shared a pizza. How much of the whole pizza did each pair eat?

A. Manny ate $\frac{1}{2}$ of a pizza and Ming ate $\frac{1}{4}$ of it.

B. Michael ate $\frac{3}{8}$ of a pizza and Frank ate $\frac{5}{8}$ of the pizza.

C. Felicia ate $\frac{1}{3}$ of a pizza. Linda ate $\frac{1}{6}$ of it.

D. Lee Yah ate $\frac{5}{12}$ and David ate $\frac{2}{12}$.

7. A. Four students each ate $\frac{1}{2}$ of a muffin. How many muffins did they eat altogether?

B. Five students each ate $\frac{1}{2}$ of a muffin. How many muffins did they eat altogether?

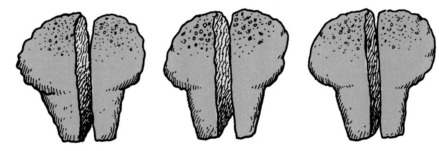

8. A. Eight students each ate $\frac{1}{4}$ of an apple. How many apples did they eat altogether?

B. Three students each ate $\frac{1}{4}$ of an apple. How many apples did they eat altogether?

C. Six students each ate $\frac{1}{4}$ of an apple. How many apples did they eat altogether?

1. Write these fractions in order from smallest to largest.

   A. $\frac{3}{12}, \frac{3}{4}, \frac{3}{3}, \frac{3}{6}$

   B. $\frac{3}{5}, \frac{3}{10}, \frac{3}{8}, \frac{3}{4}$

   C. $\frac{3}{8}, \frac{1}{8}, \frac{5}{8}, \frac{8}{8}$

   D. $\frac{1}{2}, \frac{1}{12}, \frac{5}{6}$

2. On Sunday, Shannon's family ate $\frac{5}{12}$ of a casserole. On Monday they ate $\frac{3}{12}$ of the casserole. How much of the casserole did they eat? How much is left over?

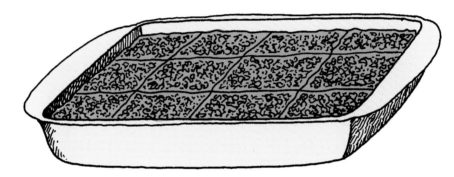

3. On Friday, a worker painted $\frac{3}{8}$ of a fence. On Saturday, he painted another $\frac{3}{8}$ of the fence.

   A. How much of the fence did he paint on the two days?

   B. How much more of the fence does he have left to paint?

4. Complete the following number sentences.

   A. $\frac{3}{4} = \frac{?}{20}$ B. $\frac{3}{6} = \frac{5}{?}$ C. $\frac{2}{3} = \frac{6}{?}$

   D. $\frac{3}{8} = \frac{?}{16}$ E. $\frac{1}{2} = \frac{?}{6}$ F. $\frac{30}{100} = \frac{3}{?}$

5. A. Four children each ate $\frac{1}{3}$ of a large cookie. How many cookies did they eat altogether?

   B. Six children each ate $\frac{1}{3}$ of a large cookie. How many cookies did they eat altogether?

Fraction Puzzles

"Today in math, you will work in groups of four to solve puzzles using pattern blocks," said Mrs. Dewey. "Each puzzle has four clues to help you find a solution. Each group member will receive one of the clues. A clue can only be shared with your group by reading it. Once all the clues have been read, the group's job is to find a solution that meets all the guidelines given in the clues."

Roberto, Nicholas, Linda, and Jackie formed a group. Each received a clue for the first puzzle. "My clue says we need to use 2 or 3 blocks," said Nicholas as he reached to get some blocks.

"Wait," said Linda, "I think we should each read our clues to the group before we start building. That way we will have all of the information we need to start."

"Great idea! Go ahead and read your clue again, Nicholas, and then we will each read ours," said Jackie.

"Now that we have all the clues, let's get started," exclaimed Nicholas.

After some work, the students found this solution:

They wrote this number sentence to represent their solution: $\frac{1}{2} + \frac{1}{6} = \frac{2}{3}$.

1. Look back at their clues and see if this solution fits all the clues they were given.

2. One of the other groups found this solution to the same puzzle.

They wrote this number sentence: $\frac{1}{6} + \frac{1}{6} + \frac{1}{6} + \frac{1}{6} = \frac{2}{3}$. Look back at the clues. Does this solution fit all the clues that were given? Why or why not?

3. Find another solution to this puzzle. Use the clues provided to make sure your solution fits all of the clues. Draw a picture of your solution and write a number sentence to represent your solution.

Homework

Solve the following problems. You may use your fraction chart to help you.

1. Put the following fractions in order from smallest to largest.
   A. $\frac{1}{5}, \frac{1}{9}, \frac{1}{8}, \frac{1}{3}$ B. $\frac{3}{10}, \frac{3}{4}, \frac{3}{8}, \frac{3}{5}$ C. $\frac{2}{3}, \frac{3}{4}, \frac{5}{8}, \frac{1}{2}$ D. $\frac{2}{5}, \frac{3}{8}, \frac{5}{12}, \frac{1}{4}$

2. Put the following fractions in order from smallest to largest.
   A. $\frac{1}{3}, \frac{1}{5}, \frac{1}{2}, \frac{1}{8}$ B. $\frac{2}{6}, \frac{2}{4}, \frac{2}{5}, \frac{2}{10}$ C. $\frac{4}{5}, \frac{4}{12}, \frac{4}{8}, \frac{4}{6}$ D. $\frac{3}{8}, \frac{3}{10}, \frac{3}{5}, \frac{3}{4}$

   E. Explain a strategy for putting fractions in order when the numerators are all the same.

3. Write a number sentence for each pair of fractions. Use the symbols <, >, or = in each sentence.

   A. $\frac{6}{8}, \frac{3}{4}$ B. $\frac{3}{5}, \frac{3}{8}$ C. $\frac{1}{3}, \frac{3}{6}$

   D. $\frac{1}{2}, \frac{5}{10}$ E. $\frac{4}{5}, \frac{5}{12}$ F. $\frac{3}{9}, \frac{1}{3}$

4. Frank and Jerome each ordered a small cheese pizza for lunch. Frank's pizza was cut into 6 pieces. Jerome's pizza was cut into 8 pieces. Frank ate 2 pieces of his pizza. Jerome ate 3 pieces of his pizza. Which boy ate more pizza? How do you know?

5. Nila and Tanya shared a sandwich for lunch. Nila ate $\frac{1}{2}$ of the sandwich and Tanya ate $\frac{1}{4}$ of the sandwich. What fraction of the whole sandwich did the two girls eat? Explain how you found your answer.

6. Lee Yah, Luis, John, and Shannon solved a fraction puzzle. Their solution is found below. If a yellow hexagon is one whole, write a number sentence for their solution.

7. Frank, Jacob, Irma, and Maya solved a fraction puzzle. Their solution is shown on the right. Does their solution fit the clues? Explain your thinking.

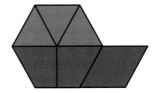

   Clue 1: The red trapezoid is equal to 1 whole.
   Clue 2: Make a shape with a value of $\frac{8}{3}$.
   Clue 3: Use at least two brown trapezoids.
   Clue 4: Do not use any blue rhombuses.

Unit 13

DIVISION

	Student Guide	Discovery Assignment Book	Adventure Book	Unit Resource Guide*
Lesson 1				
TV Survey	◎	◎		◎
Lesson 2				
Division	◎			
Lesson 3				
More Division	◎	◎		
Lesson 4				
Solving Problems Using Multiplication and Division	◎			◎
Lesson 5				
Plant Growth	◎			

Unit Resource Guide pages are from the teacher materials.

TV Survey

Mrs. Dewey shared with her class an article about the amount of television an average fourth-grader watches. Studies show that children between the ages of 6 and 11 watch an average of 3 hours of TV every day. Mrs. Dewey's class decided to find out how much TV they watch. They will record the number of minutes of television they watch for four days. Then, the class will analyze the results.

Conduct a survey to find out how much television you watch. A *survey* is an investigation made by collecting information and then analyzing it. Collect data for four days. Record the number of minutes of television you watch each day.

1. Record your data for a four-day period on the four tables on the *Daily TV Time* Activity Pages in the *Discovery Assignment Book.* One table should be used for each day. Irma's table for the fourth and final day is shown below.

Daily TV Time

	Program	Starting Time	Ending Time	Minutes Watched
Thursday	Exploring Space	3:00	4:00	60
	Milo and Bob	4:00	4:30	30
	Power Troopers	6:00	6:30	30
	Take a Chance	6:30	7:00	30
	Treasure Search	8:00	8:45	45

Day

Average Number of Minutes per Day ____157.5____

Average Number of Hours per Day _____

Total TV Minutes ____195____

Total Number of Minutes for 4 Days ____630____

2. After the four-day period is complete, find and record the following information on your copy of the *Daily TV Time* Activity Page.

   A. The total number of minutes of TV time you watched over the four days

   B. The average (mean) number of minutes of TV time per day

Converting Average Number of Minutes to Average Number of Hours

3. Irma calculated that her average number of minutes of TV time per day is 157.5 minutes.

   A. Is her average daily TV time between 1 and 2 hours or between 2 and 3 hours? How did you decide?

   B. How many whole hours of TV, on average, did she watch per day?

Irma finds her average daily TV time in hours. She knows that 60 minutes are in 1 hour. She uses the calculator to do the following problem:

| 1 | 5 | 7 | . | 5 | ÷ | 6 | 0 | = |

This is what the calculator window displayed:

| 2.625 |

4. **A.** How many full hours did Irma watch on average per day?

   B. What does the ".625" tell you?

   C. Does the answer in the calculator display agree with your estimate in Question 3A?

5. Look at your average number of minutes of TV time per day.

   A. Is your average daily TV time more or less than 1 hour? More or less than 2 hours? More or less than 3 hours?

   B. Calculate your average number of hours of TV time per day and record it on your copy of the *Daily TV Time* Activity Page.

6. Compare your average daily TV time to the data reported in the newspaper article Mrs. Dewey shared with her class. (Remember, the newspaper article reported that students between the ages of 6 and 11 watch 3 hours of TV every day.) Did you watch more or less than 3 hours of TV each day of the survey?

Making a Class Data Table

7. Share your data with the class by recording it in a class data table like the one below.

The Class Data

Name	Total TV Time for 4 Days in Minutes	Average TV Time per Day in Minutes	Average TV Time per Day in Hours
John	480	120	2
Irma	630	157.5	2.625
Roberto	165	41.25	0.6875

Use your class data to answer Questions 8–10.

8. **A.** Who watched the most TV in your class?

   B. How many minutes did he or she watch TV?

9. **A.** Who watched the least TV in your class?

   B. How many minutes did he or she watch TV?

10. What can you learn from the class data table?

11. Look at the last column in your class data table. Find out how many students' average daily TV time was between 0 and 1 hour, between 1 and 2 hours, between 2 and 3 hours, etc. Complete a table like the one below.

How Much TV Do We Watch?

_T_ **Average TV Time per Day** **(in hours)**	_S_ **Number of Students**	
	Tallies	**Total**
0 – .99	⊬⊬⊬⊬	
1.00 – 1.99	|||	
2.00 – 2.99	||	
3.00 – 3.99	||||	
4.00 – 4.99			

12. What are the two main variables we are studying?

Graph

13. Make a bar graph on *Centimeter Graph Paper* using your class television data. Label the horizontal axis with *T, TV Time in Hours,* and the vertical axis with *S, Number of Students.*

14. How many students in your class averaged between 0 and 1 hour of TV per day?

15. What average TV time is most common?

16. Describe the graph. What does the graph tell you about the amount of TV the students in your class watched?

Extension

Follow-up Survey. One month later, collect data over four days one more time. Make a data table and graph. Compare your data to the first TV Survey you completed. See if the TV Survey helped to change your habits.

TV Time vs. Reading Time. Collect data comparing the number of minutes you watch TV to the number of minutes you read every day. Graph and discuss your results. Give up television for four days and collect data on your reading habits within those four days. Discuss your results.

Homework

You will need a calculator, a *Three-Column Data Table,* and *Centimeter Graph Paper* to complete the homework.

On Monday, Mrs. Dewey's class started their data collection for TV Survey. The data collection continued through Thursday evening. On Friday, the students shared their data by combining it all on one large data table. A piece of their class data table is shown below.

The Class Data

Name and Group Number		Average TV Time per Day in Minutes	Average TV Time per Day in Hours
Ming	(Group 7)	240	
Shannon	(Group 7)	135	
Ana	(Group 7)	390	
Luis	(Group 7)	195	
Nicholas	(Group 8)	45	
Lee Yah	(Group 8)	210	
Jacob	(Group 8)	105	
Nila	(Group 8)	180	

Mrs. Dewey's students sit in groups of four. The students listed in the table above are in Groups 7 and 8.

1. Who watched more television, Group 7 or Group 8? How did you decide?

2. How many minutes of television did Group 7 watch in all?

3. How many minutes of television did Group 8 watch in all?

4. How many more minutes of television did Ana watch than Shannon?

5. Lee Yah watched about twice as much television as another student. Who? How did you decide?

6. Copy the previous data table onto a *Three-column Data Table.* Find the number of hours each student watched TV. Fill in the third column with your findings.

7. Each student in Groups 1 through 6 came to the overhead and placed a tally for themselves as shown in the following data table. Copy this data table onto a copy of a *Three-column Data Table.* Add the data for the students in Groups 7 and 8 to the table using tallies. Then, total the tallies.

How Much TV Do We Watch?

T **Average TV Time per Day** **(in hours)**	*S* **Number of Students**	
	Tallies	**Total**
0 – .99	⳾⳾⳾⳾⳾	
1.00 – 1.99	‖‖	
2.00 – 2.99	‖‖	
3.00 – 3.99		
4.00 – 4.99	⎮	
5.00 – 5.99		
6.00 – 6.99	⎮	
7.00 – 7.99		

8. What amount of TV viewing is most common in Mrs. Dewey's class?

9. Graph all of Room 204's data on *Centimeter Graph Paper.*

10. Describe the graph. What does it tell you about the amount of TV the students in Room 204 watched?

Division

Modeling Division

Ana and Roberto were given a box of 75 marbles to share.

1. Can Ana and Roberto divide up the marbles evenly? How do you know?

2. Estimate how many marbles each will get.

3. Discuss how Ana and Roberto can decide how many marbles each of them will get.

One way to divide the marbles is to pass out the marbles, keeping track of how many each person gets.

Another way is to first decide how many marbles each person will get and then pass them out. Base-ten pieces can be used to model the problem. Ana and Roberto use these base-ten pieces to represent 75 marbles. A bit is one.

4. Since there are 7 skinnies, Ana and Roberto get 3 skinnies each. How many marbles do 3 skinnies represent?

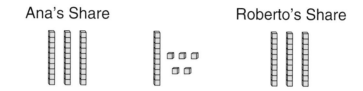

Ana's Share   Roberto's Share

There is 1 skinny left over. This skinny can be traded for 10 bits, so there are 15 bits left. Ana and Roberto get 7 bits each, with 1 left over.

So, each child receives 37 marbles.

Ana's Share   Roberto's Share

There are several ways to write 75 divided by 2 using math symbols. Here are 2 ways:

$$2\overline{)75} \qquad 75 \div 2$$

Write a story for each of the problems, Questions 5–6, and then find the answer. Be sure to explain what any remainders mean.

5. $6\overline{)78}$

6. $93 \div 4$

The Forgiving Method

Keenya said she had a third way of solving 75 divided by 2 using paper and pencil. We call this the **forgiving method.** Keenya wrote:

$$2\overline{)75}$$

Keenya then estimated how many marbles she thought each child would get. Her first estimate was 20 each. Since each child gets 20, and $2 \times 20 = 40$, 40 marbles are taken care of. Keenya wrote:

$$
\begin{array}{r}
2 \overline{)\ 75\ } \\
-\ 40\ \big|\ 20 \\
\hline
35\
\end{array}
$$

Keenya has 35 marbles left to pass out.

7. How many marbles should she give each child now? What is a good estimate?

Keenya decided to give each child 10 more marbles.

8. Why did Keenya know that giving 20 more marbles to each child is too much?

She wrote:

$$
\begin{array}{r}
2 \overline{)\ 75\ } \\
-\ 40\ \big|\ 20 \\
\hline
35\ \\
-\ 20\ \big|\ 10 \\
\hline
15\
\end{array}
$$

Keenya then chose 7. Since $2 \times 7 = 14$, she wrote:

$$
\begin{array}{r|l}
2\,\overline{)\,75} & \\
-40 & 20 \\
\hline
35 & \\
-20 & 10 \\
\hline
15 & \\
-14 & 7 \\
\hline
1 &
\end{array}
$$

Keenya saw that she could not divide further. She added up $20 + 10 + 7 = 37$. This is the number of times 2 divides 75. She finished the problem by writing the quotient on top: 37 and remainder, 1.

$$
\begin{array}{r|l}
37\ \mathrm{R}1 & \\
2\,\overline{)\,75} & \\
-40 & 20 \\
\hline
35 & \\
-20 & 10 \\
\hline
15 & \\
-14 & 7 \\
\hline
1 &
\end{array}
$$

Here is another way to do this problem using the forgiving method.

$$
\begin{array}{r|l}
37\ \mathrm{R}1 & \\
2\,\overline{)\,75} & \\
-60 & 30 \\
\hline
15 & \\
-14 & 7 \\
\hline
1 &
\end{array}
$$

The Boys' Wilderness Club from Bessie Coleman School is going camping.

9. The younger boys are sleeping in cabins. Each cabin holds 7 people. If there are 95 younger boys, how many cabins will be needed?

   A. Estimate the number of cabins. Will the number of cabins be more than 10? more than 20? more than 15?

   B. Divide 95 by 7.

   C. What does the quotient mean?

   D. What does the remainder mean?

   E. How many boys will sleep in each cabin?

   F. Is there another way to arrange the number of boys in each cabin?

10. The older boys in the Wilderness Club want to sleep in tents. The club has 9 tents. There are 43 older boys. How many boys can sleep in each tent so that no tent is overcrowded?

    A. Estimate the number of boys in each tent.

    B. Solve the problem and explain your reasoning.

Solve the following problems using the forgiving method or mental math. Record both the quotient and remainder for your final answer. Estimate to be sure your answer is reasonable.

11. $49 \div 3$ 12. $92 \div 4$ 13. $56 \div 7$ 14. $89 \div 6$

Homework

Use base-ten shorthand to model the two story problems below. Remember to describe how to use the remainder.

1. A group of campers are setting up tents. Each tent needs 6 poles. There are 32 poles in the box. How many tents can be set up?

2. Some of the campers want to go boating. Each boat can safely hold 4 people. There are 6 boats and 22 campers.

    A. Can they all go boating?

    B. Will all the boats be full?

Write a story for each of the following problems. Then, solve the problems. You may show your work using base-ten shorthand. Remember to talk about any remainder.

    3. 34 ÷ 7   4. 81 ÷ 3

    5. 67 ÷ 6   6. 75 ÷ 4

Use the forgiving method to solve the following division problems. Remember to record your final answer, the quotient, and the remainder. Estimate to make sure your answer is reasonable.

    7. 74 ÷ 2   8. 87 ÷ 3

    9. 43 ÷ 3   10. 95 ÷ 8

  11. 73 ÷ 6   12. 97 ÷ 4

13. A. The fourth-grade students at Bessie Coleman School are going on a field trip to the museum. There are 66 students and 5 adults who will be riding the bus. Each seat on the bus will hold 3 people. Use the forgiving method or mental math to divide 71 by 3. What remainder do you get?

    B. What does this remainder mean?

    C. How many seats will the bus need to have?

14. **A.** Once the students arrive at the museum, each adult will take a group of students to see the exhibits. Use the forgiving method or mental math to divide 66 by 5. What remainder do you get?

   B. What does the remainder mean?

   C. Show how you can divide the 66 students into 5 groups.

15. **A.** Jacob took pictures while at the museum. He was going to put them into a photograph album. He has 82 pictures. Each page of his album will hold 6 pictures. How many full pages will he have?

   B. Will there be any remaining pictures?

16. The museum runs a train through several exhibits. Each car holds 6 people. The train has 9 cars.

   A. Can the whole group (students and adults) ride the train at the same time?

   B. How many cars will be needed in all?

More Division

Nicholas watched 347 minutes of television in 5 days. If he watched about the same number of minutes each day, about how many minutes per day did he watch television?

1. Estimate how many minutes Nicholas watched television each day. Did he watch more than 100 minutes each day?

2. Model the problem using the base-ten pieces or base-ten shorthand.

3. Will 5 divide into 347 evenly? Why or why not?

4. What is the average number of minutes Nicholas watched television each day? Explain the remainder.

Keenya showed her method for doing division again.

How do you know what numbers to pick?

You don't always. Try to get a good estimate. The only time you have to erase is if your estimate is too big. I try to choose easy numbers at the beginning. There are many ways of getting the correct answer.

Here is one way to do the problem using paper and pencil.

```
            69 R2
        5 ) 347
          - 200      40
          ─────
            147
          - 100      20
          ─────
             47
          -  45       9
          ─────
              2
```

The answer is a little more than 69 minutes since 347 divided by 5 is 69 with remainder 2.

5. Mr. Haddad of the TIMS Candy Company has 398 Chocos to divide evenly among 6 orders.

   A. Estimate the number of Chocos each order will receive.

   B. Model the problem using base-ten shorthand.

   C. How many Chocos will be in each order?

   D. How many Chocos will be left?

   E. Do the problem using the forgiving method.

6. Joe made 282 Chocos. Mrs. Haddad had to divide them among 5 orders.

   A. Estimate the number of Chocos each order will receive.

   B. Model the problem using base-ten shorthand.

   C. How many Chocos will be in each order?

   D. How many Chocos will be left?

   E. Do the problem using the forgiving method.

7. One of the stores decided to sell Chocos in small bags. Each bag will have 6 Chocos in it. Mrs. Haddad has 96 Chocos. How many bags will she use?

   A. Model the problem using base-ten shorthand.

   B. How many bags will she use?

   C. Do the problem using the forgiving method.

Homework

Model each of the following problems in Questions 1–4 with base-ten shorthand. Then, solve them using the forgiving method.

1. 643 ÷ 5   2. 852 ÷ 3   3. 1533 ÷ 8   4. 2835 ÷ 9

Solve the problems in Questions 5–8 using mental math or pencil and paper.

5. 9076 ÷ 7   6. 2412 ÷ 3   7. 1889 ÷ 2   8. 3600 ÷ 4

Solve the following problems using paper-and-pencil methods or mental math. Remember to record your final answer. Also, if there is a remainder, remember to describe how it is used in each problem.

9. Mr. Haddad's company packages damaged Chocos in packages called "Handful Packs." At the end of the day, Carmen, an employee who packages candy, has been given 132 damaged pieces of candy. How many Handful Packs can Carmen make if each pack must contain 8 Chocos?

10. The TIMS Candy Company has 176 employees. Mr. Haddad evenly divides his staff into four categories: management, candy making, packaging, and distribution. How many employees are in each category?

11. A. Hank works 5 hours a day. He gets paid $7 an hour. How much does Hank earn in one work week (5 days)?

    B. How much does he earn in four weeks?

12. James's candy-wrapping machine grabs 6 Chocos at a time and wraps them in about 1 second. James is helping to fill an order for 4568 Chocos.

    A. How many times must the candy-wrapping machine run in order to wrap the Chocos individually?

    B. Will it take more or less time than 30 minutes to wrap all of these candies? How did you decide?

13. The TIMS Candy Company holds an annual company picnic. One hundred eighteen employees came to the picnic. Sixty-seven employees brought one guest. Forty-three employees brought two guests. The rest of the employees brought three guests. How many people attended the picnic in all?

14. Bob transports boxes of nuts for the Crunchy Nut factory. Nine individual boxes of Crunchy Nuts fit inside a carton. How many cartons will Bob need to deliver 3100 boxes of Crunchy Nuts to Bessie Coleman School for their fund-raiser?

15. A. If 7 classrooms divide the 3100 boxes of Crunchy Nuts evenly for the fund-raiser, how many boxes should each classroom get?

    B. Mrs. Randall's classroom has 32 students. If each child sells about 14 boxes of Crunchy Nuts, will they sell all the boxes of Crunchy Nuts Mrs. Randall's class needs to sell?

16. In the end, Mrs. Randall's class raised $1835. How many boxes did Mrs. Randall's class sell, if each box cost $5?

Solving Problems Using Multiplication and Division

TV Survey

Mrs. Dewey's class learned that children between the ages of six and eleven watch an average of three hours of TV each day. Use this fact to answer Questions 1–3. Practice using mental math or a paper-and-pencil method as you solve the problems.

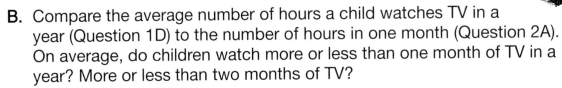

1. **A.** On average, how many hours of television does a child in this age group watch in 10 days?

   B. How many hours in 30 days?

   C. How many in 100 days?

   D. How many in one year (365 days)?

2. **A.** How many hours are there in a month which has 30 days?

   B. Compare the average number of hours a child watches TV in a year (Question 1D) to the number of hours in one month (Question 2A). On average, do children watch more or less than one month of TV in a year? More or less than two months of TV?

3. **A.** If a child watches 3 hours of TV each day, how many days would it take a child to watch 500 hours of television?

   B. How many weeks?

   C. How many months?

Reading Survey

For Questions 4–7, choose an appropriate method to solve the problem. For some questions, you may need to find an exact answer, while for other questions you may only need an estimate. For each question, you may choose to use paper and pencil, mental math, or a calculator. Be prepared to tell the class how you solved each problem.

4. Mrs. Dewey's class took a survey of the amount of time students read for pleasure in the evening. For the reading survey, they collected data for seven days. Here is Shannon's data for the seven days: 30 min, 75 min, 60 min, 45 min, 75 min, 90 min, and 45 min. Shannon averaged her data in two ways.

   A. Find the median number of minutes Shannon read for pleasure during that week.

   B. Find the mean.

5. Using the class data they found that, on average, a student in Mrs. Dewey's class reads 45 minutes for pleasure each evening.

   A. On average, how many minutes does a student in Mrs. Dewey's class read in four days?

   B. How many hours?

6. A. On average, how many minutes does a student in Mrs. Dewey's class read in 10 days?

   B. How many minutes in 30 days?

   C. How many in 100 days?

7. A. On average, about how many minutes does a student in Mrs. Dewey's class read for pleasure in one year?

   B. About how many hours?

   C. Is the amount of time a student in Mrs. Dewey's class reads for pleasure in one year more or less than the number of hours in a month? (*Hint:* See Question 2A.)

Zeros and Division

Tanya and Frank were studying their division facts. They began with 24 ÷ 4.

Frank wrote, "24 ÷ 4 = 7."

Tanya wrote, "24 ÷ 4 = 6."

She said, "One of us must be wrong. There can't be two different answers to the same division problem."

Mrs. Dewey said, "That's right, Tanya. Each division problem has a unique solution. Work together to find the correct answer. Try using fact families."

8. Write the fact family for 24 ÷ 4. Who is correct, Tanya or Frank?

Tanya said, "To find the answer to 24 ÷ 4, I look for the only number that makes $4 \times ? = 24$ true. Since $4 \times 6 = 24$, then 24 ÷ 4 = 6."

"That's good thinking," said Mrs. Dewey. "Let's use your reasoning to think about division and zero. Find 0 ÷ 24."

Tanya replied, "To find 0 ÷ 24, I find the only number that makes $24 \times ? = 0$ true. Since any number times zero is zero, $24 \times 0 = 0$ and 0 ÷ 24 = 0."

9. Use Tanya's reasoning to find 0 ÷ 5.

Mrs. Dewey said, "Tanya, now try, $24 \div 0$."

Tanya began, "To find $24 \div 0$, I find the number that makes $0 \times ? = 24$. But, no number makes this number sentence true. What do I do?"

"Since there is no solution for $0 \times ? = 24$, we say that $24 \div 0$ is undefined. In fact, if you use your reasoning with any number divided by zero, you will find the same thing. So, mathematicians say that division by zero is **undefined.**"

10. Use Tanya's reasoning to find $5 \div 0$.

"Now, think about $0 \div 0$," said Mrs. Dewey.

This time Frank began, "To think about $0 \div 0$, I try to find the only number that makes $0 \times ? = 0$ true. But, any number works. $0 \times 5 = 0$ and $0 \times 24 = 0$. Zero times any number is zero. Mrs. Dewey, I thought you said there is just one right answer. I remember you said, 'a unique solution.'"

"That's right, Frank," Mrs. Dewey replied. "Since there is not a unique solution, mathematicians say that $0 \div 0$ is undefined as well."

For each statement below, find one number that will make it true. If there is no such number, say so.

11. **A.** $8 \div 4 =$ _____ , since $4 \times$ _____ $= 8$

 B. $42 \div 7 =$ _____ , since $7 \times$ _____ $= 42$

 C. $5 \div 1 =$ _____ , since $1 \times$ _____ $= 5$

 D. $0 \div 3 =$ _____ , since $3 \times$ _____ $= 0$

 E. $28 \div 7 =$ _____ , since $7 \times$ _____ $= 28$

 F. $2 \div 0 =$ _____ , since $0 \times$ _____ $= 2$

 G. $36 \div 6 =$ _____ , since $6 \times$ _____ $= 36$

 H. $0 \div 0 =$ _____ , since $0 \times$ _____ $= 0$

Solve the following problems. When necessary, use "undefined." Justify your reasoning using related multiplication sentences.

12. **A.** $35 \div 7 =$ **B.** $0 \div 7 =$

 C. $7 \div 0 =$ **D.** $0 \div 0 =$

13. Do the division problems in Question 12 on a calculator. Explain what happens.

Homework

A Saturday Visit

Nicholas's cousin Stan came to visit on a Saturday afternoon. Solve the following problems that describe their day.

- Show your calculations using a paper-and-pencil method or explain a mental math strategy.
- Use estimation when appropriate.
- If the answer includes a remainder, explain how the remainder is used.

1. It took Stan 4 hours to get to Nicholas's house. Stan and his mother took the freeway. If Stan's mother drove 55 miles per hour, how many miles away does Stan live?

2. Stan plans to surprise Nicholas with three tickets to see the Silver Blades hockey team. If Stan's dad paid $54 for three tickets, how much did one ticket cost?

3. When Stan arrived, Nicholas was just finishing a book. Nicholas said, "This book has 273 pages. It took me four days to read it." On average, how many pages did Nicholas read each day?

4. A. The boys' mothers talked about their exercise routines while they enjoyed a cup of tea. Stan's mother burns 10 calories in 1 minute on her bike. How many calories does she burn in 20 minutes?

B. Nicholas's mother burns about 9 calories per minute on the Super Step machine. How many calories does she burn in 24 minutes?

C. How many minutes does Nicholas's mother need to use the Super Step machine in order to burn off a 340-calorie dessert?

5. A. When they got back to Nicholas's house, the boys played a board game. While playing, Nicholas had a chance to double his winnings of $2972. How much would Nicholas have if he doubled his money?

B. Instead, Nicholas landed on "Donate your earnings to 4 of your favorite charities." If Nicholas shares his earnings of $2972 equally, how much money will each charity receive?

6. Later in the evening, Nicholas and Stan played a video game involving a skyscraper. In this game you go up 18 floors if you answer all the questions in any one round correctly. If you have a perfect score after 12 rounds, you reach the top of the building. How many stories are in the building in this video game?

7. $1632 \div 8$ **8.** $976 \div 4$ **9.** $2832 \div 5$

Plant Growth

Introduction to Plant Growth

The students in Mrs. Dewey's class are studying plants and how they grow. To help the students see how plants grow, Mrs. Dewey suggested that they design an experiment that can be done in their classroom.

"Why don't we each plant a seed and then measure how tall our plants grow each day?" suggested Grace.

"That's a great idea," echoed Jerome and Maya. "Then, we can graph our data and see if all of our plants have the same growth pattern."

"That would make a good experiment," said Mrs. Dewey.

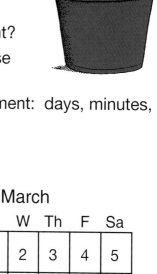

1. **A.** What are the two main variables in this experiment?

   B. What unit of measurement should the students use to measure plant height? Explain your thinking.

   C. How should students measure time in this experiment: days, minutes, hours, etc.? Explain your thinking.

   D. Which variable is the manipulated variable?

   E. Which variable is the responding variable?

"During our experiment, we will use scientific time instead of calendar time," said Mrs. Dewey. "Scientific time always starts at $T = 0$. So, in our experiment, we will start at $T = 0$ days. You will each start your scientific clock when your plant first pushes out of the soil. Let's say that this happens on March 21. We would then call this date $T = 0$ days. March 22 would then be $T = 1$ day."

March

S	M	T	W	Th	F	Sa
		1	2	3	4	5
6	7	8	9	10	11	12
13	14	15	16	17	18	19
20	(21)	22	23	24	25	26
27	28	29	30	31		

2. How is scientific time different from calendar time?

"To keep our experiment fair, there are variables that will need to be held fixed," continued Mrs. Dewey.

3. A. What variables should be held fixed in this experiment?

   B. Why is it important to hold these variables fixed?

The students in Mrs. Dewey's class decided on the following setup for their experiment. Your class may need to use a different setup.

- Each student will plant four bean seeds in a clean $\frac{1}{2}$-pint milk carton saved from the lunchroom.
- Each student will plant their seeds $\frac{1}{2}$-inch deep.
- Each student will choose one of his or her plants to measure during the experiment, cutting off any other plants that grow.
- Students will measure their plants on Monday, Wednesday, and Friday mornings and will record their measurements on a data table.
- Plants will be watered with the same amount of water after they are measured on Mondays and Fridays.

Draw

Your class will now complete a plant growth experiment like the one described by the students in Mrs. Dewey's class. Draw a picture of your experimental setup. Be sure to label the variables using symbols.

4. What variables will you measure in this experiment?

Collect

Plant your seeds. As soon as the first sprout breaks through the soil, begin your scientific clock.

- Measure the height of your first sprout to the base of the first set of leaves several times each week.
- Measure to the nearest half centimeter.
- Use a data table similar to the one shown here to record your data.
- Continue to collect data over at least 21 days.

Plant Growth

Date	T in Days	H in cm
March 21	0	0 cm
March 23	2	1 cm
March 25	4	3 cm

You will graph and analyze your data from this experiment in Unit 15 Lesson 1.

Unit 14

Chancy Predictions: An Introduction to Probability

	Student Guide	Discovery Assignment Book	Adventure Book	Unit Resource Guide*
Lesson 1				
Chance Discussions	◉			
Lesson 2				
Bean Counter's Game	◉			
Lesson 3				
Rolling a Number Cube	◉			◉
Lesson 4				
From Number Cubes to Spinners	◉	◉		
Lesson 5				
Exploring Spinners	◉	◉		◉
Lesson 6				
Make Your Own Spinners	◉	◉		
Lesson 7				
Probe Quest			◉	

Unit Resource Guide pages are from the teacher materials.

Chance Discussions

Sure Things?

Some things are **impossible.** They cannot happen. What is impossible about the picture below?

Other things are **unlikely.** They can happen, but they won't happen very often. It is unlikely that you will grow to a height of 7 feet.

Still other things are **likely.** They probably will happen, but they might not. It is likely that you will grow to a height of at least 4 feet.

Finally, some things are **certain.** They are sure to happen. It is certain that you will grow to a height of more than 1 inch.

Probability is a measure of how likely things are to happen. Events that are impossible have probability 0%. Events that are certain have probability 100%. The larger the probability, the more likely an event is to happen.

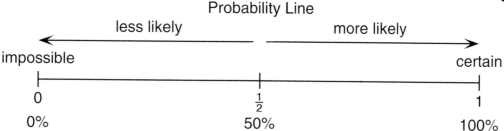

Draw a probability line like the one above. Where would each of the following events appear on the line? Use the letters to place each event on the line.

A. It will be cold tomorrow at the South Pole.

B. There is fruit in your refrigerator at home.

C. Elvis Presley will be the next President of the United States.

D. You will receive mail today.

E. The Chicago Cubs will win the Super Bowl next year.

F. You will fly to the moon tomorrow.

G. A penny will show heads when flipped once.

H. When flipping a penny, you get heads ten times in a row.

I. Monday will follow Sunday.

J. You will have homework tonight.

K. A newborn baby will be a girl.

L. It is going to snow tomorrow.

M. You will be sick tomorrow.

The letters A, B, C, D, and E on the probability line below represent five different probability categories: 0%, not likely, 50%, likely, and 100%. Look around your home. For each letter on the line, give an example of an event with that probability. Record your examples on a separate sheet of paper.

Probability Line

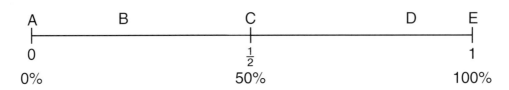

Bean Counter's Game

This is a game for 2–3 players. The object of this game is to be the first player to eliminate all twelve beans from his or her number line.

Materials

scratch paper
twelve beans or game markers per player
one number cube

Before Playing the Game

Each player first draws a line on a piece of scratch paper and then draws the six faces of a number cube as shown.

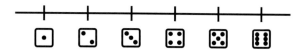

Rules for the Game

1. Each player distributes twelve beans any way he or she chooses above the drawings of the faces. Here are two examples of ways to spread the beans on the number line.

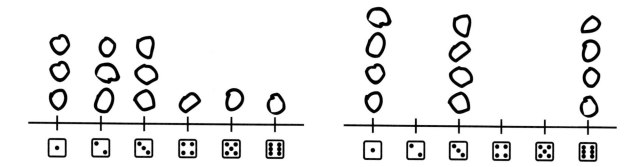

2. Decide which player will roll the number cube for the whole game. That player rolls the cube and reads the number that is face up.

3. For each roll, each player removes a bean above the matching face on the number line. If there is no bean above that face, the player removes nothing.

4. Continue rolling the number cube and removing the beans. The first player to remove all the beans from his or her board is the winner.

Rolling a Number Cube

In this lab, you and a partner will study what happens when a number cube is rolled many times. The main variables are *F*, the faces on the cube, and *T*, the number of times each face comes up.

1. Which variable is the manipulated variable?

2. Which variable is the responding variable?

3. With your partner, roll the number cube 60 times. Tally the number of times each face comes up using a table like this:

Group's Data Table

F Face	T Number of Times Face Appeared	
	Tallies	**Total**
⚀		
⚁		
⚂		
⚃		
⚄		
⚅		

Group Grand Total _____

4. A. Make a bar graph of your results.

  B. Describe your graph. For example, what can you say about the heights of the bars?

5. Combine your data with other groups to get data from the class. Record the class data on a table like this:

Class's Data Table

F Face	T Total Number of Times Face Appeared
⚀	
⚁	
⚂	
⚃	
⚄	
⚅	

Class Grand Total _____

6. A. Make a bar graph of the class data.

  B. Describe the class graph. What can you say about the heights of the bars?

  C. How is your graph of the class data different from your 60-roll group graph? Compare their shapes.

7. A number cube is **fair** if each face is equally likely to come up.

   A. What is the total number of times your class rolled the number cubes? About how many times would you expect each face to come up if each face is equally likely?

   B. Look at your class data table and graph. In general, does the data show that your class used fair number cubes? Why or why not?

8. Suppose a number cube was rolled 1000 times and a 6 came up 500 times. Do you think it is a fair cube? Why or why not?

9. Think about the *Bean Counter's Game* in Lesson 2. Based on the results of this lab, describe a winning strategy for the game.

Number Cubes and Probability

Sometimes we can only estimate the probability of an event; we can say that the event is likely or unlikely, but we don't know its probability exactly. However, sometimes we can find the probability exactly.

For example, we can find the **probability** of rolling a particular face of a number cube. Since a normal number cube has six faces and only one of those faces is ⚁, there is just one chance out of six that ⚁ will show when the number cube is rolled. The probability of rolling ⚁ with a fair number cube is $\frac{1}{6}$. This means we can expect ⚁ to show about $\frac{1}{6}$ of the time.

What is the probability of rolling a number greater than 4? Two out of the six possible faces are greater than 4, namely 5 and 6. Therefore, the probability is $\frac{2}{6}$. If we rolled a number cube 600 times, we would expect to get a number greater than 4 about 200 times, since 200 is $\frac{2}{6}$ (or $\frac{1}{3}$) of 600.

10. Probability predicts that each face will come up *about* $\frac{1}{6}$ of the time when a number cube is rolled.

    A. Did this happen in your group's 60-roll data?

    B. Did this happen in your class's data?

11. Probability predicts that a number greater than 4 (a 5 or a 6) will come up $\frac{1}{3}$ $(\frac{2}{6})$ of the time when a number cube is rolled. Does your class's data agree with this?

Answer the following questions about rolling a number cube.

12. A. What is the probability of rolling a 4? (Express your answer as a fraction.)

    B. Where would you place your answer to 12A on a probability line, nearer "1" or nearer "0"?

13. A. What are the odd numbers on the cube?

    B. What is the probability of rolling an odd number? (Express your answer as a fraction.) Explain your thinking.

14. A. What is the probability of rolling a number less than 3? (Express as a fraction.)

    B. On the probability line, would you place your answer to 14A closer to 0%, 50%, or 100%?

15. A. If Jessie rolls a 3 with a fair number cube, which of the following describes the probability of rolling a 3 on her next roll: (a) a little less than $\frac{1}{6}$, (b) equal to $\frac{1}{6}$, or (c) a little more than $\frac{1}{6}$?

    B. Why do you think so?

16. If you rolled a number cube 1200 times, about how many fives do you think would come up? Why do you think so?

Rolling a Number Cube

From Number Cubes to Spinners

Tanya and Grace want to play a game after school at Tanya's house. They read in the directions that they need a number cube to play the game, but they can't find one anywhere. Finally Tanya had an idea, "Maybe we can make a spinner that will work the same way a number cube does when we play the game. All we need is a paper clip, a pencil, some paper, and a protractor."

1. What is the probability of rolling each face on a fair number cube?

2. What would a spinner look like that would give the same results as a number cube?

3. How many regions would be on such a spinner?

4. What would be the measure of each angle on the spinner?

5. Create a spinner which will give the same results as a number cube. Use the *A Spinner for a Number Cube* Activity Page in the *Discovery Assignment Book* and a protractor to help you.

6. Test your spinner. Spin your spinner 60 times and record the number of times the spinner lands in each region.

7. Share your data with the class. Record your data on a class data table.

8. **A.** Make a bar graph of the class data.

   B. Describe the graph.

9. Compare the graph of the class data for the spinners to the graph of the class data for the number cubes in the lab in Lesson 3.

   A. How many bars does each graph have?

   B. Are the shapes of the graphs similar to one another?

10. Will your spinner give the same results as a number cube? Why or why not?

From Number Cubes to Spinners

Exploring Spinners

Exploring Spinner 1

You and a partner are going to spin 40 times using Spinner 1. You will need a copy of Spinner 1 from the *Discovery Assignment Book* and a piece of *Centimeter Graph Paper* to complete this part of the lesson.

Spinner 1

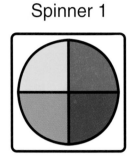

1. Draw the following data table on your own paper and use it to record your data.

Spinner 1 Data

Region	Predicted Number of Times Spinner Will Land in Region (Out of 40)	Number of Times Spinner Landed in Region (Out of 40)	Class Data: Total Number of Times Spinner Landed in Region (Out of _____)
Yellow			
Red			
Blue			
Green			

   A. Before you begin, predict the number of times the spinner will land in each region. Record your predictions in the second column of your data table.

   B. Spin 40 times and record your results in the third column of your data table.

2. Are your results for Spinner 1 close to your predictions? Why or why not?

3. Predict what a graph of all the class data will look like when each group adds their data to a class data table. Show your prediction using words or a drawing.

4. Add your group's results for 40 spins to the class data table. Then, record the totals from the class data table in the last column of your data table.

5. Make a bar graph of the class data.

6. Is the shape of your predicted graph for the class data similar to the shape of the class graph?

7. Draw a probability line on your paper. Each of the following statements has a letter in front of it. Use the letter to place the statement correctly on the line.

   A. The probability of the spinner landing on yellow.

   B. The probability of the spinner landing on green.

   C. The probability of the spinner landing in a purple region.

   D. The probability of the spinner landing in a region other than yellow.

8. Choose the probability that will correctly complete this statement: The chance of spinning yellow is (a) one in four, (b) one in six, or (c) three in four.

9. Write the probability of spinning yellow as a fraction.

10. What is the probability of the spinner landing on yellow **or** green? The word "or" has a special meaning in math. This question asks for the probability of the spinner landing in the area covered by stripes in the picture.

11. Write the probability of the spinner landing on red, blue, or green.

Spinner 1

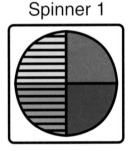

Exploring Spinner 2

You and a partner are going to spin 40 times using Spinner 2. You will need a copy of Spinner 2 and a piece of *Centimeter Graph Paper* to complete this part of the lesson.

12. Draw a data table for Spinner 2 just like the table for Spinner 1.

    A. Before you begin to collect data for Spinner 2, predict the number of times the spinner will land in each region. Record your predictions in your data table.

    B. Spin 40 times and record your results.

Spinner 2

13. Predict what a graph of the class data will look like. Show your prediction with a drawing or use words.

14. Add your results to a class data table. Then, record the class data in your table.

15. Make a bar graph of the class data.

16. Is the shape of your predicted graph for the class data similar to the shape of the class graph?

17. Compare the class graph for Spinner 1 to the class graph for Spinner 2. How are they alike? How are they different?

18. A. The regions on Spinner 1 all have the same area. How does that affect the shape of the graph?

    B. The regions on Spinner 2 do not have the same area. How does that affect the shape of the graph?

19. Find the probability of Spinner 2 landing:

    A. On red.

    B. On yellow.

    C. On green.

    D. On green or yellow.

    E. On red or blue.

    F. In an orange region.

    G. In a region that is not red, yellow, or green.

Probability Problems

20. **A.** When you spin this spinner, what is the probability that this spinner will land on A?

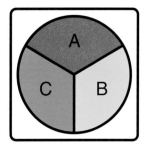

    B. Danny spins the spinner 150 times. About how many times do you expect it to land on A?

21. Tim painted 3 sides of a cube red and 3 sides blue.

    A. What is the probability that a red side will come up when the cube is rolled?

    B. Tim rolls the cube 5 times and it comes up red each time. What is the probability that it will come up red on the next roll?

22. **A.** What two ways can a nickel land when it is tossed into the air?

    B. What is the probability that a nickel will land "heads up" when it is tossed in the air?

    C. Jenny tosses a nickel 100 times. About how many times do you expect it to land heads up?

23. Abby wanted to invite a friend over to play, but she couldn't decide who to call. She put the names of Erin, Whitney, Tess, and Sam into a hat, closed her eyes, and pulled out a name. What is the probability that she chose Tess?

24. Peter, Nick, and Nate play a spinner game. Before playing, they agree that Peter will have Region A, Nick will have Region B, and Nate will have Region C. If the spinner lands in a player's region, he scores the point or points for that region. Do you think this is a fair game? That is, do you think each boy has an equal chance of winning? Explain your thinking.

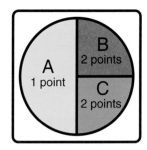

Make Your Own Spinners

Professor Peabody is inventing games for children to play. He needs a different spinner for each game. Each spinner will be divided into regions with different areas.

I. Design a spinner for Game 1. Professor Peabody wants the spinner to make data like this. Use the *Blank Spinners* Activity Pages from the *Discovery Assignment Book* to make your spinners.

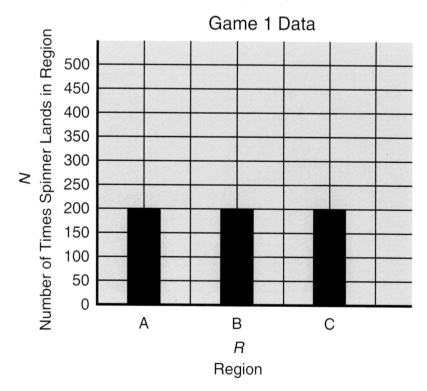

Game 1 Data

---

2. Design a spinner for Game 2 that you think will make data like this.

Game 2 Data

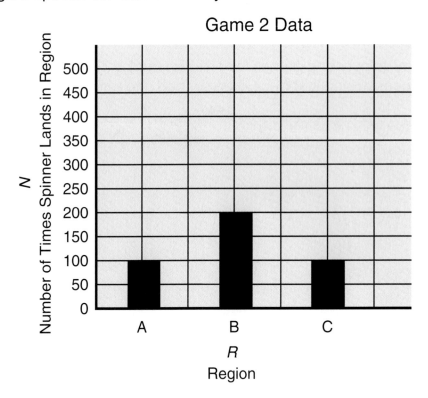

3. Design a spinner for Game 3 that you think will make data like this.

Game 3 Data

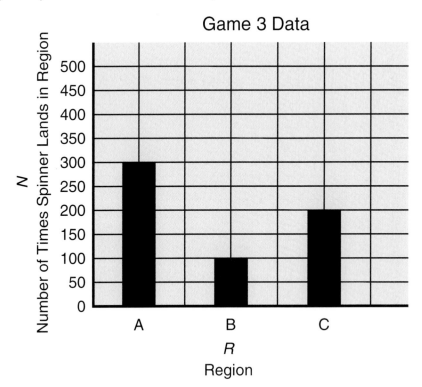

Make Your Own Spinners

4. Design a spinner for Game 4 that you think will make data like this.

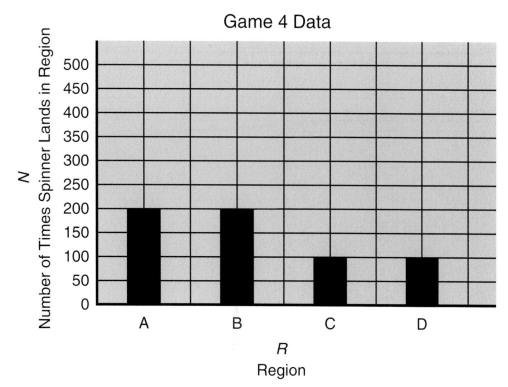

Game 4 Data

5. Choose one spinner. Test your spinner by collecting data and making a graph of the data.

A. How many times will your group spin your spinner?

B. Is the shape of your graph similar to the shape of the graph in the question for the spinner you have chosen? Why or why not?

Unit 15
Using Patterns

	Student Guide	Discovery Assignment Book	Adventure Book	Unit Resource Guide*
Lesson 1				
Plant Growth Conclusion	◎	◎		
Lesson 2				
In the Shade of the Old Meranpi Tree			◎	
Lesson 3				
Planet Gzorp	◎			◎
Lesson 4				
Function Machines	◎			
Lesson 5				
Taste of TIMS	◎			◎
Lesson 6				
Patterns and Problems	◎			

*Unit Resource Guide pages are from the teacher materials.

Plant Growth Conclusion

In Unit 13 you started the *Plant Growth* lab. When you finish collecting data, review the data for your plant. Here is a fourth grader's picture of the lab.

Use your *Plant Growth* picture to help you answer these questions.

1. What is the manipulated variable?

2. What is the responding variable?

3. What variables are held fixed?

4. Make a point graph of the data in your data table. Plot time on the horizontal axis and height on the vertical axis.

Use the graph to answer the following questions:

5. If there is a pattern to your data, fit a line or curve to the data points. Describe the shape of your graph.

6. How does your graph compare to those of your classmates?

7. Use your graph or data table. What was the height, *H,* of the lowest leaf at time *T* = 5 days?

8. Use your graph or data table. On what day was the height, *H,* of the lowest leaf equal to 10 cm?

9. What was the height of the lowest leaf at the end of your experiment?

10. A. What does your graph look like when your plant is growing fastest?

    B. What does it look like when it is growing slowest?

11. Write a paragraph that tells the story of your graph. Use your answers to Question 10 to help you. Include the following information: On which days did your plant grow the most? On which days did it grow the least? How did your plant grow in the beginning, middle, and end of your experiment?

12. What do you think the data would show if you continued to record the growth of the plant?

13. Which graph, Graph A or Graph B, looks more like the graphs of the plants in your class?

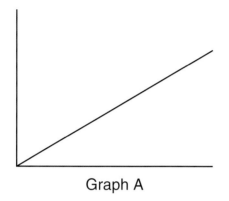

Graph A

Graph B

14. Compare your graph with some of the other graphs you have drawn this year. How are the graphs different? How are they similar?

15. Shannon and Jerome graphed the growth of their plants. What do the graphs tell you about how the plants grew? Using the graphs, tell as much as you can about how Shannon's and Jerome's plants grew. Compare the stories of the two graphs. How were they the same and how were they different?

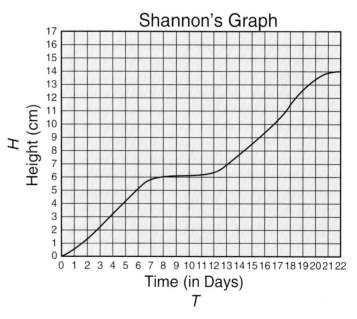

Shannon's Graph

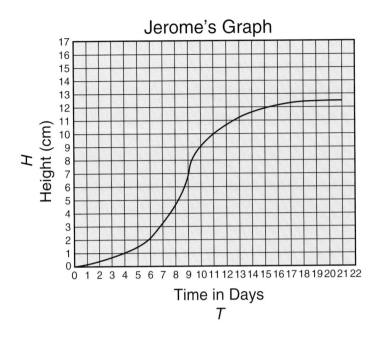

Jerome's Graph

Height (cm) H

Time in Days T

Homework

You will need a piece of *Centimeter Graph Paper*.

1. Grace planted a sunflower seed. She waited until it sprouted and measured its height every few days. She measured the plant at the same time each day, 8 A.M. Here is her data table. Make a graph of Height (in cm) versus Time (in days) of her data on *Centimeter Graph Paper.*

2. What was the height of the plant at the end of the experiment?

3. On which days did the plant grow the most?

4. On which days is the graph the steepest?

Date	T Time in Days	H Height in cm
10/19	0	0
10/21	2	$\frac{1}{2}$
10/23	4	1
10/26	7	6
10/28	9	10
10/30	11	12
11/2	14	16
11/4	16	18
11/6	18	19
11/9	21	19

5. Here is the graph of Professor Peabody's plant growth data.

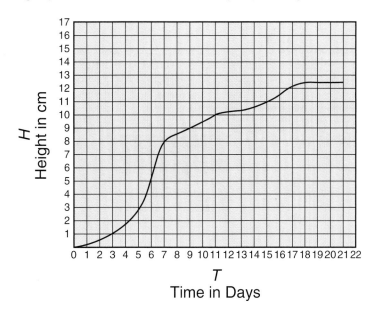

T
Time in Days

Professor Peabody's mouse, Milo, chewed up his data table. Make a data table like the one below and fill in the missing information using the graph.

T Time in Days	H Height in cm
0	
2	0.5
3	
	3
7	
8	
9	
	10
	10.5
19	

Planet Gzorp

Far, far away, there is a planet called Gzorp. You can find many strange and beautiful things on Gzorp. The plants and animals on Gzorp are especially weird. Some of them are made of all squares!

This is an Add Three Gator.

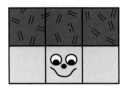

This is a Square Turtle.

And, this is a Triangle Fish.

Add Three Gator

The plants and animals that are made of squares grow by adding more squares. Different kinds of plants and animals add squares differently. For example, a 1-year-old Add Three Gator looks like this:

When it is 2 years old, it looks like this:

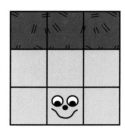

When it is 3 years old, it looks like this:

It keeps growing, getting three squares larger each year. The dark blue squares show the squares it grows each year.

1. Create a data table like the one below showing the age in years and the size in squares for Add Three Gators between the ages of 1–7.

Add Three Gator Growth

Age in Years	Size in Squares
1	3
2	
3	
4	

2. Do you think an Add Three Gator that is as old as you is very big? Find out. Record the data for this Add Three Gator in your data table.

3. Use your data table to find out how many squares a 6-year-old Add Three Gator has.

4. How many squares does an 11-year-old Add Three Gator have? Tell how you solved this problem.

5. How old is an Add Three Gator that has 66 squares? Tell how you solved this problem.

6. If an Add Three Gator has 100 squares, about how old is it? Tell how you solved this problem.

Square Turtle

A Square Turtle grows into a bigger square each year. These are 1-, 2-, and 3-year-old Square Turtles.

7. **A.** Draw a 4-year-old Square Turtle.

   B. Write the number of squares it has in all.

   C. How many squares does it have on one side?

8. **A.** How many squares does a Square Turtle have on one side when it is 5 years old?

   B. How many squares does a 5-year-old Square Turtle have in all?

9. **A.** Create a data table for Square Turtles between the ages of 1–10.

   B. Describe patterns you see in the table.

Square Turtle Growth

Age in Years	Size in Squares
1	1
2	
3	
4	

10. How many squares would a 22-year-old Square Turtle have on one side?

11. **A.** If a Square Turtle has 36 squares, how old is it?

    B. If a Square Turtle has 169 squares, how old is it?

12. **A.** How many squares does a 10-year-old Square Turtle have?

    B. How many squares does a 75-year-old Square Turtle have? Tell how you know.

13. Estimate the age of a Square Turtle that has 1000 squares.

Triangle Fish

A Triangle Fish is a sea creature on Planet Gzorp. It lives in families. A family of Triangle Fish is shown below.

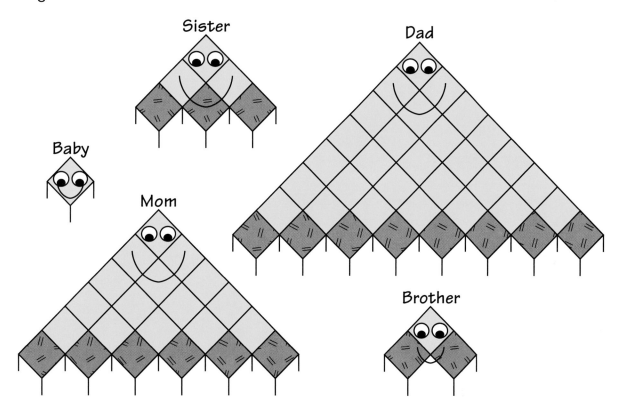

14. How old are the children in the Triangle Fish family?

15. How old are the parents?

16. **A.** Create a data table for Triangle Fish between the ages of 1–10. [*Hint:* A four-, five-, and seven-year-old Triangle Fish are not shown in the family.]

    B. Describe in words how a Triangle Fish grows.

17. **A.** How many squares does a 10-year-old Triangle Fish have?

    B. How many squares does a 15-year-old Triangle Fish have?

Triangle Fish Growth

Age in Years	Size in Squares
1	1
2	
3	
4	

18. **A.** If a Triangle Fish has 36 squares, how old is it?

    B. If a Triangle Fish has 210 squares, how old is it?

    C. If a Triangle Fish has 465 squares, how old is it?

19. How could you find out how many squares there are in a 48-year-old Triangle Fish? Estimate the answer.

20. Estimate the age of a Triangle Fish that has 20,100 squares.

Homework

You will need a calculator to complete this homework.

1. How many squares does a 30-year-old Add Three Gator have? Show your work.

2. Estimate the age of an Add Three Gator that has 5000 squares. Tell how you made your estimate.

3. How many squares are on one side of a Square Turtle that has 81 squares in all?

4. How many squares does a Square Turtle have on each side if it has 361 squares in all?

5. How many squares does a 30-year-old Square Turtle have? Show your work.

6. Estimate the age of a Square Turtle that has 7500 squares. Tell how you made your estimate.

7. Estimate the number of squares a 25-year-old Triangle Fish has.

Function Machines

Irma and Luis are exploring their Auntie Pat's attic one day.

Irma: "Hey, Luis, look at this!"

Luis: "It looks like some kind of machine."

Irma: "Yeah, but what is it?"

Irma: "It says Double Machine. What do you think that means?"

Luis: "Maybe it doubles stuff."

Irma: "Look at all these cards with numbers on them. They look as though they fit in the slot."

Luis: "Let's try it!"

They put in a card with 25 on it and turned the crank. With a lot of coughing, sputtering, and choking, the machine spits out a card saying 50.

Irma: "It really works!"

Luis: "This machine could help us double all kinds of numbers."

1. Irma and Luis tried the double machine on lots of numbers. They put their results in a data table like the one below. Make a data table like this one and fill in the blank spaces.

Doubling Machine

Input	Output
25	50
7	14
14	
	30
100	
	100
	7
N	$2 \times N$

Luis: "Say, Irma, I found another machine over here, but I can't read the label."

Irma: "Let's try it out and see if it works."

Luis: "I put in 10 and out came 20."

Irma: "It looks like another doubling machine. Let's put in 20."

Luis: "30 came out, so it can't be doubling."

2. Make a data table like the one below and fill in the missing entries.

Mystery Machine

Input	Output
10	20
20	30
5	15
17	27
	45
25	
0	
	39
N	

3. What does the mystery machine do? There are many ways to answer this question. You can write the answer in words: The mystery machine is an "add ten machine."

You can write the answer in symbols. If we use *N* to stand for the Input number, then:

$$\text{Output} = N + 10$$

4. If you are given an output number, how can you find the input number?

Here are two more function machines. The one in Question 5 multiplies the input number by 10 and then subtracts 5. The machine in Question 6 subtracts 5 from the input number. Set up two-column data tables like the ones below and fill in the missing values.

5.

Input	Output
1	5
2	15
3	25
4	35
	55
15	
	205
100	
N	$10 \times N - 5$

6.

Input	Output
12	7
11	
	5
9	
	3
	2
6	
	0
N	$N - 5$

Guess My Rule

This is a game for two or more players. The players will need a *Two-column Data Table*. They can use calculators if they like.

- One player is the Function Machine. The player thinks of a rule and writes it down on a piece of paper but doesn't tell it to the other players.
- The other players take turns, each one giving the Function Machine an input number and writing it in the data table. The player who is the Function Machine tells the other players the output number and writes it in the data table.
- A player may make one guess describing the rule during his or her turn.
- The first player to guess the rule is the winner. In the next round the winner becomes the Function Machine.

In Questions 1–2, use the Input-Output Patterns to complete each data table.

1.

Input	Output
3	10
10	
	27
53	
	200
	1000
100	
N	N + 7

2.

Input	Output
1	30
2	
3	
4	
5	
10	120
	100
N	10 × N + 20

Here are data tables for two function machines. Find the Input-Output patterns. Use the patterns to fill in the blanks in each data table. Describe the Input-Output patterns using words or symbols (or both).

3.

Input	Output
1	12
2	24
3	
4	48
5	
10	
	240
N	

4.

Input	Output
20	41
15	31
10	
	11
0	
2	5
	101
N	

5. Make a data table like this on your paper. Make up your own values for the input and output columns which follow a rule. Write the rule in symbols in the last row.

Input	Output
N	

6. Play *Guess My Rule* with a family member.

Taste of TIMS

Weight and Mass

Professor Peabody is having trouble telling the difference between weight and mass. He knows that **mass** is the amount of matter in an object and that **weight** is a measure of the pull of gravity. But, it's hard to tell the difference on Earth. So, he decides to travel to the moon to see what happens to his weight and mass.

Professor Peabody weighs 148 pounds on Earth. He discovers that his **weight** on the moon is less than his weight on the Earth. Why do you think this happens?

The moon's gravity is weaker than the Earth's. Because there is less gravity pulling on Professor Peabody, he has less weight.

Now, he checks his mass.

His **mass** has stayed the same! Why do you think this has happened? Why didn't Professor Peabody's mass change when the gravity changed?

Taste of TIMS

Shannon used the sandwich she brought for lunch to do an experiment. She placed her sandwich on a two-pan balance and used standard masses to find its mass. Then, she took a bite out of her sandwich and found the mass of the remaining sandwich. Shannon kept taking bites out of her sandwich, each time finding the mass, until her sandwich was gone.

Repeat Shannon's experiment using a sandwich of your own.

Draw a picture of the experiment.

1. What is the manipulated variable?

2. What is the responding variable?

3. What variable or variables are fixed during the experiment?

 **Collect**

4. Collect data for 1, 2, and 4 bites. Record your data in a table like the one shown below.

N Number of Bites	M Mass in Grams
0	
1	

 **Graph**

5. Make a point graph of the data in your table.

 **Discuss**

6. If the points suggest a line, draw a best-fit line. If they suggest a curve, draw one.

7. **A.** Use your graph to predict the mass of the sandwich after your third bite. Write down your prediction.

   B. Did you use interpolation or extrapolation to make your prediction?

8. **A.** Use your graph to predict the mass of the sandwich after your sixth bite. Write down your prediction.

   B. Check your prediction. Is your prediction close to the actual mass?

9. Predict how many bites it would take for you to eat your entire sandwich. Check your prediction and finish your sandwich.

10. Find the mean number of grams eaten with each bite.

11. Plot your partner's data on your graph. Compare your graph and data with your partner's. How are they the same? How are they different?

12. **A.** Who has a bigger bite size, you or your partner?

    B. Which student had the larger sandwich?

13. Two students' lines for the experiment are shown below. Tell a story for this graph. Include in your story which student had the sandwich with the most mass and which student took bigger bites.

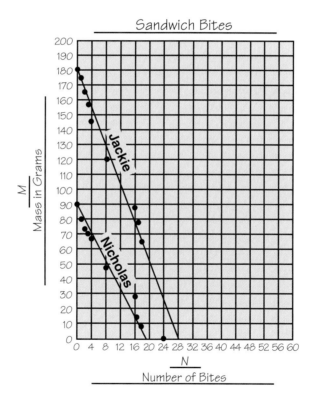

14. Three pairs of students do a similar experiment. They mass a sandwich, then record the mass after one bite, two bites, and four bites have been eaten.

   A. Tell what is the same and different for each graph.

   B. For each pair, what does the graph say about the mass of each sandwich?

   C. For each pair, what does the graph say about the size of the students' bites?

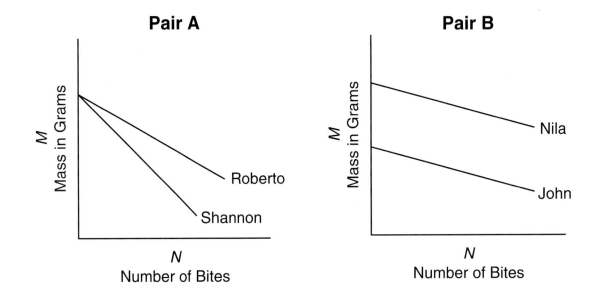

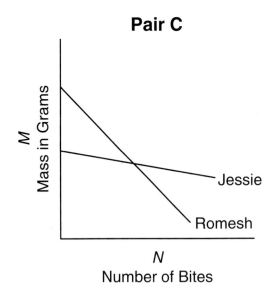

15. Romesh did the *Taste of TIMS* lab with an apple. He plotted his data in a graph. Tell a story about the graph.

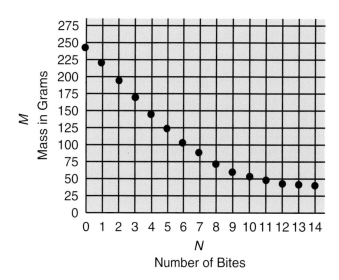

Homework

You will need a sheet of *Centimeter Graph Paper.*

1. Professor Peabody used the *Taste of TIMS* lab to see how long it took his mouse, Milo, to eat a dish of food. He recorded the data in a table. Plot a graph for Professor Peabody's data.

2. Predict the mass of the food left in the dish after 3 days.

3. Predict how many days it would take Milo to eat the entire dish of food.

4. What is the average amount of food eaten each day? Show how you got your answer.

N Number of Days	M Mass in Grams
0	114
1	103
2	91
4	67
6	43
8	22

Patterns and Problems

You will need a piece of *Centimeter Graph Paper* and a calculator to complete these problems.

1. Ming's function machine triples a number, then subtracts three. Jackie's function machine doubles a number, then subtracts two.

Machine X

Input	Output
1	0
2	3
3	6

Machine Y

Input	Output
1	0
2	2
3	4

A. Which data table is Ming's?

B. Which data table is Jackie's?

2. Maya's and Roberto's function machines have different rules.

A. Help them complete their data tables for the numbers 0–5.

Double Plus Two

Input	Output
0	
1	
2	

Add 1, Then Double

Input	Output
0	
1	
2	

B. What do you notice about Maya's and Roberto's data tables? Explain.

Patterns and Problems

3. Jacob's function machine is missing its rule. Help Jacob find the rule for his function machine.

Input	Output
0	5
1	7
2	9
3	11
4	13
5	15

Give a title for the data table that shows the rule.

4. Nila's sandwich has a mass of 153 grams. She took one bite and the mass of her sandwich is 122 grams.

   A. If each of Nila's bites has the same mass, what is the mass of two bites?

   B. How much mass will three bites have?

   C. How many bites can Nila take until her sandwich is gone?

5. John's sandwich has a mass of 139 grams. He took one bite and the mass of his sandwich is 109 grams.

   A. If each of John's bites has the same mass, how many bites can John take until his sandwich is gone?

   B. Who has a bigger bite size, Nila or John?

6. Irma has organized her plant growth data in a table. Plot Irma's plant growth data on *Centimeter Graph Paper*.

Plant Growth

Day	Height (in centimeters)
0	0
4	2
5	4
7	8
8	12
11	14
15	15
17	15

A. How many centimeters did Irma's plant grow by Day 6? Show your work.

B. Use your graph to predict how many centimeters Irma's plant will grow by Day 18.

7. Frank organized his plant growth data in a table. Plot Frank's plant growth data on the same piece of *Centimeter Graph Paper* as Irma's. Describe the differences and similarities in their graphs.

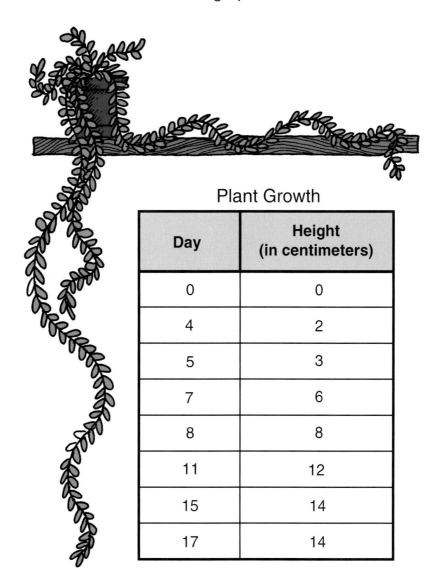

Plant Growth

Day	Height (in centimeters)
0	0
4	2
5	3
7	6
8	8
11	12
15	14
17	14

Unit 16

Assessing Our Learning

	Student Guide	Discovery Assignment Book	Adventure Book	Unit Resource Guide*
Lesson 1				
Experiment Review	◎	◎		
Lesson 2				
Problems and Practice	◎			
Lesson 3				
Area vs. Length	◎			
Lesson 4				
The Many-Eyed Dragonfly				◎
Lesson 5				
End-of-Year Test				◎
Lesson 6				
Portfolios	◎			

Unit Resource Guide pages are from the teacher materials.

Experiment Review

Professor Peabody loves to play with his toy cars. He likes to see how far each of his cars can roll down ramps that are set at different heights.

Watching his toy cars roll down ramps reminds Professor Peabody of an experiment he did several months ago.

Discuss

1. Which lab do you think Professor Peabody is thinking about?

2. Answer the following questions about the lab in Question 1. You may look at the lab pages in the *Student Guide* or your portfolio to help you.

   A. What variables did you study in the lab?

   B. Did you have to keep any variables fixed, so that the experiment would be fair? If so, which ones?

   C. Did you measure anything? If so, what did you measure? What units did you use?

   D. How many trials did you do? If you did more than one trial, tell why.

   E. Describe the shape of your graph. Use words or a sketch.

   F. What were the most important problems you solved using your data?

3. Look at the picture of Professor Peabody on the opening page of this unit. This picture, the labs in your portfolio, and the *Student Guide* can help your class make a list of the labs you completed. For each lab, answer each part of Question 2. Use the *Experiment Review Chart* in your *Discovery Assignment Book* to help organize the information.

Problems and Practice

Use appropriate tools such as paper and pencil, calculators, or pattern blocks to solve the following problems. For some problems you need to find an exact answer, but for others you need only an estimate.

1. **A.** Tanya and her sister planted a rectangular flower garden. The garden plot is 4 feet wide and 6 feet long. What is the area of the garden plot?

   B. Tanya wants to put a fence around the garden. How many feet of fencing should she buy?

2. A rectangle is made of 36 square-inch tiles. Sketch all the possible rectangles. Write a multiplication sentence for the number of tiles in each rectangle.

3. Jessie recorded the time she spent watching television over a four-day period. Her data is recorded in the table below.

Day	Minutes of Television
Monday	240 minutes
Tuesday	210 minutes
Wednesday	255 minutes
Thursday	90 minutes

   A. Find the median number of minutes Jessie watched television during these four days.

   B. Find the mean number of minutes Jessie watched television during these four days. Give your answer to the nearest whole minute.

   C. What is the total number of minutes Jessie watched television during these four days?

   D. How many total hours of television did Jessie watch over the four days? Give your answer to the nearest hour.

4. Shannon helped her mom sell donuts at the Farmer's Market. Each donut costs $0.50. If Shannon sold 67 donuts and her mom sold 43 donuts, about how much money did they collect?

---

5. A. Show each of the decimals below using base-ten shorthand. The flat is one whole.

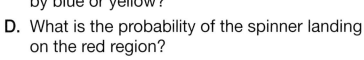

0.45   0.68   1.04   0.1   0.05

B. Arrange the decimals in order from least to greatest.

6. Ana and Nila are using the following spinner to play a game.

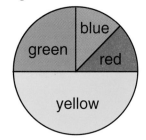

A. What fraction of the spinner is green?

B. What fraction of the spinner is red?

C. What fraction of the spinner is covered by blue or yellow?

D. What is the probability of the spinner landing on the red region?

E. What is the probability of the spinner landing on the red or the blue region?

F. What is the probability of the spinner landing in a region other than the green region?

7. A. Irma and Maya are working with pattern blocks. They call the yellow hexagon one whole. Maya builds a shape using three green triangles, one red trapezoid, and one blue rhombus. Write a number for Maya's shape.

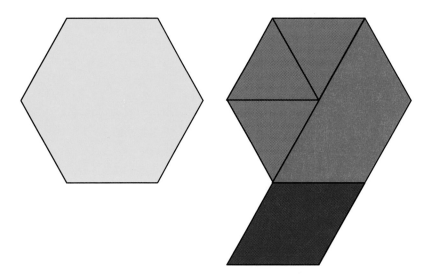

B. Write a number sentence to show Maya's work.

8. Jerome, Shannon, and Nicholas each play on a different soccer team. They have played the same number of games. Jerome's team won $\frac{5}{6}$ of their games. Shannon's team won $\frac{3}{4}$ of their games. Nicholas's team won $\frac{7}{12}$ of their games.

   A. Put the fractions in order from smallest to greatest. You can use your Fraction Chart from Unit 12.

   B. Which team had the best record?

9. Linda made the following function machine. Copy the table. Help her complete her data table using her rule.

Double, then subtract 3

Input	Output
4	5
7	
8	13
	21
N	

10. A. Grace's sandwich has a mass of 142 grams. She took one bite and then found the mass of the remaining part of the sandwich to be 110 grams. If each of her bites is the same size, what will be the mass of the sandwich after Grace has taken a total of three bites?

   B. How many total bites will it take Grace to eat all of her sandwich?

11. Jackie and her sister are planning a party at a local indoor play park. They plan on inviting six people besides themselves. The total cost of the party is $96. How much will the party cost per person?

12. Michael, Jackie, Shannon, and Frank each brought a sandwich for the lab *Taste of TIMS.* Instead of finding the mass of each sandwich, they found that the total mass of all four sandwiches was 592 grams. What is the average mass of each sandwich?

13. Tanya's mom is working in an office supply store. Yesterday, a shipment of assorted notepads arrived at the store. There are 36 notepads in each box. The store received 28 boxes. How many notepads did they receive?

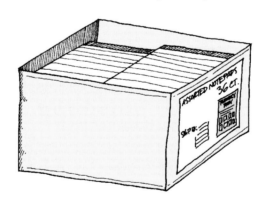

Area vs. Length

Michael and Jessie were looking through their portfolios. Michael pulled out the *Perimeter vs. Length* lab. Jessie did too. They compared the types of airplanes they chose to study. Michael studied the commuter plane and Jessie studied the long-haul jet.

1. Look back at the *Perimeter vs. Length* lab in your portfolios or Unit 2 Lesson 2 in the *Student Guide.* What plane did you study?

2. What variables did you study?

In Unit 2, you helped Myrna find the perimeter of runways so that lights could be strung all around them. You chose one of the following planes to study:

*   The light planes are the smallest airplanes at the Antopolis airport. They need runways that are 1 inch wide.
*   The commuter planes need runways that are 2 inches wide.
*   The short-haul jets need 3-inch-wide runways.
*   The long-haul jets need 4-inch-wide runways.
*   The heavy-transport planes need runways that are 5 inches wide.

Myrna needs your help again. The runways at Antopolis Airport need to be coated with a special paint to seal the cracks. To buy enough paint, Myrna needs to find the area of each runway, no matter how long.

Use the TIMS Laboratory Method to help Myrna. You will work on runways for only one kind of plane. Your teacher will help you choose.

You will use square-inch tiles to make several runways of different lengths for your kind of plane. For each runway, you will record the length and the area in a data table. Then, you will graph your data and look for patterns.

3. Draw a picture of the lab. Be sure to show the two main variables, Length (*L*) and Area (*A*). Also show your kind of airplane and how wide your runways will be.

You will use square-inch tiles to make several runways for your kind of airplane. With your group, decide how long to make your runways. Do not make runways that are longer than 10 inches or you may have trouble graphing your data.

4. Make your runways. Record the length and area of each runway. Keep track of your data in a table like the one shown here.

Runway Data Table for _____
(Type of Plane)
Width = _____

W **Width of Runway** **(in inches)**	*L* **Length of Runway** **(in inches)**	*A* **Area of Runway** **(in square inches)**

5. **A.** What is the manipulated variable?

   B. What variable is the responding variable?

   C. What variable stays the same for all of your runways?

6. Graph your data. Put Length (*L*) on the horizontal axis and Area (*A*) on the vertical axis.

7. Look at the points on the graph. If the points form a line, use a ruler to draw a line through the points. Extend your line in both directions.

Questions 8 to 12 are for runways the same width as yours.

8. How wide are your runways?

9. What is the area of a runway that is 4 inches long?

10. Find the area of a 12-inch-long runway. Show how you found your answer.

11. What is the area of a 100-inch-long runway? Explain how you found your answer.

12. Give a rule for finding the area of a runway for your type of airplane, no matter what the length.

13. Explain the difference between inches and square inches.

14. Professor Peabody tried to help Myrna. He worked hard and studied runways for three kinds of planes: light planes (1-inch-wide runways), short-haul jets (3-inch-wide runways), and heavy transports (5-inch-wide runways). Unfortunately, Professor Peabody forgot which line on his graph he drew for each kind of runway. Which line did he draw for each kind of runway? Explain how you know.

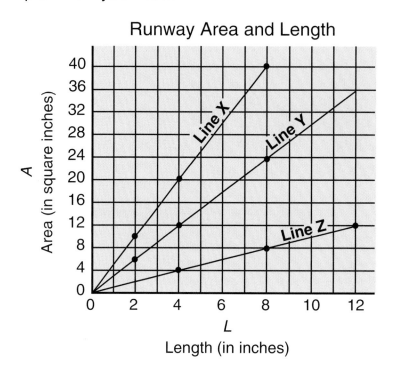

Runway Area and Length

15. Write a letter to Myrna about your kind of runway. Tell her what kind of plane your runways are for and explain what you learned about the area of your runways. Explain how you can find the area for your kind of runway, no matter what the length. Use the Student Rubric: *Telling* to help you organize and write your letter.

Portfolios

Look at the work in your portfolios. Compare work from the beginning of the year to work you have just completed. Have you improved?

I have. I used to just write down answers. Now I show my work in lots of ways: I draw pictures, write sentences, make graphs…

I can't wait to show my portfolio to my mom and dad. They will be amazed.

1. Choose items from your collection folder to add to your portfolio. Choose items that are similar to the work that is already in your portfolio. Here are some examples of things you can choose:

   A. The *Experiment Review* from Lesson 1 of this unit.

   B. The solution to a problem you have solved. For example, you may choose to include your solutions to the problems in *The Many-Eyed Dragonfly.*

   C. A lab you have completed. *Area vs. Length* is a good example.

   D. Items your teacher recommends.

2. Add the name of each new piece to your Table of Contents. Include a short description of the work and the date it was finished.

3. Write a paragraph comparing two pieces of work in your portfolio that are alike in some way. For example, you can compare two labs or your solutions to two problems you have solved. One piece should be new and one should be from the beginning of the year. Use these questions to help you write your paragraph:

   • Which two pieces did you choose to compare?
   • How are they alike? How are they different?
   • Do you see any improvement in the newest piece of work? Explain.
   • How could you improve your newest piece of work?

Student Rubric: Knowing

In My Best Work in Mathematics:

- I show that I understand the ideas in the problem.

- I show the same mathematical ideas in different ways. I use pictures, tables, graphs, and sentences when they fit the problem.

- I show that I can use tools and rules correctly.

- I show that I can use the mathematical facts that apply to the problem.

Student Rubric: Solving

In My Best Work in Mathematics:

- I read the problem carefully, make a good plan for solving it, and then carry out that plan.

- I use tools like graphs, pictures, tables, or number sentences to help me.

- I use ideas I know from somewhere else to help me solve a problem.

- I keep working on the problem until I find a good solution.

- I look back at my solution to see if my answer makes sense.

- I look back at my work to see what more I can learn from solving the problem.

Student Rubric: Telling

In My Best Work in Mathematics:

- I show all of the steps that I used to solve the problem. I also tell what each number refers to (such as 15 boys or 6 inches).

- I explain why I solved the problem the way I did so that someone can see why my method makes sense.

- If I use tools like pictures, tables, graphs, or number sentences, I explain how the tools I used fit the problem.

- I use math words and symbols correctly. For example, if I see "6 − 2," I solve the problem "six minus two," not "two minus six."

Index

This index provides page references for the *Student Guide.* Definitions or explanations of key terms can be found on the pages listed in bold.

A

Addition
 with base-ten pieces, 78–80, 84–85
 multidigit, 174
 paper-and-pencil, 79–80, 84, 174
Angle, 41–56, **42,** 243–250
 acute, **50**–51, 54–55
 comparing, 43–44, 53
 drawing, 47, 54
 measuring, 243–250
 obtuse, **51,** 54–55
 in pattern blocks, 55–56
 right, **48**–49, 54–55
 in shapes, 45–46, 56
 vertex of, 243
Area, 28–38, **29**
 counting square units, 433–436
Arm span, 20–23
Average, 12, **13,** 22, **125**

B

Bar graph
 interpreting, 5, 9, 11, 14. *See also* Labs
 making, 4, 10. *See also* Labs

Base (with exponents), 113
Base-ten
 division, 364–378
 multiplication, 298–303
Base-Ten Board, 68
Base-ten pieces, 68–85
 bit, **68**
 flat, **68**
 pack, **68**
 skinny, **68**
Base-Ten Recording Sheet, 68
Base-ten shorthand, 71–85, 280–282, 285–287
Best-fit line, 123–124

C

Categorical variable, 7, 20
Certain event, 385
Center of turning, 251–254
Centimeter, 272
Circumference, 132
Comparing
 angles, 43–44, 53
 fractions, 351–352, 354
Convenient number, 202, 203
Cubic centimeter, 216
Cubic foot, 220

Data analysis, 16–17, 20–23
Data collection, 2–10, 18, 20–23
Data collection and analysis, 258–363. *See also* Labs
Data table, 18, 264. *See also* Labs
Decimals
    hundredths, 283–287
    tenths, 276–282
Decimeter, 271
Degrees, angle measure, 47–48
Denominator, 276, 326
Dividend, 58
Divisible, 184
Division, 235, 364–370
    divisibility patterns, **184**–189
    facts, 58–63, 234–236
    forgiving method, **366**–370
    paper-and-pencil, 366–373
    by zero, 375–376
Division sentence, 58–60, 104
Divisor, 58, 235–236
Doubles, 154, 156–158

Edge, of a 3-dimensional shape, **256**–259
Equilateral triangle, 241
Estimation
    benchmarks, 169
    length, 35
    of products, **202**–206, 306–307, 311, 315
    of quantities by comparing, 162–167
    sums and differences, 171–174
    ten percent as a measure of closeness, 166–168
    using convenient numbers, 202–206
Even number, 98
Experiment review, 232–233, 430
Exponent, 98, 101, **113**–115, 155–158
Extrapolation, 124

Face, of a 3-dimensional shape, **256**–259
Fact family, 59, 63, 99, 234
    division, 58–60
Factor, 103–106, 109, **184**–189
    division, **61**
    prime, **110**–115
    tree, **111**–115
Fair number cube, 390
Fewest Pieces Rule, 74–75, 281
Fixed variable, 141
Fractions, 326–355
    addition, 348–349
    addition and subtraction, 333–335
    comparing, 336–338, 345, 351–352, 354
    equivalent, **343**–345
    pattern block, 346–352
    problems and puzzles, 353–355
    strips, 326–332
Function machine, 411–416, 424–425
Functions, 406–414

Games
    9 to 5 War, 175–176
    Bean Counter's, 387
    Draw, Place, and Read, 159
    Fill It First, 221–222
    Floor Tiler, 107–108
    Frabble, 339–342
    Guess My Rule, 412
    Hundredths, Hundredths, Hundredths, 286–287
    Operation Target, 183, 224
    Product Bingo, 116–117
Graphs. *See also* Bar graph, Point graph
    interpreting, 36, 403–404, 421–423. *See also* Labs
    making. *See* Labs
Gzorp, 406–410

H

Height, 20–23
Hindu-Arabic numbers, 65–67
Horizontal axis, 5–6

I

Impossible event, 384
Interpolation, 124
Intersecting lines, 238

J

K

L

Labs
    Area vs. Length, 435–438
    Arm Span vs. Height, 17–23
    Bouncing Ball, 139–145
    Downhill Racer, 288–295
    Perimeter vs. Length, 31–36
    Plant Growth, 379–381, 402–405
    Rolling a Number Cube, 388–391
    Taste of TIMS, 419–423
    Volume vs. Number, 225–229
Length, 31–38
    metric measurement, 270–275
Likely event, 385
Line segment, 239
Lines
    intersecting, **238**–242
    parallel, **238**–242
    perpendicular, **238**–242
    rays, **240**–242
    segment, **239**–242
Liter, 219

M

Manipulated variable, 140
Mass, 417–423
Mean, 125–138
Measurement, length, 270
Median, 13, 125–131, 138
Meniscus, 221
Meter, 270
Milliliter, 219, 273
Money, 24, 60, 63
Multiple, 98, 185
Multiple trials, 141
Multiplication, 96–101, 298
    all-partials method, **197**–201, 305–307, 313–316
    array model, 96–108, 234
    break-apart products, 298–303
    break-apart strategy, 190–192
    by 1, 61
    by zero, 61
    compact algorithm, 308–312, 317–321
    facts, 58–63, 234–236
    Facts I Know chart, 62
    multiples of ten, 193–195
    number sentence, 303
    round numbers, 207–210
    turn-around facts, **61**
Multiplication and division facts, 234–236
Multiplication sentences, 100

N

Negative numbers, 86–91, **87**
Nets, 258–262
Number
    even, **98**
    odd, **98**
    prime, **98, 104**
    square, **98**
Number cubes, rolling, 387
Number lines, 169–171, 173
Number sentence, 199
    division, 58–60, 104
    multiplication, 100, 303
Numbers
    negative, 86–91
    positive, 88–91
Numerator, 276, 326
Numerical variable, 7, 20

Odd number, 98
Order of operations, 180–183, **223**

Parallel lines, 238–242
Parallelogram, 241
Patterns and functions, 406–410
Percent, 10% as a measure of closeness, 166–168
Perimeter, 28–38, **29,** 31–38
Periods for place value, 150–153, **151**
Perpendicular lines, 238
Pictures, in Labs, 17. *See also* Labs
Place value, 68–85
    big base-ten pieces, 157–159, 159–161
    big numbers, 157–161
    decimals, 276–287
    Fewest Pieces Rule, **74**–75
    ordering numbers, 160–161
    periods, 150–153, **151,** 152–155, 158–159
    reading and writing numerals, 150, 152–155,
        157–159
Point graphs
    interpreting and making predictions, 120–124,
        146–148. *See also* Labs
    making, 157
    powers of two, 155
Polygon, 247
Portfolios, 39–40, 233, 439
Positive numbers, 88–91
Powers of two, 155–156, 156–158
Predictions, 143–145. *See also* Labs
    making, 120–124
    using graphs, 120–124
Prime number, 98, 104
Prism, 256–267, **259**
    drawing, 257
    volume of, 263–267
Probability, 384–399, **390**
    as a fraction, 390–391
    and spinners, 392–399
Probability line, 385–386
Product, 61, 107–108
Protractor, for measuring angles, 244–245

Quadrilateral, 56, 247
Quotient, 58, 235–236

Ray, 240
Responding variable, 140
Roman numerals, 64–67
    subtractive principle, **66**
Rounding, 170–171. *See also* Convenient number

Shapes, geometric, 240–241
Square inch, 29
Square number, 98
Student Rubric: *Knowing,* 441
Student Rubric: *Solving,* 442
Student Rubric: *Telling,* 443
Subtraction
    with base-ten pieces, 80–85
    multidigit, 174
    paper-and-pencil, 82–85, 174
Survey, 3
    hours of TV watched, 358–363
Symmetry, 251–255
    line, **251**–254
    turn, **251**–254

Temperature, 137
TIMS Laboratory Method, 17. *See also* Labs
Triangle Flash Cards, activities with, 61–62
Turn-around facts, multiplication, **61**

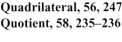

Unlikely event, 384